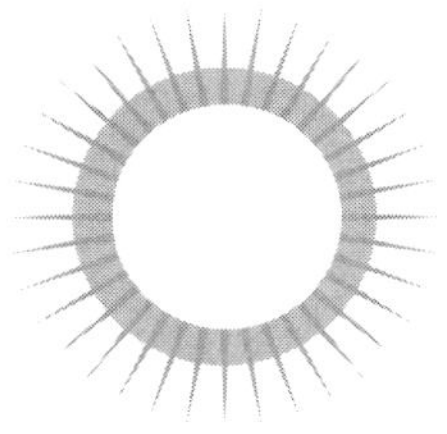

Public Art
Thinking Museums Differently

Hilde Hein

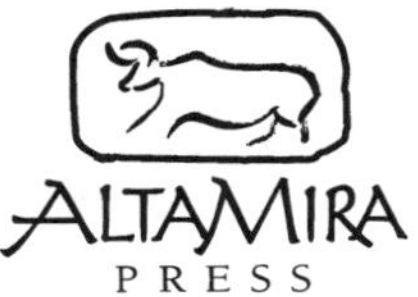

ALTAMIRA PRESS

A Division of

ROWMAN & LITTLEFIELD PUBLISHERS, INC.

Lanham • New York • Toronto • Oxford

AltaMira Press
A division of Rowman & Littlefield Publishers, Inc.
A wholly owned subsidiary of The Rowman & Littlefield Publishing Group, Inc.
4501 Forbes Boulevard, Suite 200
Lanham, MD 20706
www.altamirapress.com

PO Box 317
Oxford
OX2 9RU, UK

British Library Cataloguing in Publication Information Available

Library of Congress Cataloguing-in-Publication Data

Hein, Hilde S., 1932–
Public art : thinking museums differently / Hilde Hein.
p. cm.
Includes bibliographical references and index.
ISBN-13: 978-0-7591-0958-2 (cloth : alk. paper)
ISBN-10: 0-7591-0958-3 (cloth : alk. paper)
ISBN-13: 978-0-7591-0959-9 (pbk. : alk. paper)
ISBN-10: 0-7591-0959-1 (pbk. : alk. paper)
1. Art museums—Philosophy. 2. Public art. I. Title.
N430.H45 2006
708.001—dc22 2006008509

Printed in the United States of America

∞™ The paper used in this publication meets the minimum requirements of American National Standard for Information Sciences—Permanence of Paper for Printed Library Materials, ANSI/NISO Z39.48–1992.

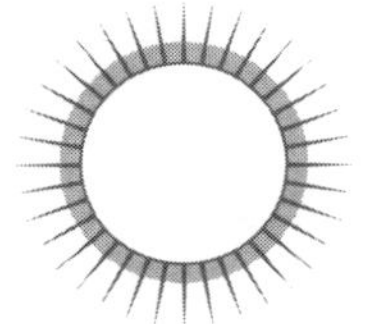

Public Art

Thinking Museums Differently

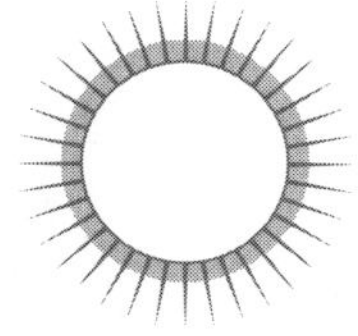

Contents

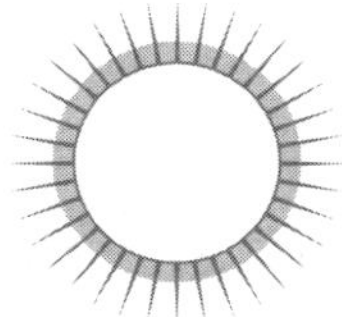

List of Illustrations

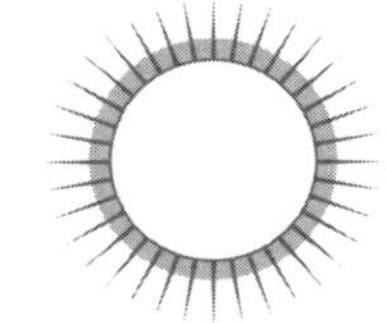

Preface

Historians of museums dispute their subject's origin. One history recalls temples to the muses, "sacred groves," and ancient academies of learning where scholars came to contemplate ideas. An alternative version focuses on natural and man-made objects accumulated in privately owned medieval collections and Renaissance cabinets of curiosities, where rare and wondrous specimens were preserved for the studious enjoyment of selected patrons. Still others trace the museum's descent to the relatively recent institution that came into being together with the inception of the modern nation-state. Each genealogy frames its subject differently, underscoring those features that seem most consistent and continuous with a favored representation of what the museum is today. This book is not a historical examination of the museum's past; neither is it a project of institutional history. Instead of seeking sources, I offer a proposal that bespeaks the museum's future. It intervenes among current controversies concerning the museum's function and prospects and suggests a mobile model through which these might be advanced.

In a previous book, *The Museum in Transition,* I joined the museum discourse at the stage where object centeredness was yielding priority to the prevalence of experience-orientation and a focus on people. I date the initial murmurs of this trend to the 1960s, when a confluence of economic, political, social, and ethical pressures drove a number of institutions and many individuals to radically reassess and reconfigure themselves. My concentration on museums as exemplars of this movement derived from my observation of the Exploratorium, the San Francisco museum that launched my abiding fascination with museums of all kinds. Here I encountered an explicit and fundamental concern with experience but also, and necessarily, the recognition that experience is stimulated in people through their exposure to things in the world and the relations among them. The Exploratorium set out deliberately to design and organize exhibits meant to generate experiences that foster understanding of the world beyond the museum. The aim was not to produce a surrogate world; neither was it to create gratuitous experiences without worldly reference. The museum was to be a center of things that would encourage learning and would empower people to achieve its fulfillment.

In principle, eliciting experience has always been the objective of museums. Art museums, in particular, take pride in their nurturance of aesthetic gratification and the heightened insights that follow from the experience of art. Science and history museums, likewise, knowingly rely on empathy and aesthetic acuity to bolster their cognitive program. Empirical science is grounded in the priority of experience. But the placement of experience front and center as the objective of the museum, displacing the primacy of the collection, was a mid-twentieth century innovation, and its impact has been profound.

One consequence of that shift of attention was the apparent demotion of objects to secondary status as instruments—vehicles for the delivery of experience rather than as ends unto themselves. This was understandably disconcerting to art world connoisseurs who exalt the work of art for its intrinsic and irreducible value. That conviction deterred art museums from jumping uncritically upon the experiential bandwagon. Although they too eventually adapted to the participatory ethos, they could not endorse a move seemingly warranted by the focal shift, namely, the recourse to simulation. If the heart of the museum was no longer to be the authentic object—"the real thing"—then whatever could evoke an equivalent experience might serve as well. Many museums of all types were cast adrift in search of a new center. Exciting technologies enabling them to elicit and reproduce dramatic experiences, authentic in their own way, were appearing at an unprecedented rate, and visitors were responding enthusiastically to them. Museums were turning into popular places to enjoy instead of silent cathedrals of learning. Although no less pedagogically impelled than before, they had assumed a learner-oriented stance that purported to be nonlinear, nonauthoritarian, and democratic. Visitors would be free to create their own experience. But wasn't that a recipe for anarchic confusion?

What remained to identify the museum as a unique institution with a distinct purpose? What achievements would mark its success?

As these perplexities became more troublesome, I turned back once again to the foundational issue of the concept of the museum. In the earlier book, I had declaimed against the promotion of random experience toward no specific end and warned against market-driven "experience merchandising." Now I could see that a broadened approach to the museum's performance was needed. Experience is central, but it need not be generated at the cost of object orientation: On the contrary, I believe the two elements are both vital and mutually invigorating. Moreover, experiential diversity entails a supportive context enriched by robust reference that includes but is not limited to material realia. Experience rarely occurs in a vacuum.

I persist in advocating that museums should emphasize their differences. They are bound by professional standards, but these do not legislate standardization of content, style, or ideological conformity. Museums are not like other institutions with which they share legal and tax-exempt status. They have little in common with prisons, graveyards, and hospitals, and the tropes of incarceration and protective custody used to compare them diminish the museum's true potential. Museums can diverge radically from one another, and through juxtaposition of their own resources, they can modify themselves significantly. They are actors, not stages, and can play many parts without loss of integrity. They are not aptly described by metaphorical reductions to sacred or morbid places full of fascinating things. Such characterizations limit the museum's agency and are seriously out of date. Neither is the museum merely an epistemological technology devised to covertly instill discipline or convey a foreordained set of ideas. Museums are good to think with and not only to indoctrinate. The versatility of their parts welcomes controversy and rightly stimulates repeated exploration.

Pursuing an independent line of interests, I had been thinking about another aesthetic puzzle that, like the museum, exploded conventional static categories. I wondered about public art, whose recent practice seemed to outrun its perceived identity. Generally neglected by aestheticians, public art was portrayed dismissively by them in opposition to the objects kept in museums—or in private sanctuaries—and destined for subjective contemplation by individual appreciators. This gradation was bewildering to me since many of the objects sequestered in museums had, in a previous life, embellished places of public worship or official edifices used for the administration of public affairs. Others had adorned open urban spaces and served secular and ceremonial functions remote from the very notion of art, if not of aesthetic pleasure. Why had their placement within the museum transformed them into objects of private satisfaction rather than public use, turning them into "private art"? The museum now appeared to be a switching station, an anomalous public construction with the avowed purpose of facilitating and ministering to private, subjective experience—somewhat like a public bathhouse. Ironically, the collectivization of these private experiences was necessitated not by economic expediency, which it also served, but by the validation it assured to the privatized experience that it rendered. It occurred to me that the privatized experience that takes place in the museum derives its legitimacy from the publicity of the institution that presents it. Without such public sanction, subjective pleasure would be merely the satisfaction of personal appetites. Warranted judgment, embodied by the museum, carries more weight than singular preferences.

I have no objection to individual gratification, but the museum has a grander function comprising its public identity. Might there be, I wondered, a correspondence between the museum, a public entity that privatizes, and public art, an apparent contradiction if the appeal of art is inherently a private affair? I struggled with the idea that public art derives its nature, but not its existence, appositionally with reference to the exclusive practice of the museum. This notion is worrisome since the phenomenon of public art precedes museums and their content by several centuries—regardless of how the museum is defined. Logically, if not chronologically, we may characterize public art as nonprivate art. It is not destined for private absorption. Public art belongs to the public sphere independently of specific authorship and addresses itself to an audience of societal units, sometimes cohesively but also disruptively. Thus it fractionates as readily as it consolidates social entities—publics, not individuals.

Conjecturing further, I decided to juxtapose museums with public art, not intending to declare the one a species of the other, but in order to consider the common elements of their nature. This led to an exploration of the uses of public art throughout its history. I had done preliminary work including a published essay in 1996 and preparation of an edited volume on public art. Enormous changes in the art form had taken place within recent decades, and public art was rapidly gaining widespread attention on many fronts. In effect, the distinction between public art and private art was blurring as earth art, environmental art, and politically infused art manifestations were spilling into and out of the museum and onto the highways and byways of the world.

The pace at which these developments were happening exceeded the rate of comparable change in museums. Whatever their motivation, museums are inevitably encumbered by the weight of buildings and objects, of bylaws, donors, payrolls, and boards of trustees. They cannot shift gears without massive lubrication. Nonetheless, there were resemblances to the dynamics of public art, and that is what intrigued me. Perhaps the more volatile features of public art could shed light on the slower-paced trajectory of the museum. In this book I explore the affinity between museums and public art. I argue that museums are changing more ponderously and with less clarity of purpose but in a direction similar to that of public art. Most notably, I see both as actors that no longer presume a ready-made audience with a more or less fixed disposition. Rather, they set out to construct multiple publics of limited duration and variable character. The ephemeral object and elusive agent prevail over the stability and constancy still symbolized by traditional museum architecture and the pedestaled equestrian statue.

Because of their unequal agility, the dynamism of public art is more evident than that of the museum, where resistance is also more pronounced. Factionalism is also inevitable. Its presence in public art can be comparatively easily managed, since there is room in the world for conventional statuary and ornamentation alongside proliferated civic interventions that simmer and boil and soon disappear. Museums, however, still confront mutually exclusive options and long-lasting decisions. I do not mean to underestimate those constraints but rather to point to a trend toward their diffusion.

At the same time, I see merit in that trend because it permits the museum to adjust to new pressures and assume responsible agency even as it endorses the participation of unfamiliar agents. Appearing as an actor with conviction while catalyzing change is preferable, I think, to waffling in indecisive passivity, mistaking equivocation for the opposite of the authoritarian didacticism that it seeks to disavow. My aim in this book is to speak favorably of the movement toward committed temporality and impermanence while acknowledging the difficulties that museums face in achieving it. I emphasize the permeability of museum walls, the instability of their process, and the fluidity of the publics they construct. My hope is to distinguish authenticity from longevity and to ground the fleeting experiences prompted by the museum in distinct and sustainable values.

While I was writing this preface, a friend drew my attention to a phenomenon that skirts the boundary between museums and public art, displaying their proximity. It is the "Extra Mile Project" in Washington, D.C., sponsored by the Points of Light Foundation. Initially conceived by its founder, John Johansen, as an interpretive museum with videos and hands-on exhibits, the plan was scaled back to become a more modest sequence of bronze medallions set into a mile-long segment of sidewalk near the White House, to honor America's tradition of volunteerism and its unmonumentalized heroes. Pedestrians come upon these medallions at their feet by chance as they glance down upon such figures as William Edwin Hall, founder of the Boys and Girls Clubs of America, and Linda and Millard Fuller, founders of Habitat for Humanity. Open-ended by design, the walk may take years to complete, as new candidates are presented. A kind of street art, this project also approaches the genre of the museum, in particular, the memorializing variety that is currently in fashion.

While this is a small-scale example of the union of museum with public art that I envision, it conveys the mobile intention of public-construction common to both. It briefly unites people in a common interest. Many people with whom I have discussed the idea of assimilating museums to public art immediately assume that I am referring to museum architecture and cite examples of striking museum edifices that clamor for attention and have received a great deal of it. But architecture, whether deferential or challenging, is not what I have in mind. Indeed there is considerable controversy over the place of architecture in museum design and function. While some critics argue that ostentatious buildings undermine or clash with their content, others defend structures that amplify the space of museums, complement their holdings, and expand visitor experience. I do not enter these discussions, for my interest is not in the museum as statuary or as a location in space. Instead, I present the museum as a temporal process, changing its state as it acts with variable intention. By viewing the museum through the fluid lens of public art, I hope to affirm that dynamic identity.

I have benefited from the help of a number of people and institutions in developing this theme. I am grateful to the Women's Studies Research Center at Brandeis University and its director, Shulamith Reinharz, for the endorsement which emboldened me to begin and stick with my self-appointed task, and to Mitch Allen, the founding director of AltaMira Press, who listened to a rambling account of my idea as we walked along the pre-Katrina New Orleans waterfront—and thought it promising. Grace

Ebron and Jason Hallman helped me through the editing phase. Hafthor Yngvason, former director of public art of the City of Cambridge Arts Council, and now director of the Reykjavik Museum in Iceland, was an invaluable source. We never completed the book of writings on public art that we hoped to edit, but our many planning sessions were an education and inspiration for me. My friends Barbara Sandrisser and Robert Tsukayama escorted me all over Washington, D.C., to photograph public art and have consistently plied me with good company and excellent dinners, as well as literature on promising topics. Anne Serafin, Pam Allara, and Josephine Simon read and critiqued segments of early drafts. My writers' group at the Women's Studies Research Center at Brandeis read and very critically discussed two chapters in progress. Jane Roland Martin bore with me through traumatic writing and editorial crises. Barbara Sandrisser, Marling Mast, and Eleanor Rubin provided me with photographs, and Professor Joseph Agassi of Tel Aviv University gave me philosophical references I needed. When it looked as if the Vietnamese images by Martha Winnaker that I had seen were lost, James Tatum and Michael Boehm provided me with more-recent replacements. Elaine Gurian and Annie Storrs were valuable museum resources, and I am grateful to the Brandeis IT service for helping me reconcile images in various media and rescuing me from several computer catastrophes. I was pleased to present a brief digest of my thesis at a conference on Permanence/(Im)permanence at Carnegie-Mellon University, and I thank Judith Schachter, her staff of conveners of that event, and my fellow panelists and discussants. Seeking images to include in this book has been a fascinating journey that drew me into a new world visually and technologically, and I am grateful for the kindness of strangers along the way. Finally, my thanks to the many friends and acquaintances, in and out of museums who have shared my interest, accompanied my wanderings, and listened to me as I worked through my thoughts. They have impelled me to become as clear and articulate as I can be, and I hope to live up to their effort.

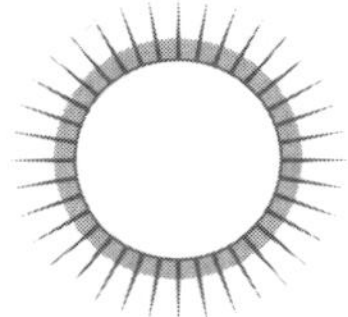

Introduction

I was one of the thousands of people drawn to New York by the Christo *Gates* project in February 2005. Billed as "the biggest public art event the city has ever seen," it was surely colossal, but that was not the sole source of its fascination.[1] The long-awaited event arrived in Central Park as an unexpected antidote to September 11, 2001, bringing joy in place of the persistent gloom. Strangers talked to strangers, photographed one another, and sat together on park benches taking in the sounds of the flapping fabric and the play of light upon it. Although some purists question whether *The Gates* is art and others challenge its merit, there is no doubt that it is public. More importantly, it constructed a public out of the mass of individual visitors who came to experience it. However briefly, we—most of us perfect strangers to one another—came together in fellowship. We were not a local community: neither were we joined in a common mission, but *The Gates* created a bond amongst us whose impact remains powerful while baffling to skeptics.

When a friend asked me afterwards what I thought of *The Gates*, I began by telling her about the light, air, sound, and color; the breeze; the cheerful people wearing "saffron" accessories; dogs in fashionable vests; children in strollers; bicycles; and the urban hawk Pale Male—whose reconstructed nest at an apartment across the street drew a long queue of tourists to a strategically located telescope.[2] As I went on and on, she finally interrupted to say, "But you're telling me about everything else. What about the art?" "That is the art," I answered. The art is its gestation, history, the public it gathers and reactions it evokes, and the memories it leaves behind. It is a process, not a thing. Like Christo's earlier wrappings, constructions, and curtains, this environmental transformation is a cultural drama whose meaning attaches to all of the political, economic, social, and environmental issues of our time. The spectacle affects us without text or aesthetic manifesto through every sense and instinct, recalling the forms and histories of all art.

Who could have predicted the events, twenty-six years and more in the making, that forged *The Gates* community today? It made people happy, and we needed that now. Whether experienced at ground level for easy eye-catching and eavesdropping, or from a distance, or from above, or, less intensely, even through images, *The Gates* was a gathering current. Its site was a vast open-air stage that excluded no one and where every object became a prop. There was no scripted plotline to define beginning, middle, and end, but an environment virtually sculpted to affect "an experience" that immersed participants, leaving them with a sense of value somehow consolidated in memory.[3]

Its presence prolonged, diffused, and etherealized, *The Gates* was reflected in the pyramidal windows of the Metropolitan Museum, caught in scattered glimpses from within, and again, viewable among excited companions from the regal height of the museum's rooftop. The Met glowed in its fragile presence, as the colorful banners flickered ahead and then danced out of sight, melding the museum into the spectacle of moving figures and masses. *The Gates* extended the museum's glamor, and the two constructions merged into a single, vibrant work of art.

Emerging from the park afterwards, visitors joined a celebration that continued into the streets and whose ending is indeterminate. One grew sensitized to ripples, street noises, tones, and patterns ordinarily unnoticed, vernacular reminders, oddly Zen-like, that divulge possibilities still uncontemplated. As public art, *The Gates* project is at once a souvenir of the present moment and a monument to events of past and future yet commemorative of neither heroes nor victims.

The art of Christo and Jeanne-Claude commands attention; it does not inspire indifferent responses. Cohorts of both devotees and denouncers appear everywhere, broadcasting their contradictory opinions. Intrigued by the enthusiasm that such art elicits and by its nonviolent, yet outspoken loyalists, I have been moved to study public art more closely. A probe of its history and development over the past century reveals astounding reversals and transformations that, I believe, are also present but in less clearly articulated form in other cultural destinations. Examining the trajectory of public art might, therefore, illuminate the slower-paced journey of the museum.

Traditionally the museum is represented as an institution, magisterial, materially solid, and sometimes spectacular, whose function is to collect and keep (curate) works of art among other types of objects and artifacts and to promote knowledge about them. Notwithstanding this stable and lordly calling, the museum is, in a sense, imperceptible; it is the invisible eminence that wields power to move and reassimilate us. This is the power of art. An unmediated aesthetic presence insinuates itself into our being, causing us to see and understand things differently.[4] Unlike most works of art, however, the museum—until recently—possessed an aura of legitimacy and the authority to bestow or withhold judgment upon the objects under its control. Its anonymous and indirect validation enhanced the aura of specific and fallible authorship. The guaranteed authenticity of the museum's content, promissory of truth, uncoupled the museum from responsibility for what it represented or the need to vindicate it. But, concealed behind the assurance of detached objectivity, contemporary critics have disclosed the museum's unwillingness to acknowledge its own cognitive and moral preconceptions.[5] These have never been absent and are not absent now, but they are changing, and the direction of their current movement mirrors that of public art, which has always been exhortative.

As an actor whose history includes molding and guiding people's thoughts and actions, the museum cannot suddenly reverse itself and license subjective experience. Assuming the mantle of pluralism and democracy, many museums now avoid absolute declarations of "unvarnished truth" and offer the option to "make what you will" of a vast variety of experiential stimuli, but the museum owes the public the additional truth of its own purpose-driven core, which it typically continues to withhold. I believe this reticence is due more to ambivalence and confusion than to guile on the part of museum leadership. The effect upon the public, however, is bewilderment.

Museums pronounce education to be a major component of their mission and rely on exhibits and charismatic personnel to achieve it. The formative impulse goes beyond overt instruction, however. Aesthetically conveyed throughout, it is transmitted substantially through the deployment of objects and the conduct of people. The shaping of publics is not accidental; it is what museums have always done. Today's publics are more numerous than those of the past, the techniques of their assemblage more complexly industrialized, and their effects more unpredictable. Conventional behavior by visitors can no longer be assumed. Traditionally an attitude of respectful decorum was expected of them; one did not romp through a museum.[6] Contemporary museum behavior has become more relaxed, in part as a result of new expectations fostered by museums and by their advertised openness. Participation in the form of "hands-on" activities, interactive exhibitions, and theatrical devices displaces more passive presentations such as dioramas and docent lectures. We cannot be certain of the actual range of responses to these early devices, but present-day visitors are encouraged to ask questions and express opinions. This is no trivial innovation; it represents a differently constructed view of what an audience is and should be—one that is not awed by the museum but acquits itself as equal. This posture embodies a political perception, also embraced by the museum, which parallels actual social change. It reflects the egalitarianism also nurtured in the public art of recent decades.

The traditional museum's uniqueness relative to other institutions derived from the mute materiality of its contents and their precious irreplaceability.[7] The museum's dedication to objects also singled out the institution ethically: where else could you even consider the rescue of an inanimate thing over a human being in the event of catastrophe? In the museum you were supposed to save the Rembrandt painting from the flames, not the director or the visitors. Museums were special: guardians of objects deemed fixed in significance, they embodied the wisdom and culture of earlier generations and other worlds. Things were valued as meaningful objects, which people came to honor and learn from. Infused with what has since been called "methodological fetishism," the objects took on a social life separate from that of the genius of the people—creators, users, and collectors, who successively encountered them. The things, therefore, linked people unconsciously, through and across civilizations, and promoted experiences that were collectively enhancing and collaboratively enhanced.[8] The things gained new and additional value as museum objects that even the most priceless of them would have lacked in their prior incarnation. And the museum, as purveyor of such prized items and protectors of their corporeal soul, also acquired a spiritually elevated status.

That peculiar object-centered fixation shifted toward the end of the twentieth century, when a preference for process over stasis also emerged. Now museums declared themselves visitor- or, more broadly, people-centered. Instead of hiding in secluded parks and behind grand and intimidating facades, where unseen curators grind their lives away in research, museums professed to be at the heart of communities with which they earnestly sought interaction and with whose interests they identified. Even the most object-rich and traditionally oriented museums abandoned their lofty isolation and announced their purpose to be face-to-face engagement with the public. This public was deemed coequal, neither devoid of cultural enlightenment nor in need of spiritual uplift but wanting only the stimuli to experiential expansion.

The causes, reasons, motives, and merits behind this shift have been well analyzed by museographers and cultural historians, but the museum continues to be depicted popularly and in practice as a magnificent locus for people to encounter things. That model hardly extends the museum's business beyond fussing over material objects and fixed interpretations and persistently underestimates the dynamic relationship between the museum and the public. It misconstrues the role played by the public. At the same time, it fails to note that the contemporary museum manages experience as subtly as it formerly transmitted knowledge. The disembodied agency of the museum suffuses and sometimes preempts the will of particular individuals.[9]

I concentrate here on the unique ability of the museum to change the way people think and feel, affected indirectly through the manipulation of things.[10] Seeing an exhibition is not merely observing a group of objects: the same objects differently assembled or under other circumstances will be differently seen and differently understood. An unstated intentionality expressive of the museum nevertheless underlies specific curatorial and design team projects. This purposiveness cannot be encapsulated in mission statements or year-end reports, for it is not a deliberate program but comes across much as a person's character is revealed through habit and gesture—and actually comes to be only as the conduct of the agent happens over time. This museum persona, like that of an individual person, is the foundation of action rather than a sum of particular acts, and it flavors every act (or exhibition) the agent performs. We judge the agent in its perceived light and not in virtue of any single act or professed conviction.

The museum, of course, is not a person in a strict sense. It does not think, bleed, or feel, but it does act purposefully and is far from passive. The attribution of creative power and attendant moral responsibility to it relates to my proposal to assimilate the museum to public art.[11] I view the museum as an artifact, a product of collective human design, that bears aesthetic and cultural interest but is unlike the works of art that are typically displayed on the interior walls of an art museum. I therefore call the museum "art," but not "museum art," which is destined to be privately contemplated. If it makes sense to consider the museum "art" at all, then surely it is "public art." The museum is inherently public, a gathering place that publicly generates private experiences. Anomalously it assembles people in a public space, where, in a manner distinct from that of simultaneous yet independent theater attendees, they engage individually in nonsynchronized exchanges. Hovering over those subjective events and orchestrating them is the museum's presence, which fuses elements unanticipated even by itself. Innumerable past encounters and features of the immediate environment conspire to produce impressions that are public by virtue of their collaborative origin and destination and private chiefly in their experiential confinement. All things considered, it seems to me that the museum has more in common with the aesthetic productions scattered in profusion throughout the world than with those treasures sheltered within its premises, which, in this book, I will call "private art" or sometimes "museum art."

Public art, unlike the more sequestered private art, appears in pedestrian places, like playgrounds and shopping malls, along highways and the ordinary junctures of life. Even when its purpose is to celebrate heroism and transcendence, it aims to speak to common people and is meant to bring them together. Of late, it has descended from the pedestal that separates art from the public and incorporated the public more closely into itself.[12] This merging symbolizes a new perception and attitude toward collaboration, mutual illumination, and understanding. It repudiates the hierarchical structures of a society that "talks down" to people and purports to educate them by "filling up" empty cavities with prescribed lessons. Public art in the late twentieth century fostered active participation rather than submissive reverence. It encouraged self-respect and emboldened grass-roots creativity. Controversial from the outset, it was not, nor is it now, universally accepted, but it launched an activist consciousness and a burst of populist aesthetic expression that coincided with people's demand for social empowerment.

Related to the social proliferation of public art was its material dispersal—from recyclable stuff to random sounds and ordinary movement. Replacing solid, stationary monuments that massively occupy space, fleeting shafts of light, and precariously heaped piles of junk—doomed to disintegrate—now designated the fate of matter, the passage of time, the elusiveness of memory, and the fallibility of judgment. But these things are rarely understood alike; an agile public art delivers them fractionated to resonate uniquely in each perceiver's heart. The new public art is mobile and practical. It exposes the ordinary, provokes criticism, and subjects itself to question as it probes outward and inward, releasing fresh ideas. Such volatility is a fertile model for the museum, which, likewise, is reexamining its own foundations and reconceptualizing its future.

Public art solicits self-reinvention. Rejecting a monolith does not sanction unlimited license, but it encourages experimentation, dialogue with critics, and bold exposure. These are tactics, not ends in themselves or ultimate solutions. In practice, public art has ventured in collaboration with environmental enterprises and landscape and maintenance projects (such as waterworks, transportation, and sanitation systems). Some public art is all but indiscernible from urban amenities such as park benches, gardens, and bus stop shelters. Some productions disappear after a few hours, lasting only for the duration of a river trip or a street procession, and some are dispersed into cyberspace immediately.[13]

Less dramatically perhaps, the museum is taking similar steps toward ephemerality. Its movement is held in check by its historic association with permanence and truth—not to mention the sheer bulk of massive buildings and objects. A growing professionalism and a corps of certified exhibitioneers may also interfere with taking risks freely. Heavily obligated museums, without independent means, are indentured to sponsors and must navigate the shoals of partisan opinion in order to achieve an acceptable level of discretion.[14] While I do not mean to endorse indiscretion or to dislodge conventional respect toward the museum, I want to vindicate a regard for material things that also affirms the brevity of their endurance, their inevitable decomposition, the volatility of their value, and some doubt about their significance.

In this book, I challenge the foundational tenets of the museum, notably *ars longa, vita brevis*. Hippocrates' dictum notwithstanding, twenty-first-century art is disintegrating and blending with life. Museums are relinquishing their claims to the immutable and universal. Instead of transmitting eternal values to the public, they seek to resonate with transient ideas and to stimulate sympathetic vibration. I hope to make this motion less random. Simply jiggling with the times is not acceptable. I use public art as a model, understanding that museums cannot and need not strive to equal the ephemerality of a parade or a vapor trail. Nonetheless, museums can commit to short-lived realities and provisional truths without violating a sacred trust. Collectively and individually, they should stand firmly, but not fixedly, behind what they choose to say—and they should say something.

I begin, in chapter 1, with an exploration of the concept of experience as traditionally analyzed. Museums have always evoked experience, but until recently have not declared this to be their primary objective. I maintain that experience is intrinsically private and subjective, hence inevitably plural, and that designing its production on a massive scale neither is nor ought to be the museum's ultimate goal. Whatever might qualify as a singular or shared "public experience" can only be engineered and is therefore ethically and aesthetically suspect as conducive to a lobotomized society whose members have lost their critical faculties.

Chapter 2 is an extended analysis of the concepts of public and private and examines the difficult relationship between them. I briefly survey the history of the notion of *the public* (not to be confused with a public or with the adjective "public"). I also introduce the term "private art" and argue that, while it is a late arrival upon the world's art scene, it has—in the Western world, which gave birth to the museum—become the standard against which art in general is measured. Ranged against that standard are various nonprivate art forms, including public art, which, until recently, did not figure, as such, in the canon determined by the art world.

In chapter 3, I extract the concept of public art from a history of its recognized instances. While this is a question-begging procedure, and some of the examples I discuss might be challenged, my aim is not lexical certainty but a workable demarcation between public art and private art in the absence of clear definition. I claim that their difference is social, not political, in that constructing a public is an essential component of public art. Private art, in contrast, courts public reception indifferently and nonessentially. Both types of art are potentially but not necessarily political. Apart from their social meaning, public art and private art are alike in their disposition of matter and form. I trace a brief history of public art in America up to its radical redefinition and social redirection in the 1960s.

Chapter 4 picks up where the preceding chapter left off, examining events of the 1960s that pertain to the changes in public art. In particular, I stress the prevalent decommodification of art, its dematerialization and impermanence. While many of these features also appeared as contingent aesthetic devices in private art of the era, they were explicitly and intentionally emphasized by public artists in the context of constructing a public. For the creators of private art this was not an issue, since their use of aesthetic experimentation need not take the public into account.

Chapter 5 begins with conventional descriptions of the museum as a uniquely distinguished place, in which cultural artifacts are preserved, studied, and exhibited. I discuss some standard definitions and a variety of critical assessments of the museum that have been made by museum insiders and by cultural critics from an external perspective. Following my observation in chapter 1 that museums are undergoing radical self-assessment and significant change, in this chapter I selectively discuss some whose development coincides with transformations concurrently pursued by contemporary public art.

Chapter 6 expatiates on the museum's resolution to focus on people rather than things. I suggest that this objective posits a false dichotomy, since museums cannot be exclusively about either people or things but necessarily depend on both. Like public art, the museum supervenes upon objects and people, interlacing them in a redefined time and space. Dramatically reaching out, museums assemble and mediate, gathering publics that find and recognize themselves aesthetically linked in a social unit.[15] Empathic indirection, not direct discourse, is the solder that joins them, and their fusion may be weak and temporary. It can be discordant or even explosive, but its aesthetic scaffolding offers shelter and museums can afford to be somewhat adventurous under its protection. Although unable to be as radically inventive as public art has been, museums are adopting similar innovative approaches that stretch their conventional description almost—but not quite—to the breaking point. In my opinion, their credibility is jeopardized more by holding back and failing to declare themselves than by taking positions boldly.

The experience of public art is instructive. It has not been uniform, and it has been controversial. Forthright museums can expect similar conflict, but that is a mark of their vitality. While not an end in itself, dispute is a means to achieving plateaus of clarity. Museums have the opportunity to sharpen attentive interest in a world where uncertainty and differences are prominent and often frightening. The path taken by public art does not erase difference; it leads to a relaxation of uniformity and conformity. It enables people to live compatibly with disunity, surrounded by hypothetical conditions. This nomadic promotion of "what if . . ." does not negate the affirmation of value but renders it meaningful. It averts the condescending tolerance of "diversity" and the disingenuous pronouncement of fundamental "oneness." The museum makes room for dissonance.

Chapter 7, the conclusion, offers an example of a museum that is purely ephemeral, blurring the distinction between museum and public art in all but name. I do not think its kind will displace the audacious museum designs that are being realized at this moment. But they too are a form of public art, intended for permanence, which is sometimes abbreviated. They speak to more than housing for objects: with enormous optimism, they propose to construct a public of all the people of the world.

Shortly after my experience with *The Gates*, I took part in the ceremonial dismantling of a mandala, a sacred sand painting laboriously constructed by Tibetan nuns at Wellesley College's Davis Museum and Cultural Center.[16] Visitors made their way in and out of galleries of abstract, pop, and conceptual art before crowding into the bare room in which the nuns had spent a week praying and creating the mandala. The mandala, mounted on a raised platform at the center, was composed of brightly colored Tibetan sand mingled with pale sand from Cape Cod to signify peace and healing in east and west. It was cordoned off from the circle of camera-snapping viewers seated on camp stools or jostling for positions behind them. The nuns were now reversing their earlier construction process, gathering in a circle, again to chant prayers and to re-collect the sand into small vessels. Robed in saffron, like *The Gates*, the nuns played trumpets and Tibetan percussion instruments. Their task completed, they circled the room three times with their burden and, pied piper-like, led the crowd of onlookers out of the museum, zigzagging through the wooded wintry landscape to a bridge overlooking Wellesley's lake. From there, with more chanting, they poured the libation of sand into the water. It scattered like feathers in the wind as it descended and was gone. As I reflected upon dust returning to dust, someone behind me spoke regretfully of the ephemerality of "all that work." That was a voice of solid American pragmatism with an alternative set of cultural values.

Pondering this religious observance, some members of the audience questioned its place in an art museum. Is the performance of a religious rite art? Does it "belong" in a museum? Was this "event" a cultural artifact displayed as performance rather than in the usual museal manner as static metonymic fragments?[17] Was this exhibition an instance of avant-garde curatorial audacity that engaged the public experientially, or was it an embarrassing moment of "postcolonial othering" in which a sacred ritual was objectified? Could it be public art—theatrically converging upon the landscape where it concluded? I wondered too about these boundaries and their transgressions, and as I questioned people, I found little agreement and less consciousness of the radical conceptual assumptions at the heart of their puzzlement.

These and related preoccupations have moved me to write this book. I believe that a new phenomenon is gestating in cultural institutions, but its coming to birth is difficult. Apart from museum workers, museologists, and museographers, most people still regard museums as static structures, places where things are kept to be studied and enjoyed, much as books are preserved in libraries (without the privilege of taking them home). The variety of civil events that also take place in museums (and libraries) is taken as incidental, a secondary byproduct that draws attendance to exhibitions and makes good use of the spacious and impressive architecture. Perceived as underutilized real estate and tourist attractions, museums are appreciated as community resources, but however sensational their structure, they are not understood as art, much less as public art.

Notes

1. The work consisted of 7,532 metal and vinyl "gates" supporting 116,389 miles of saffron (orange) fabric placed at intervals throughout twenty-three miles of footpaths that crisscross Central Park. Some 640 paid workers helped install it, and another 340 people were on hand in the park as "ambassadors" to answer questions and fix glitches throughout the sixteen days of the project.

2. The nest had been removed when the hawk and his mate left untidy droppings and unfinished meals on the street below, but after a torrent of popular protest it was restored with fortifications.

3. A woman quoted in a *New York Times* article (February 13, 2005) mused: "It will be fascinating when they're gone." Remaining as a presence in imagination, even the negative space of its absence will continue as a monument of sorts. A progeny of diminutive and homemade imitators of *The Gates* was immediately engendered and distributed by Web around the world, prolonging the work's ephemeral reality.

4. In this, museums are unlike typical institutions—banks, hospitals, universities, and research centers—which are overtly directive, with explicit didactic functions related to their primary objectives.

5. At this point, I am avoiding explanations in terms of caste, class, tribal or doctrinal difference, or the attribution of deception, affirming minimally that authenticity is not identical with truth.

6. Recent studies claim that visitors rarely spend as much as a minute per object. This infuriating statistic is reached, however, by averaging the number of items in the museum against total time spent by visitors in the museum. Many visitors do saunter past objects casting rapid glances here and there, stopping only briefly to look carefully, but many others choose purposefully to examine particular objects with protracted attention. Few scoot by on roller skates, but strollers and noisy children are common, and decorum is no longer what it used to be. In fact, there have always been pockets of independence,

where people make use of the museum to indulge in their own, peculiarly appreciative, pastimes.

7. Department stores, hospitals, graveyards, and churches—all of which have been likened to museums—also value objects, but they do not assign paramount value to them. Museums proudly did that but no longer do so without serious soul searching.

8. The expression, coined by Arjun Appadurai, in *The Social Life of Things: Commodities in Cultural Perspective* (Cambridge, 1986) points to a condition different from that identified by Marx as "commodity fetishism" (the mystification of human labor that has gone into the making of objects). Appadurai refers to a mutual synthesis between inanimate objects and human subjects, such that their alleged dualism is denied. Theoretically, human actors encode things with significance, but in practice we learn from things how human life is organized, and this perpetually changing mutual construction defines both elements.

9. A minority of museums is overtly activist in collaboration with other agencies that are striving to alter public behavior. Some aquaria and natural history museums, for example, are working as ecological and environmental change agents, health advisors, etc. They are not "neutral" and do not pretend disinterested objectivity but represent themselves as public citizens with explicit reform agendas. This collective stance on the part of a museum is not to be confused with the individual engagement of its workers, which may or may not conform to the museum's objectives. From a traditional perspective, the explicit abandonment of "neutrality" is a threat to the museum's fundamental identity. Currently, a few agenda-driven private museums are also emerging to advance specific doctrines such as "intelligent design."

10. Other means, such as words, physical coercion, influence peddling, money, or other rewards and punishments are not excluded, but they are not the unique domain of museums.

11. The attribution of a persona, and therefore of a moral identity, to the museum was also an important feature of my previous book, *The Museum in Transition: A Philosophical Perspective* (Washington, D.C.: Smithsonian Institution Press, 2000).

12. A great deal of public art has never been exalted. It appears on postage stamps, money, deeds and warrants, and most official signage, but figuratively speaking, these too were "pedestal art," often featuring images of heroes and classical deities. Today, the public domain is filled with common cartoon characters, cute animals, and toys.

13. Some short-term projects are based upon years of preparation that engages the work of researchers, public officials, and volunteers. Conforming to Christo and Jeanne-Claude's representation, all this is integral to the work of art and so extends both its duration and outreach. See also Mags Harries and Lajos Heder's 1999 temporary installation *Bronx River Golden Ball* (New York), in which a large

ball was accompanied down a ten-mile stretch of river, stopping at points for celebration and environmental observation. viz. *Reaching Water*, CAC Gallery, Cambridge, Mass.: Cambridge Arts Council (2004).

14. Independently funded and operated museums, such as the Bob Jones University Museum, in Greenville, South Carolina, which claims to have the largest collection of religious art in the Western Hemisphere, have no such constraints. Its guidelines are therefore able to instruct visitors that "you may enjoy and learn something from the depiction of a religious legend, but you find salvation only in Jesus Christ. . . ." viz. Sarah E. Worth, "The Ethics of Exhibitions: On the Presentation of Religious Art" in *The Journal of Aesthetics and Art Criticism* 62, no. 3 (2004).

15. Arthur Danto is mistrustful of an identity politics that usurps the sensibility that gave birth to the museum and now transforms it. He is right that what will emerge is not the museum as we know it, but the hybrid offspring coming to birth might also reinvigorate the museum concept. "Museums and the Thirsting Millions," *After the End of Art: Contemporary Art and the Pale of History* (Princeton, N.J.: Princeton University Press, 1998).

16. Davis Museum, February 20–March 1, 2005.

17. Christian and Jewish sacramental objects are often preserved in museums, both as art and artifact, but I have never seen a seder celebrated or a baptism performed inside a museum. Perhaps secular weddings take place in rented museum space alongside birthday parties and corporate dinners, but since the days of private cabinets, the guests do not eat from the royal china or sit on collectible roped-off chairs.

The Experiential Museum

The metaphysical experience is at the mercy of the physical event.

—TOM STOPPARD

A great trip is not about the destination; it's all about the experience.

—PETER GREENBERG

The Meaning of Experience

Experience happens everywhere and at all times, sometimes with life-transforming intensity and sometimes beneath notice. Both cherished and feared, it defines us yet may also destroy us. To experience is to be, though the converse is not true. Experience does not exist unattached. Wherever there is experience, there must be something that experiences, a subject for which the experience is an object. In a nutshell, this is what Rene Descartes's famous dictum, "I think, therefore I am" is all about.[1] The phrase has been taken to affirm substantively more than it strictly entails. It does not imply that you or I exist, but it does seem to warrant belief that having experience requires an entity that experiences. A little bit of experience can go a long way. It suggests the possibility of reflective self-knowledge. No wonder we seek and prize it.

So what is experience? A vast literature details types of experience, but can experiences be enumerated? Measured? Compared? Are they distinct like grains of sand or uncountable like drops in a glass of water? Can they be "marked off" on a scale? Do they have fixed duration? Do they occur in sequence or simultaneously? Or are they merged in an infinite present? Do they endure beyond their "having?" Where do they go when completed? Can they be repeated or revived when past? Can they be conjured at will, or do they "just happen?" Are they retained in memory or foreseen in hope? Do they "belong" exclusively to whoever "has" them or can they be shared? Can they be bought and sold? In short, there is much to wonder about what experience is, how it comes about, where it leads, and what to do with it.

Most of our experience is routine, too familiar to elicit attention. We inhale and exhale noticing only if we are short of breath or asthmatic, in which case every gasp for air is an acutely felt triumph that preempts the act of breathing itself. Only the disruptions in the constant stream of sights, sounds, and other events stand out as "experiences"; yet the normal as much as the abnormal and unusual is experienced. The philosopher John Dewey described experience as a process with several phases.[2] One is instrumental, serving as means to an end, and we are inclined to overlook it in favor of the final phase that absorbs and fulfills it. Having mastered the skills of lifting a spoon to one's mouth, of chewing and then swallowing, we cease to attend to these operations and focus on the end in view, eating, which may, in turn, be ignored as a means to other ends and experiences. We are aware of the intervening stages only if they are disabled and we need to relearn them.

Dewey called some of our experiences *consummatory*: in these, means and ends are no longer differentiated. There are a felt unity and completeness that are satisfying. We remember such experience not as a sequence of antecedent and consequent moments but as a single totality, individualized and self-sufficient. The experience is complete unto itself: Dewey denotes it "an experience." It is a fusion of the experiencing person, the subject, and that which is experienced, the object—a complex of environmental conditions, subjective apprehensions, and cognitive and emotional responses, all suffused with a pervasive quality that is prototypically aesthetic. These experiences, even when bitter or sad, are uniquely gratifying; they add zest and vitality to every aspect of human life. The enjoyment of art is a special instance of consummatory experience but not the only one. An exquisite dinner, a terrible fright, a fascinating conversation, or a moment of solitude—all qualify as examples of such aesthetically integrated experiences. They are not rare but are too often underappreciated.

Dewey disagrees with those philosophers who pronounce aesthetic experience to be irreducible to ordinary biological, emotive, or cognitive conditions. These theorists claim that only certain circumstances or types of objects can initiate the aesthetic experience, which they identify with a unique subjective state of mind that sets the aesthetic constellation apart from ordinary living. Dewey's view of consummatory experience depicts it as organically grounded and continuous with the whole person. In a sense, each of us is the sum of experiences we have accumulated over a lifetime. They shape us as we shape them, constantly becoming who we are. The experiences we acquire are not "out there" to be picked up like seashells but congeal within us through our transactions in the world. They are not delivered to us ready-made but are undergone; they exist in their undergoing and persist in what we subsequently undergo. Some experiences conflict and contradict others: defying the laws of logic, they challenge us to resolve them, evoking interest and wonder, another level of experience.

Most accounts of experience concur that it is generative and often transformative. However we are changed by or grow through experience, the process is invariably mediated by something—a challenge, falling in love, a dream, a tragic accident, a text or image—something that is translated to become specifically one's own, for experience is never generically apprehended. I suggest that the museum is an agent that mediates experience, publicly presiding over and bringing into focus objects and ideas—occasionally incompatible ones—to make them accessible as private experience.

Origin of the Experiential Museum

If human flourishing depends on our growth through experience, we rely on various institutions to help us cultivate the ability to gain and utilize it. Museums have been resources that harbor objects extracted from someone's experiential domain and introduced into someone else's. What, then, can be meant by the term "experiential museum" above and beyond the pallid observation that people have experiences in museums as they do elsewhere? The current expression is meaningful only against the background of the traditionally designated "collection-based" museum. The latter term encapsulates the notion that the soul of a museum is its collection and that therein lies its identity. Collections have been the foundation of museums for several centuries. They were understood to be what the museum was about. Some museums preserved the trophies of conquest; others featured natural rarities, and still others the fruits of human artifice. Most were assembled under the guidance of some encyclopedic or philosophical classification system and were committed to its demonstration. Every museum embodied the passion of its founders and excited that of disciples. Some of them stirred up violent theological and scientific controversies. There is no doubt that they stimulated a host of intense experiences, yet no one would have designated them "experiential museums." They were not "about" experiences, although having and remembering interesting experiences were certainly among their benefits. Experience, as such, however, can be neither collected nor stored. The memory of its accumulation and delight in possession of a collection are experiences that enhance its value to someone, but they are not on display in the museum. While an ever-present potential of the museum, experience was not its goal, nor was it considered the motivation for collecting or the lure that enticed visitors into the museum. Experience was a welcome adjunct to the real business of the traditional museum, which centered upon the collection. Today, the focus is reversed and museum collections are perceived as instrumental to the production of experience.

In America, the language descriptive of museums began to change some time in the late 1960s or early 1970s. A number of factors played a part—the general irreverence toward property of the 1960s, the antiauthoritarianism that associated museums with a privileged elite, the civil rights and antiwar struggles, the early women's movement, and the cultural rebellion of young people. Collecting material objects according to hierarchical rankings seemed offensive on all fronts. But some reversals were specific to the museum world itself. Stephen Weil, writing in 1990, refers to "an emerging new paradigm," a term he attributes to the Dutch museologist Peter van Mensch, who highlights communication as a primary function of museums.[3] This marked a new awareness of the inseparability of the museum's interpretive and exhibition functions, but it does not yet valorize the knowledge, values, and skills that visitors bring to the museum. Although the focus on communication acknowledged that things do not speak unequivocally for themselves, the museum continued to regard itself as a transmitter of knowledge about something, a one-way process whose success lies in its (largely immeasurable) ability to control the receptive experience of an audience. At this point, the challenge to the museum was to present objects—still the central concern—in a manner that would mediate and convey an intended message. Interpretation was the significant concept, while the audience remained a monolithic and essentially passive unknown. The problem perceived was how to impart ideas to the public successfully, not how to receive and incorporate ideas that would reflect a collaborative endeavor.

Audience surveys were rare before the twentieth century. Some studies tracked visitor movement through the museum and recorded visitor behavior. In the 1930s, demographic studies had categorized visitors, but interviewing them was not common before the 1960s and was rarely interactive. The 1960s and 1970s witnessed an explosion of new survey and assessment techniques, many of them adapted from social science and commercial resources. Importantly, they solicited not only information about their subjects' reaction to exhibits, whether or not they had been "correctly" apprehended, but also addressed the wants and interests of the public. Museums were becoming cognizant—and cared—about the disconnect between their own intention and expectations and the perceptions of their visitors. Armed with better observation practices, exhibit designers worked hard to figure out how to transmit their ideas more effectively, but they were not yet prepared to give up control to the point of allowing visitors to "make meaning" entirely on their own. The "voice" of the museum was still that of a benign but authoritative educator with a lesson to deliver. The quality of the "museum experience" might be a persuasive means, but it was not yet an end.

Children's museums were among the first to take the particular character of their audience seriously. Although they had existed as didactic institutions following the old model for nearly a century, they entered a new phase in which the changing needs and capacities of the children whom they served became central issues.[4] They still collected and displayed objects, but as the makeup of their communities shifted, so did their educational imperatives. Adapting to preliterate and multilingual audiences, they had to rely on experiential procedures that were culturally nonrestrictive.[5] Gradually they began to appreciate the creative impulses of their new public. Science museums, likewise, took off in a new direction in the 1960s. Breaking away from a pattern of depicting the accomplishments and products of science, they began treating objects as instruments to be used in the teaching of scientific concepts. The artifacts collected or, more often, designed and constructed in the museum held value as devices that visitors could manipulate to help them grasp concepts rather than as evidence of fact or tributes to the genius of the past. Objects now were treated as source material meant to generate inquiry rather than as illustrations of established ideas or devices to demonstrate truths.

There was precedent for this approach in Europe. The German Museum for Masterworks of Natural Science and Engineering, known simply as the Deutsches Museum, was conceived prior to World War I but not realized until afterward. The purpose of its founder, Oskar von Miller, was to teach industrial history and scientific principles in the museum by means of demonstrations and visitor-participation devices. The museum was severely bombed during World War II but gradually rebuilt itself with a new collection of participatory exhibits designed to illustrate modern scientific concepts. Popular science education was also the motivation behind the Palais de la Decouverte, founded in 1937 in Paris. It held few historic artifacts but featured constant experimental demonstrations performed by university students and was intended as a sort of living textbook of science, complete with laboratories.[6] These museums, which focused less on relating facts or history than on engaging the public in the practice of science, had a great influence on the development of science museums in the United States. Following World War II, a growing awareness of the importance of technology and the role of science in public policy making led to more museums whose primary aim was to teach *how*, not *what*. The very nature of their subject matter was experimental and so challenging to the "hands off" policy of traditional collection-based museums. Of the artifacts the new type of museum contained, a large proportion was deliberately designed to be touched, cranked, listened to, or somehow manipulated. They were neither rare nor precious but were useful for the kind of "hands on" teaching that was soon to win attention among liberal educators.

So far did such applications deviate from the classical model of the museum, that the new science centers were initially denied status as museums by the American Association of Museums (AAM). They responded by creating their own advocacy organization, the Association of Science and Technology Centers, in 1974, and ultimately were accredited by the AAM as well. Twenty years later, their activist, "participatory" style had become normative throughout the museum world. The museum had become a resource for rendering experience communicable and comprehensible—or that was its claim. In the face of the invincible privacy of experience, the museum had recreated itself as a phenomenological springboard for the transcription of experience in the validating presence of a public.

Common to these innovative museum approaches is the transfer of interest from the collection of material objects held by the museum (and their attendant care) to the manner in which museum visitors were to make use of them. Both children's museums and science centers were as dedicated as ever to the goal of educating their public; what had changed was the pragmatics of how that aim was to be accomplished. The difference stemmed in part from a profound theoretical reassessment of what knowledge is and correlatively of learning and teaching. The passivity implicit in the system of pedagogy prevalent prior to the 1960s—the so-called "banking model" of deposit and investment—presumed that learners were empty receptacles differing only in capacity. Now they were viewed as variegated, textured beings, marked by their own history and experience and by the constructive proclivities they brought with them into the museum. In order to reach their visitors, museums must therefore study them. Museums were thus a part of the broader revolution of the era whose slogans professed to put people before property and, not incidentally, to valorize experience as a teaching tool.

But museums necessarily retained their historic loyalty to the things they preserved and held in trust. The demotion of objects from intrinsically valuable collectibles to instrumental devices ran against the grain. It happened gradually and in stages, augmented by America's throwaway economy and the ease with which young people's affection gravitated toward the virtual world revealed by computers. The decline of the object continues today in rhetoric that retails dematerialized assets and experiences, but it began mildly in the museum and somewhat awkwardly, with educationally motivated attention paid first to visitor-sensitive language and next to visitor-centered exhibition content.

Their ambition to reach out and educate wider audiences stimulated museums to scrutinize the public more carefully and to accommodate to it. Under pressure also from external funding sources that demanded indicators of success, museums needed more progressive planning programs. At the same time, educators were gaining influence within the museum and were proposing a variety of experimental and interactive teaching strategies. Teachers had always been the undervalued interface with the public, a vantage that was now anxiously sought. Visitor surveys and assessments were undertaken, interpretive texts and labels revised; soon, visitor input was consulted in the design and presentation of exhibitions.[7] Exhibition development ceased to be the exclusive and sometimes unwanted responsibility of curators. Teams including designers and "audience advocates" in addition to subject specialists negotiated the complex project of designing exhibitions.[8] Discontented critics of the innovative trend opposed it as "dumbing down," an abandonment of the museum's scholarly responsibility that threatened its authority. But proponents welcomed the steps toward two-way communication that, they hoped, would increase the numbers of and open doors to a greater variety of museum visitors. The public now was clearly recognized as a part of the equation, although the full extent of its stakeholding was not yet realized. Neither was its plurality or its difficulty.

The unfamiliar concept of "museum literacy" had to be absorbed. This was guided by an emerging new populist historiography based on ordinary artifacts rather than on documents. Drawing from the techniques of anthropology and archaeology to carve out the field of material culture studies, researchers in museums were well placed to advance the new historical ideas and vernacular research paradigms. Historians, who had long thought of museums chiefly as material repositories, now turned to their methodologies as well. The stories extracted from things were far from univocal and even more perversely context dependent than written records. They inspired sophisticated museum interpretation and imaginative narrative that relied increasingly on often discrepant oral histories taken from "ordinary" people.[9] Visitor responses to the new exhibits diverged wildly. What had formerly appeared a straightforward explanation of an object that needed only to be well articulated to be grasped now was revealed as a minefield of hypotheticals. No single source could authenticate it; no standard method could legitimate it. A statement by Patterson Williams, then an educator at the Denver Art Museum, signals a crucial transition: "To call for museum literacy . . . is to call for a theory of instruction focused on teaching visitors how to have personally significant experiences with objects."[10] Working collaboratively with selected members of the public, a few museums adopted an open-ended strategy for producing exhibits consistent with an "experience-driven paradigm." No longer sidelined as passive observers, visitors were now at the center of instruction sites, collaborating with museum workers as participant learners. The next move was to make museums personally significant—in the words of Lois H. Silverman, "everyperson his or her own interpreter" engaged in the process of "making meaning together."[11]

The new emphasis on subjectivity and personal experience, concentrating on the wants, history, and interests of the individual viewer, diminishes the perspective of curatorial expertise and scholarly knowledge. Its effectiveness challenged along with its former invisibility, the traditionally omniscient persona of the museum gave way to a polyphonic voice found offensive by some and empowering by others. Defending the move as a triumph for critical independence and creative imagination, the partisans of experience depicted the museum as forum, as catalyst, and as provocateur, a vital site of disputation and dissent in a sea of conformity. Its critics glimpsed the specter of Disneyland and the supermarket. Living on the barricades of the contemporary culture wars, the museum was forced to become self-reflective.

History and Justification

The history of explicitly experiential museums is short, although the exhibition of objects meant to be experienced is as old as museums themselves. No one doubts the passionate engagement of collectors, nor is the tender solicitude of classical curators and conservators a lesser experience. Experiences of pride, greed, envy, competitiveness, love, and intellectual curiosity all have their place in the world's museums. Not everyone who enters them undergoes the same experience, yet the Napoleonic expectation that visitors to the Louvre could be converted from subjection to citizenship through exposure to France's royal treasures suggests remarkable faith in the unequivocal persuasive power of the museum experience. Inviting the public to share experientially in national pride is unlike a declaration of an inviolate truth; it is a calculated appeal to juicy, self-interested acquisitiveness.[12] We may assume that it worked.

The self-identified "experiential museum" reverses classical priorities by promoting the thesis that objects are elements of, and frequently necessary to, the having of experience. Experience is not reducible to its material substrate, but neither is it entirely independent of it. Imagination, unaided by something to fasten upon, is rarely sufficient to contrive a genuine museum experience.[13] Classical museums relied on beauty or oddity or the sumptuous splendor of things to supplement interest in the knowledge they conveyed, while today's museums use auxiliary technologies to trigger the experiential arc that imagination completes.

Born of the interaction between an occasioning object and a perceiving consciousness, experience is altered by affective or cognitive interventions. Museums of the late twentieth century set out to remake themselves into a new dialogic kind of institution by foregrounding aspects of visitor experiences and legitimating them. The claim to endorse the visitor's experiential freedom purported to deflect attention from the museum's own cognitive coerciveness, but this presence cannot be altogether erased, since a part of the baggage that visitors bring with them is the indelible sense of museum authority. The museum's sudden self-effacement is confusing and leads visitors to feel abandoned.

Museums that stress the inherent multivalence of objects to sanction their own manufacture of dramatic experiential enhancements jeopardize the interpretive freedom they pretend to encourage. If, as suggested, all points of view truly were equally valid, then, paradoxically, they would all be equally trivial. Why favor any one in particular? And, while contrived experiences cannot be literally false, they can be fraudulently induced or dangerous. Experience turns out to be even harder to control than meaning, which readily bends to instruction.

Hardly a museum today can stand entirely aloof from the new experiential paradigm, although some resist applying that language to themselves. Selected critics deplore what they call a universal "aestheticizing" tendency that seems attached to the elevation of experience as an end in itself.[14] Indeed, if sheer stimulation were the aim, the real world offers no lack of it. If they are to escape mere redundancy, museums must frame the world in ways that illuminate it. But that entails intentional stylization, as museums have always provided. Only now do they contemplate the practice with ambivalence and embarrassment.

Like a missing puzzle piece, the experiential gambit seemed to fill a gap in conceptualizing the museum. The excitement of experience galvanized the museum world, which sprang to action. Experience is indeed an "eye-opening" force. Who has not suddenly grasped an idea through personal experience that he or she intellectually had understood only vaguely? "Aha! Now I get it!" We memorize rote formulas and "rules of thumb" in school and find them utterly meaningless until experience brings them home. They magically make sense when one applies them. Experiential learning is not a form of proof, however: it is no substitute for argumentative understanding, but it is a tasty aperitif. It opens the mind and readies it for deeper knowledge. Well introduced, experiential exhibitry enlivens the museum climate without spoiling the claim to cognitive advancement. Well administered, experience adds a dramatic twist and brings a gratifying sense of reality to animate descriptive discourse. By validating visitor experience, museums underwrite both individualism and pluralism and energize the interactivity of exhibits.

The inherent authenticity of experience is an additional merit, close to the heart of the classical museum. Authenticity with reference to the provenance of objects is a byword of museum collection. Fakes and frauds are the bane of curatorial reputations, and the effort to certify "the real thing" is never ending. Comparatively speaking, the authenticity of one's own experience is much easier to defend than that of an object. It is undeniable—whether or not it conforms to anything in the world—for no one else has access to it. Yet, although incorrigible, experience is an unreliable guide to any certainty beyond itself. Exploring the gulf between experience and truth might be a very good point of departure for museum pedagogy, but few have ventured to follow it.[15]

It is hard to accept the idea that incorrigible experience has little to do with warranted judgments of fact or value, yet truth is not assessable by the strength of conviction. Feeling certain is a subjective state that is independent of the certainty of what is believed. We are constantly reminded of the merits of learning from experience, and the urge to believe is powerful, but sometimes it needs to be resisted. Museums would do well to apply their history of persuasive authority to cross-examining experience, rather than merely fashioning and celebrating it. Some are beginning to probe experience by testing what can be unlearned from it, and for this task, they are better equipped than institutions burdened with formal curricula.

Experimenting with Experience

Here I will consider two early examples of museums that explicitly declared themselves "experiential." Both approached experience as a means to an end and not as an end in itself. There are significant differences in their objectives, but each departed intentionally from the prevailing paradigm of the collection-centered museum. Each had its reasons.

The Exploratorium, San Francisco's Museum of Science and Art, was founded in 1969 by the physicist and science educator Frank Oppenheimer. Alarmed by the inadequacy of science teaching in America, he wanted to make science more accessible and interesting to the public. The proposal that he brought to potential supporters was for a museum in which people could learn through directly experiencing and manipulating things instead of being told about them. The public was to interact with objects much as experimental scientists do in the natural world or in a laboratory. The objects displayed in the museum were therefore designed to be handled and used. Many were donated scientific apparatus, obsolete technical equipment, or replicas fabricated by the museum's machine shop from textbook models. Beginning with inexpensive, jerry-built, and found materials, the Exploratorium eventually housed over 6,000 objects, but they were hardly a collection in the traditional sense. In fact, defying the convention of the unique and irreplaceable object, the museum staff published a series of "cookbooks" with recipes that explained for the benefit of other museums exactly to what end the exhibits were constructed and how to replicate them. The true museum content, this implied, was not the artifacts as such but rather what took place when people interacted with the exhibits. That was to be an experience. In Deweyan fashion, it would point beyond itself to additional experience and prepare the learner for new understanding.

Writing two decades later, Oppenheimer's friend and colleague Philip Morrison said: "The museum is itself openly subjective. . . . The crux is perception; here learning is direct, experiential. . . . It is that feeling of shared experience that dominates the subjectivity of the research worker and the serious student of science, and here it is offered over and over again to everyone who will try."[16] Note the emphasis on "shared experience," for it was a presumption on the part of the museum founders that, though the visitor's initial encounter was individual, a common logic would follow such private experience. In the end, learners were expected to reach fairly predictable knowledge, since, let us recall, they were not performing groundbreaking experiments that would revolutionize science. They were exploring "the known," but experience would help them understand it. Faith in the observer's ability to profit from experience was the ground of the museum and anchored a hope for human empowerment. Truth arbitrarily dispensed by authority seemed a dubious path to enlightenment, for it weakened confidence in one's own judgment, but conclusions thoughtfully extracted out of one's own experience might lead to learning and, indeed, open the way to genuine knowledge.

The process would be educational. Clearly there were rules of practice and skills that must be mastered: Seeing (touching, hearing) alone is not believing, but it is a plausible point of departure. Sensation is a signal that sets off inquiry as far as the inquirer is able to follow it. One inducement employed by the Exploratorium was strictly phenomenological; visitors were plunged into (or exposed themselves to) an experiential situation by activating an apparatus. The idea was not to stop with the ensuing experience—although that might be fun and did satisfy many visitors—but to go on to an analysis of how and why that observation or experience takes place (again, assuming its conformity to a standard pattern). Exhibits were produced and arranged in groups that reinforced and amplified the original experience, so that visitors could follow "threads" of reasoning suggested by the sequence of experiences or by the young explainers who stood by to help. Visitors were, of course, free to wander independently, selecting their own experiential stream, but Oppenheimer himself believed that there is an order of nature to be discovered that could be traced through successions of experiences analytically scrutinized. He welcomed fanciful alternative theorizing up to a point but tended to be impatient with "wow-enthusiasts" who disregarded the "how" and even more so with those who settled for explanations he considered absurd or irrational and for which no corroborating evidence would be relevant. It was, he insisted, vital that exhibit apparatus be designed to permit accurate and detailed observation, never simplified so as to guarantee the "right" result."[17] Experiences were anticipated, but not preordained. Confusion was tolerated; dissimulation was not, for it would defeat the cognitive point.

The Exploratorium's featuring of experience was much heralded throughout the museum world but not well understood. Many imitators fastened upon the physical interactivity of exhibits and the idea that visitors touched them to make something happen. They ignored the rationale and exaggerated the manipulation. Visitors also, especially children, delighted in pushing buttons, twirling dials, and pressing levers, sometimes without attending to the effects that actually followed. Experience as such was often taken to be the point of the exhibit—seeing an image, lifting a weight, hearing a sound. But the intention of the Exploratorium was not just to make people do something previously forbidden in museums or to make something happen but to implant curiosity and follow it up with exploration: What are the conditions that produce an after-image? How does a lever amplify force? Why does a tone change over distance? The next move, abetted with additional exhibits, was to probe for an answer to the questions generated when something did happen. Failing to understand the entire project, many museums fixed upon the answers and short-circuited the experiential discovery process built into the Exploratorium design. Some museums simply equated experience with animated demonstrations.

Other museums chose to leave questions wide open, wishing to avoid the appearance of authority that might be implied in the analytic sequence of the Exploratorium style. Offering sensations or dilemmas, they gave little further guidance but encouraged visitors to invent their own stories. Unlike the Exploratorium's presumption of a rational path to shared understanding, these museums focused on difference and individualism, urging their visitors to be creatively independent. These museums also tend to deal with huge social issues such as racism, environmental deterioration, and disease that do not lend themselves easily to progressively illuminating experiments. They frequently turn visitors back upon themselves, dramatically asking how they feel and how individuals might improve the world through personal effort. What links these museums to the Exploratorium concept is only their shared conviction that museums must achieve their educative function interactively by enlisting visitors experientially.

My second model of an experiential museum is the U.S. Holocaust Memorial Museum in Washington, D.C., which was officially dedicated in April 1993, after fifteen years of difficult gestation. It was designed to take American visitors on a narrative journey that would induce a profound emotional and moral experience.[18] The very space of the museum and its architecture were meant to isolate the interior from the comforting presence of the Mall outside. The forbidding brick and towers were to concentrate and intensify visitors' experience of anguish. Unlike most history or archaeology museums, the Holocaust Museum is not primarily committed to describing the culture of a people, although it is an archive and research center. Its artifacts are comparatively few and were chosen for their profoundly evocative and commemorative value rather than for their descriptive function. The objects are not props; they are genuine actors in the story the museum tells, which evokes horror, sadness, and perhaps hope in visitors. Notably, this museum is a memorial, a house of memory, intended not to glorify the fallen victims or their liberators but to evoke empathy, preserve faith in human nature, and issue a warning against its subversion.

Like the Exploratorium, this museum demands collaboration on the part of museum-goers. Visitors must be actively engaged, not by pushing buttons or performing physical operations but by yielding themselves compassionately with heart and mind to the unfolding narrative. There is much information to be absorbed by the attentive inquirer, but the displays carry a burden beyond evidence. They impart "the shiver of contact," impelling visitors empathically to "touch the Holocaust as an outpost of memory."[19] While that lesson is cognitively vague, the museum expects affective consensus to be achieved through the power of its moral and emotive impact. Unlike the Exploratorium, the Holocaust Museum does not anticipate agreement based on reason or logic—although one might hope for common decency. It is meant to be "visceral," indeed almost preemptive of thought.

The Holocaust Museum is deliberately disorienting. Its materials and the organization of its spaces confuse, constrict, and alienate. Visitors squirm in discomfort, and there is little chatter among them. In silence, they move as if herded by a malevolent force. The planners understood that interludes for restorative meditation would be necessary, and so visitors pass in prescribed sequence through what the designer, Ralph Appelbaum, called "a play in three acts" (with intermissions) prior to emerging again into ordinary life on the Washington Mall. To further heighten their experience, visitors were initially presented with a card upon entering, with a photo and biography of a person more or less like themselves, with whose fate they might identify as they took in the exhibition. That process proved to be impracticable with the volume of traffic and was subsequently discontinued, leaving visitors to imagine the experience of the Holocaust on their own and think about it afterward.

Thus, while the Exploratorium employs subjective experience to promote cognitive inquiry that is shared and impersonal, the Holocaust Museum draws on resonant personal experience to commemorate "suffering experience" and to reflect morally upon the conditions that bring it about.[20] Neither museum regards experience as an end in itself or, strictly speaking, as what is on display; both view it as instrumental to accomplishing purposes that differ sharply from one another in the two cases. Although the commemorative imperative sometimes takes precedence over the educational voice in the Holocaust Museum, both museums are unabashedly didactic. There are things too painful or too difficult to be shown; hence, some issues are left unexplored or ambiguous, but more emphasis on experiential exhibitry would probably not have resolved that problem.[21] For both the Exploratorium and the Holocaust Museum, the evocation of experience seems a credible procedure, one of several devised to implement the complex goal of learning. Neither museum is content simply to impart information or to document facts in the hope that visitors will assimilate them to achieve understanding. Both institutions preserve continuity with the traditional object-oriented museum while moving forward into a new dimension of interactivity. Each of them is dedicated to the pedagogic principle that true learning, both cognitive and affective, begins with the learner's own effortful experience. The museum can only stimulate and enrich that result.

Experiencing Art and the "Museum Experience"

Reliance by museums on experience for their effect is not new. By and large, museums have always employed the latest technological devices that will ensure the most thrilling experience, whether they be wraparound sound effects, realistic dioramas, or dramatic spectacle.[22] It is no coincidence that museums lately have looked to theme parks for practical advice on how to manufacture experience more efficiently. That is the business of amusement parks, but typically it has not been the business of museums, since business was not what they were about. Creating experience has been auxiliary to, and sometimes only an embellishment of, the museum's real objectives.

Ironically, those institutions that today are most reluctant to call themselves "experiential museums" are the very ones that purport to deliver the most profoundly transformative experience of all, namely, that of great art. The art historian James Elkins complains that today's art museums, in league with professional art historians, have abandoned the intimate, engulfing experience that pictures once provided and replaced it with a duller, socially calibrated surrogate. With our senses shielded in intellectual armor, we now view paintings in safety and comfort, look at them with emotional distance, and see only what is denoted on the museum label.[23] Museum labels generally conform to a theory. Even the bare-bones attribution—artist, date, and national origin—betrays a conceptual frame to which visitors unconsciously adapt their perception. We examine the works judgmentally and comparatively but rarely admit to being moved by them. None of the professionally approved modes of signage contemplate why art matters or how it should be important in people's lives. We learn to evaluate rather than feel in the presence of art. Surprisingly, nonetheless, Elkins's research turned up a number of people who reported deep, tearful experiences, incomprehensible even to themselves, in front of particular pictures. Due to their public façade, museums are not friendly places for self-transformative experiences, agrees David Ross, former director of the San Francisco Museum of Modern Art—yet "you should leave the museum reeling and thinking," he says,[24] and some people certainly do.

James Cuno writes in a similar vein of the museum's responsibility to offer the public the opportunity "to stop before works of art . . . and be absolutely arrested by them, to experience them as being outside ourselves, as they really are *in themselves*—an experience that holds promise of decentering us at a radical moment of unselfing."[25] The experience of art, he says, is capable of changing us from who we were and causing us to "leave at a different angle." His fellow museum directors agree with him but, to varying degrees, point out that in the rush to offer too many things to too many people, museums have undermined that primary objective. Philippe de Montebello, director of the Metropolitan Museum, writing in the same volume, despairs of the confusion between experiencing works of art and the museum as an experience in and of itself. Visitors arrive today, he says, expecting a "museum experience" of which the art is a regrettably shrinking part. He notes an unfortunately expressed advertisement for the newly refurbished Victoria and Albert Museum that promotes "a very nice café with art on the side."

Art museums have always been about experiencing art, but there are many ways of doing that. The intention of formalists, including many of the current elder statesmen of the art world, was distinctly experiential. They rejected the referential storytelling and historicizing of a prior era as incidental to art, preferring more immediate, abstract meditations. But in one or another sense, art has been dedicated to some type of experience—if only pride in ownership of an expensive commodity. Arthur Danto notes the "Bonaparte mentality" that gave its form to most modern national art museums, including not only the Louvre but also the Prado and the Riijksmuseum, and that surely was the triumphal plan of Hitler's aborted Führermuseum. No doubt a heady experience. As Danto puts it: "The possession of art was a symbol of authority . . . and the violent seizure of someone else's art was, like raping his women, a symbolic appropriation of his authority and the metaphorical demonstration of his impotency."[26] Admittedly, we are speaking here of an indirect experience, the joy of its possession rather than delight in the art as such. But perhaps this is no less obliquely relevant than the moral inspiration or, alternatively, the erotic arousal for which art has also been celebrated. If the exact nature of the experience that art elicits is hard to pinpoint, all the more so is the satisfaction derived from that experience. Perhaps satisfaction—fill in the kind—simply is the experience, sufficient unto itself.

Art in the 1960s became differently experiential as audiences were asked to "complete" works of art through their own physical presence—by walking through or around them, viewing themselves reflected in them, interacting with other viewers, or creatively participating in "happenings" and other interactive art forms. Contemporary social and postmodern theoreticians, who read art as a text, find meanings there that are not directly experienced but intellectually inferred with the help of independently possessed information. They are reacting to the apolitical claims of formalists and the political pronouncements of a later breed of artists. Sometimes, in turning art back upon itself or its history, however, we re-experience it in new ways, extracting an emotive bonus from the experience of its political or referential content.[27] We get a "charge" from it. The turbulence of the last decades of the twentieth century shook up conventional notions of art, leaving the field open to new arrivals and so to new ways of experiencing them. Women and other outsiders, who did not share the canonic experience of its conventional patrons or did so only at a remove, sought their own validation in newly conceived or historically neglected art forms. They too offered something transformative but quite unlike the experiences promised heretofore. While their achievement is by no means universally acknowledged, they have taught (some of) us to think about art differently and thus, in many instances, to experience even old art anew.

Similar influences have affected the way in which history museums and historic sites deal with experience. Responding to trends in tourism and travel as well as to technological innovation, even the most conventional sites have reinvented themselves. The leading factor for change, however, is the new social history that highlights women, people of color, immigrants, and working-class themes that traditional history overlooks. Independent of their quality and the merit of their message, museums that treat these subjects are forced to be experiential and experimental because of the relative paucity of relevant documentary materials. They rely on the power of artifacts and reconstructions, for unlike "official history," which is replete with chronicles and analytic texts, "people's history" is preserved chiefly in ordinary objects, many of them tattered and worn. Their material worth is minimal—few are constituted of precious substances, but their mnemonic and affective potential is strong. They are capable of evoking powerful emotive experiences—some distasteful—or simply of providing pleasing entertainment. Museums combine the display of these objects dramatically with real or projected human interactions. Perhaps of all types of (adult) museums, history museums are most at risk of crossing over into the realm of pure spectacle, competing with theme parks as agreeable distractions.[28]

In principle, social history and house museums could profoundly challenge the conventions of museum history and form. Their intersection with "ordinary lives" inevitably mingles public culture with very private experience. It is impossible, for example, to represent women's history without exploring in uncomfortable detail the intimacies of family dynamics, obstetrics, and child-rearing. No one is untouched by these topics; everyone is engaged, but traditional museum fare has excluded or sanitized them. Putting the implements of domestic abuse and servitude under their noses exposes people to experiences as banal and as brutal as the Holocaust. The museums that strive to bring forth such experience are in an anomalous position: What they purport to reveal has been culturally disguised and protected while collectively enforced. To animate an experiential response that goes beyond sentimentality or passive sympathy, museums must combine the resourcefulness of the Exploratorium and the Holocaust Museum. They must generate both understanding and practical intelligence.

Few museums have undertaken to expose concepts that are regularly misrepresented or suppressed, and those that do have met with limited success. Most confine themselves to sustaining received sentiment colored by gentle bursts of irony. At best, they invite us to imagine ourselves into other times and places and cast us briefly into the (polished) shoes of others.[29]

I do not mean to denigrate museums' historical reconstructions. My concern is that current excitement within the museum community over the liberating potential of experience seems to promise something more radical than what museums have actually accomplished. In the experiential museum, visitors are said to be free to "make meaning," while cognitively linear museums of the past were supposedly more doctrinaire and restrictive.[30] My response is that museums have always fostered experience and that today's museums that place experience front and center are no less didactic than their predecessors and as likely to limit or distort the meanings they sanction. No museum can prohibit a visitor's atypical experience, but all museums anticipate and strive to husband a fairly uniform range of reactions to their exhibits. That is perfectly reasonable. Unusual responses, however, merit exploration. They are interesting not for their phenomenological uniqueness or as celebrations of personal freedom but for the enhanced understanding they might yield of the circumstances that brought them about and caused them to differ from the alleged norm. Are these physiological? Environmental? The result of upbringing or culture? Do they reflect differences of class or political conviction? What can we learn from these differences? Unless museums go beyond the sheer fact of experiential individuality, to investigate its vast penumbral hinterland, there is little value in being the occasion of an experience.

I believe that museums are actors that incorporate things and ideas and bring them publicly together. The museum is one of a number of cultural resources that mold the thinking of private individuals collectively as members of civil society. Shaped by exposure and acculturation (which also excludes some people from the museum altogether), individuals undergo experiences that are strictly their own. Yet the meanings these acquire are not generated by the individual alone. They intersect in a public sphere composed of influential institutions like the museum and other extended selves. The museum might be better described as a site of confluence, rather than of collection. Neither experiences nor the people who have them are collectible, and those objects assembled derive their value from the confluence of experience and ideas. In its public capacity, the museum is responsible for ordering, sustaining—sometimes restraining—and materially enhancing the volatile private events that experiences ultimately are. Given no more than the irreducible privacy of individual experiences, the museum could have no effect in the world, but, by acting creatively to yoke together multitudes of such private events, the museum synthesizes a plurality of public entities.

To advance that project, I turn next to the concepts of private and public and the complex interactions that constitute them not as polar opposites, but as historically codependent contraries whose complementarity creates the world we inhabit.

Notes

1. Rene Descartes, *Discourse on Method*, pt. 4, 1637.

2. John Dewey, *Experience and Nature* (Chicago, 1925).

3. Stephen Weil, "Rethinking the Museum: An Emerging New Paradigm," originally published in *Museum News* (1990).

4. Michael Spock, interviews by Donald Garfield in *Museum News* 72 (November–December 1993):34.

5. Mindy Duitz tells the moving story of how the Brooklyn Children's Museum, founded in a neighborhood dominated by white middle-class immigrants, transformed itself more than a half-century later when its population consisted chiefly of Caribbean and African-American families with a high rate of under- and unemployment. "The Soul of a Museum: Commitment to Community at the Brooklyn Children's Museum," in *Museums and Communities: The Politics of Public Culture*, eds. Ivan Karp et al. (Washington, D.C.: Smithsonian Institution Press, 1992).

6. Victor J. Danilov, *Science and Technology Centers* (Cambridge, Mass.: MIT Press, 1982).

7. Minda Borun, "Naïve Notions and the Design of Science Museum Exhibits," *Curator* 36 (1993): 201–19. The practice of building exhibit prototypes and observing audience use of them before completing a final design gained currency but was later undermined by the appearance of professional exhibit design companies to whom exhibit projects were outsourced.

8. In a later phase, marketing experts joined the exhibition team, but in the early stages, learning, not selling, was the critical objective.

9. Material culture criteria of reference were multifaceted with respect to material, place, design, time of origin, and function but were slow to admit such dimensions as politics, class, gender, and race.

10. Patterson Williams, "Object Contemplation: Theory into Practice," *Journal of Museum Education* 9 (1984).

11. Lois H. Silverman, "Making Meaning Together: Lessons from the Field of American History," *Journal of Museum Education* 18 (1993).

12. Carol Duncan, "Art Museums and the Ritual of Citizenship," in *Interpreting Objects and Collections*, ed. Susan M. Pearce (London: Routledge, 1994).

13. There are museums of the mind, but they are solipsistic unless some physical medium records and reports their message.

14. The expression seems to originate with Walter Benjamin, who points to the inevitability of war entailed by fascist efforts to render politics aesthetic. "The Work of Art in the Age of Mechanical Reproduction," in *Illuminations* (New York: Schocken Books, 1969). A variant view is expressed by Wolfgang Welsch in *Undoing Aesthetics* (London: Sage, 1997): "Public space today . . . is as such already hyperaesthetic, even before art comes into it." His response is a brief for disruption—not to say "uglification"—a figurative shaking of the public by the scruff of its neck to awaken it from its stupor.

15. It is much more usual to portray the gulf between appearance and reality, although appearance is less certain than experience and reality no more accessible than truth.

16. Philip Morrison, foreword to *The Exploratorium: The Museum as Laboratory*, by Hilde Hein (Washington, D.C.: Smithsonian Institution Press, 1990).

17. To illustrate: an exhibit called Critical Angle lets visitors rotate a transparent plastic semicircle so that a light beam that passes through it is refracted. As the light reaches the surface at different angles, a rainbow appears. As it spreads over the disk's round surface, the angles at which the light beams emerge have become shallow, bending back toward the surface of the disk, and at a critical point refraction becomes total reflection. The beam reflected back into the disk is white. If the disk is turned slowly, the rainbow dims and its colors disappear one by one. The critical angle is that point at which all the light is reflected. The exhibit was designed to permit visitors to rotate the disk, not just to but beyond the critical angle and to use it as a lens that plays with the light to achieve other effects. Nature is not so accommodating as to reveal only what the experimenter expects to see. There are other interesting surprises to be found and explained.

18. Edward T. Linenthal, *Preserving Memory: The Struggle to Create America's Holocaust Museum* (New York: Penguin, 1995).

19. Linenthal, *Preserving Memory*, 154.

20. Interjecting my own personal experience, I think I was most profoundly moved by an exhibit of *zyklon B* canisters. About the size of a beer can, these were mechanically perforated by a machine and deposited into a tube that fed into the killing chambers. What stunned me was a few raggedly perforated edges of cans indicating that, in cases of malfunction, someone had taken the trouble—and risk—to intervene by hand personally, making sure the object would do its deadly job. What kind of mind could be so dedicatedly meticulous or so numbed?

21. The failure of the United States to bomb Auschwitz is a case in point. viz. David Wyman, "Why Auschwitz Was Never Bombed," *Commentary*, May 1978.

22. Panoramas including sound and motion were popular museum spectacles in the 1820s, and dioramas were introduced at the Milwaukee Public Museum in 1830. viz. Edward P. Alexander, *Museums in Motion* (Nashville: American Association for State and Local History, 1979).

23. James Elkins, *Pictures and Tears: A History of People Who Have Cried in Front of Paintings* (New York: Routledge, 2001).

24. Salmagundi #139, Conference at Skidmore College, "An Age of Museums?" April 2001.

25. James Cuno, ed., *Whose Muse? Art Museums and the Public Trust* (Princeton, N.J., and Cambridge, Mass.: Princeton University Press and Harvard University Art Museums, 2003). (Italics in original.)

26. Arthur C. Danto, *Masterpiece and the Museum* in *Encounters and Reflections: Art in the Historical Present* (New York: Farrar, Straus and Giroux, 1986).

27. Enjoyment of art's irony, a privileged experience available to a select few, inclines to be self-congratulatory and to invoke a sense of superiority. It entails cognitive understanding as a primary response and is experiential only at a secondary remove. Arguably, it is not a direct reaction to the art at all but is an exultation of one's own cleverness.

28. Were they less intimidated by controversy, history museums might stir more profound emotive experiences. The dismal outcome of the 1995 Smithsonian *Enola Gay* exhibition, among others of the same vintage that were defeated by museum sponsors, suggests that the risk of antagonizing supporters trumps both experiential intensity and educational depth. For discussion of some of these cases, see Mike Wallace, *Mickey Mouse History and Other Essays on American Memory* (Philadelphia: Temple University Press, 1996).

29. On a recent visit to a sixteenth-century slave embarkation castle in Ghana, I experienced something of the fearsome chill that a "chosen" woman might have felt. A second-story balcony of the castle overlooked an open plaza that adjoined the dungeon where women were kept for months in darkness to await the arrival of the slave ship that would carry them away from all they knew and loved. Having been selected from among others granted a moment of sunlight in the courtyard outside their prison, the woman would be prodded up a narrow stairway, which I also climbed. As she approached the top, the dirty boots of her captor would confront her and then the repellent figure of the stranger who would use her for his pleasure. What were her expectations and what ploys available to her? One can only imagine. One would not re-enact the experience. A recently opened exhibition on slavery at the New York Historical Society approaches the subject, as will the promised Museum of African-American History to be constructed in Washington, D.C.

30. See, for example, Lisa C. Roberts, *From Knowledge to Narrative: Educators and the Changing Museum* (Washington, D.C.: Smithsonian Institution Press, 1997).

The Private, the Nonprivate, and the Public

The mass is a matrix from which all traditional behavior toward works of art issues today in a new form. Quantity has been transmuted into quality.

—WALTER BENJAMIN

In practice . . . private "arousal" and public "mobilization" cannot be confined to their proper spheres: rape and riot are the "surplus" of the economy of violence in public and private images.

—W. J. T. MITCHELL

The idea of public may manifest itself through congregation and gathering, through habit or ritual, by action or location, but the genesis of the public occurs within each of us where the turbulent and often conflicting forces of private impulse and common good reach some détente, some symbiotic coexistence.

—PATRICIA PHILLIPS

Reversals of Private and Public

Whoever visits a museum enters a public space in the company of unknown individuals, each of whom undergoes a uniquely private experience. The confluence of such private events, held in tension by the museum, generates many publics that come and go, dissolve and reform, perpetuating patterns that persist in the world independently of the museum.

"Public" and "private" are correlative and covariant terms set in contrast on a scale of human construction. They do not exclude but entail one another, for a public is composed of elements that presuppose a whole, and privacy is defined relative to the public from which it secedes. Liberal societies today treat the individual self as fundamental, representing it against the backdrop of a fictionalized public world. But an alternative and equally plausible theory holds that private selfhood is a fiction that emerges out of a prior organic whole. Some cultures consider the liberal perspective aberrant. To them, the isolated self is pathologically extracted from an integrated totality that properly confers identity on its component parts. Privacy is not universally esteemed, nor are its merits indisputable. According to Hannah Arendt, the Greek city-state consigned all activities related to individual life and the survival of the species to an inferior, private domain that people inhabit out of necessity, not choice. The public sphere, or political domain, was the realm of freedom, where equals lived among equals, neither ruling nor ruled. This idealized condition, attended by wealth and health, presupposed mastery of the necessities of life and therefore independence from the inequities and violence of the private domain.[1] A later version of the human condition depicts the (private) family as social archetype, a household headed by a paternalistic autocrat. This compression of whole into part rejected the classical distinction between private and public, eliminating both spheres and leaving a massively tiered despotism replicated in cellular miniature. *Res Publica* endured chiefly as an ideal embodied in the person of the leader.

The concept of the "public" reappeared in Western society centuries later in conjunction with a newly emergent segment of society. This nonconforming minority, lacking political authority, sought commonality at a level that transcended purely practical and survival-oriented subjection. Differing from otherworldly split-off groups (though its intent was not necessarily irreligious), its union was an expression of resistance against the futility of subjective life, a quest for transcendence to be found in public recognition and achievable only in public. Aware of the pluralism arising from its different social positions and the resulting variety of its perspectives, an enlightened and educated group of people set itself apart from both the authority that reigned over it and the restrictive household structure that confined it. In Europe, people found relief from their dual subjection in the "public house" and the salon, where men of arts and letters met to talk of common interests.

According to Jurgen Habermas, the kindling of self-consciousness in the eighteenth century inflamed principled opponents of arbitrary authority and not merely rebellious victims. Increasingly confident of their own exercise of reason in matters of commerce and economic administration, these dissenters cast themselves loose as a forum where private people insisted that public authority legitimate itself before the newly defined public. No longer generalized as "mankind in general" or "the world under God," this limited public was an outspoken critical entity composed of private people relating to one another voluntarily through the use of reason, rather than as subjective creatures driven together by identical needs.[2] As yet apolitical, these private persons assembled independently of social rank, drawn by the power of the "better argument" determined by reason, which came to displace the sacramental status of social hierarchy.

The rise of this public, with its conviction that reason is a universal human faculty,[3] led to a commodification of culture, making it in principle, accessible to everyone (on payment of admission or purchase) and leading to a decline of patronage. Art and literature became elective objects of free choice, subject to shifting preference. A new breed of critics and arbiters of taste arose to serve as mentors to a public hungry for counsel on the exercise of choice. Their medium was the press, issuing pamphlets and newspapers that promoted and published critical debate. Educated public opinion was to be a vehicle and organ of reliable common sense that would form a bulwark against the corruption of power, whether of the people or their overseers. Enlightenment optimism promised the triumph of this public and the eventual resolution of private differences under a reign of reason.

History, however, was to prove otherwise. It revealed that, without private property, including personal capacities and skills that have exchange value in society, an individual is forced to barter away his freedom for survival. Within a century, the aura of reason had disintegrated, and a more negative image of public opinion as the subjective opinings of the many prevailed. Now the public sphere was suspect, and the esteemed status of personhood reverted to the private individual. The aristocratic Alexis de Tocqueville warned against public opinion as a threat to the state, and even liberals such as John Stuart Mill stopped short of advocating universal suffrage for fear of its irrational power.[4] The public, nonetheless, achieved a political voice—that of a majority made up of a multitude of individuals.

Ironically, the freedom Aristotle attributed only to persons in public life was now ascribed to the privatized and property-holding individual. It was private property, mostly land, not public participation, that enabled individuals to overcome necessity and so grounded their identity. The glorification of privacy, sentimentalized as intimacy and subjectivity, was the triumph of Romanticism. The United States Constitution, created at the end of the eighteenth century, protects "the right of people to be secure in their persons, houses, papers, and effects, against unreasonable searches and seizures," but it was not until the end of the nineteenth century that control over personal information about oneself and one's reputation was considered a protected right, like that of private property.[5] Today, we hold personal privacy—the right to engage in self-regarding conduct without intervention from government—as a priority (although it is imperiled by alleged risks to security). Privacy as the right not to be bothered or intruded upon enhances the freedom of privileged individuals but not without additional protection provided by a profoundly politicized public sphere. We tend to associate "public" with government, especially in matters of sanctions and funding, but private discipline and philanthropy are equally influential and sometimes prevail over government.

Writing early in the twentieth century, John Dewey considered a public to be a temporary protopolitical aggregation of persons, neither the whole of a community nor officially appointed by it but defined collectively by the indirect effects upon it of certain events or large-scale transactions.[6] Publics, he believed, are generated by such things as a declaration of war, epidemics, and new technologies—but also by factory closings, strikes, and highway programs. People are affected differently as private individuals from how they are affected as part of a public and so must understand their several functions contextually. The media and a variety of cultural institutions distinct from government are the means by which members of a public address one another. Their separate autonomy was therefore crucial, Dewey maintained, for it kept the private pursuit of personal interest apart from political governance. Between the poles of the personal and political was the public sphere, where debate, rather than competition among special interests, could achieve effective action independently of and sometimes in opposition to prevailing political authority. Note that this model does not prohibit individuals from pursuing their own interests; that is their right as private persons. But it is not their function to do so as members of a public, where no private interest should dominate. In Dewey's view, democratic government has the responsibility of serving the public good as distinct from the particular interests of any individual or group within the whole. But government does not define the good; that is accomplished in the public sphere. Public institutions, likewise, whether or not they are agencies of government, should serve the well-being of society as a whole and not that of a select few. With due regard for their stunning paternalism—all too evident with hindsight—we might imagine that the nineteenth-century philanthropists who founded our cultural institutions truly believed they were inspired by public spirit rather than personal interest and were acting for a common good. Social improvement through public uplift was their expressed goal. Public parks and gardens, museums, and recreational centers were perceived as beneficial to society because they cultivated popular taste and inculcated discipline. Civic-minded private donors supported them, while local governments and the public, with notable exceptions, embraced them.[7]

This benign characterization of public and private symbiosis is no longer plausible. The public sphere has disintegrated into an arena of competing private interests. It has become a rhetorical marketplace presided over by a government bureaucracy that answers to manipulated public opinion. Persuasive haggling, not rational debate, determines that opinion. Decisions of public import are reached by acclamation, reflecting manufactured wants and gratification of consumers rather than a projection of rational thought upon the public good. Public figures are reduced in stature to private proportions, while those allegedly responsible for elevating them nitpick through their intimate data, savoring it vicariously.

Over a half-century ago, the sociologist C. Wright Mills coined the term "the power elite" to warn Americans against the trajectory he saw them following along a path toward submission to totalitarianism. Above all, he deplored the eclipse of the public, which he saw as giving way to the *mass*. He characterized a community of publics as follows:

> (1) There is roughly the same proportion of givers to receivers of opinion. People speak to and listen to each other. (2) Communication is so organized that receivers can easily and without reprisal answer back to publicly expressed opinions. (3) There are easily accessible outlets for acting on opinion formed by such discussion—even against prevailing authority. (4) Authoritative institutions do not penetrate or obstruct the expression of opinion. The public is autonomous.

A public, so qualified, is capable of deciding its good and imposing its will on the government elected to protect it. The opposite conditions prevail in a mass:

> (1) Fewer people express opinions than receive them; they are delivered impersonally to millions of viewers over national networks and prepared by professional opinion makers. (2) It is difficult for receivers to answer back immediately or with any effect. (3) Responsive action is rigorously controlled. (4) Agents of the authorized institutions penetrate the mass and interfere with the formation of independent opinion through discussion.

Under the second set of conditions, the public has been reduced to an aggregate of individuals who respond passively to the suggestions given to them by controlled media. They are no longer rational; neither are they motivated by or capable of reflecting upon the public good. Their private wants and desires are manipulatable, so that they do not even act out of genuinely personal interest, let alone that of the whole. They have sacrificed autonomy at both the private and the public levels; indeed, they have become automatons. But unlike the robots of science fiction, they believe in the legitimacy of the system that rules them.[8]

An earlier depiction of the mass by Siegfried Kracauer (1929) prefigures its descent into tyranny and anticipates its dehumanized acquiescence to the *Ratio* of capitalism. Empty abstraction takes the place of reason and is paired against extremist romantic cult mythologizing. Kracauer draws upon a timely aesthetic metaphor, American chorus-girl revues: "These products of American distraction factories are no longer individual girls, but indissoluble girl clusters whose movements are demonstrations of mathematics. . . . The regularity of their patterns is cheered by the masses, themselves arranged by the stands in tier upon ordered tier." Both viewer and viewed are seen to be the abstracted building blocks, not of a natural community but of an artificial mass of functionally linked individual elements, like the prongs of a rake. They are reduced to become units of a system, whose charm is its calculability unknown to its trained components. It is an end in itself, a self-replicating ornament.[9]

Nonjudgmental definitions of the concept are rare. One that professes to understand the mass purely numerically is given by Noel Carroll, who conceives the mass in terms of its access to and reception of goods, rather than its control over them. Masses, he says, "are reached by vast delivery

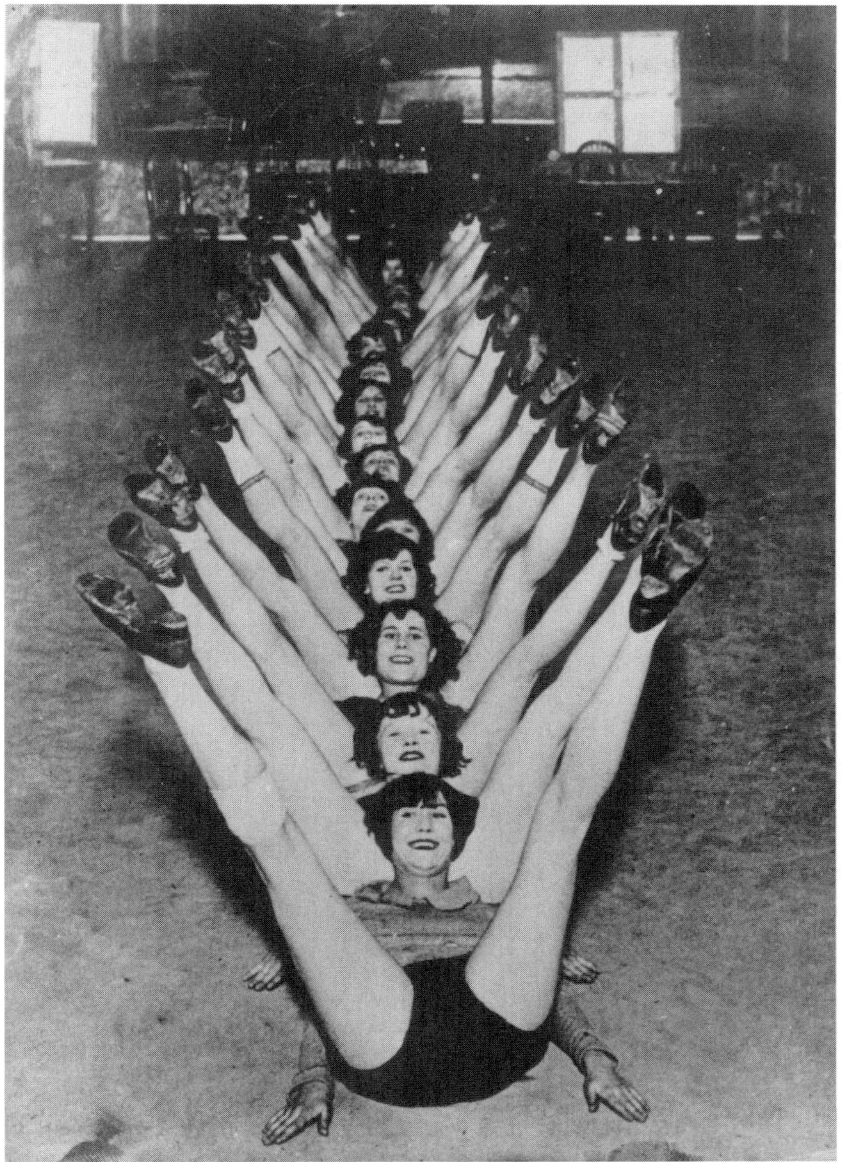

"Girls at a Rehearsal" (Ullsteinbild, Berlin, Germany). "Tiller Girls" cited as mass art in Siegfried Kracauer, *The Mass Ornament* (1929).

systems that are able to reproduce or present the same performance or the same object to more than one reception site simultaneously."[10] I will return to this topic later. Here, I introduce the mass only to include it in a selective survey of public/private syntax, as one among other forms of the nonprivate.

My aim in this book is to understand the museum as an institution that is *both* public *and* private and to do so in light of a type of art whose definition seems to assume a distinction *between* public and private. This distinction is elusive. Ordinary discourse deals with things that are *either* public *or* private—lives, interests, property, affairs, business, language. The concepts appear to be mutually exclusive, and people do intuitively resonate with the grammar of exclusion. Perhaps they are mistaken. I have underscored the confused history of the paired terms in the hope that further exploration will illuminate the concept of the museum—an institution whose public identity lies at the root of its private function and effectiveness.

Vagaries of Meaning

Some languages speak less ambiguously: "public" means open and accessible, though not always free, while "private" means closed, secret, and hidden.[11] "Private" is a term of exclusion that tells people to keep out. Because it suggests large numbers, "public" sometimes implies a lack of discrimination and oversight. Public drinking fountains and recreation areas may be unclean. On the other hand, since in public one is on view and exposed to scrutiny by others, conduct that is permitted in private may be forbidden in public. There are public dress codes. Services to the public can be provided by private as well as publicly owned institutions (e.g., churches, philanthropic organizations, and family foundations), but they generally derive some public benefit thereby (e.g., tax reduction) and so are subject to public regulation. Public agencies are often, but not always, initiated by governments, although their operation may be subcontracted and privately run.[12] Government subsidy, if not actual operation, has come to be the hallmark of what is understood to be public, and in order to be eligible for public support, organizations must comply with certain conditions. Privatization frees them from those restrictions but instead can render them the vassals of corporate interests and private ambition. Government support is a controversial issue in liberal societies, for it suggests endorsement and threatens interference. Proponents of public subsidy for cultural and educational institutions maintain that these are critical to the maintenance of communitarian values, but their opponents argue that the practice inevitably favors a monolithic majority and ignores the diverse preferences of minorities.[13]

Employed as a noun, the term "public" is relative. It references one group of people to another and not always the same one. Like "laity," it designates as outsiders "the public"—those who are not part of a given profession or persuasion. Thus, physicians and priests may be part of the museum-going public, while museum curators and directors are among the public that attends churches and sits in hospital waiting rooms. Publics in this sense are constantly resifted and recomposed, and everyone belongs to several of them. As a result, adherents to distinct publics may be faced with contradictory demands, a problem of moral prioritizing that can be deeply troubling and leads to professional and legal conflicts. The public is sometimes an audience that takes part in an event and is bonded by that experience (e.g., fellow dog-show exhibitors), but with events as colossal as televised Olympic Games or wars, the public is neither proximate nor simultaneous and has little community of interest beyond the immediate outcome—which is assessed oppositely by opposing sides. Moreover, the media-public engages in spectatorship separately, its members detached from one another and often alone.[14] Nevertheless, the concept of "the public" carries a hint of cumulative energy capable of conjuring images of a mob. As described above, it can be pacified and its collective strength so manipulated that members move as a mass, obediently in lockstep, in unconscious mimicry of one another. The communities to which we belong are more articulated. Usually they include us intentionally and often through our choice, but we are part of the public (or a public) to some degree by accident.[15]

No substantive expression "the private" corresponds to "the public" in the manner just discussed.[16] This is interesting from the perspective of gender, for the public is implicitly a male construction, though comprised almost equally of women. The private sphere remains conceptually feminine and, though associated with interiors, represents the consummate outsider status relative to the public sphere. Feminists of the 1960s declared the personal political, and the private public, in defiance of a male-constructed dichotomy that kept women out of public life. A torrent of feminist theory since the publication of Simone de Beauvoir's *The Second Sex* has shown how the doctrine of dual spheres emanated from a male perspective and worked to the detriment of women. It has shown, in addition, that the appeal to privacy as an essential claim to immunity from public intervention can be divisive and dangerous.[17] As a condition opposite to the public, privacy is a fiction, and the sanctity of the private realm is delusional. Actual practice, historical and contemporary, has invariably integrated all human conduct—reproduction and production, domestic work and commerce, custom and law. Public mechanisms have always controlled "intimate" relations and continue to do so as they grow increasingly technologized. No aspect of life is impervious to surveillance, whether by way of traditional devices such as gossip and rumors or by less personal instruments such as health codes, marketing studies, social science surveys, or government licensing. If ever there was a time when a man's home was his castle, the walls now are thoroughly perforated. Where privacy was a function of protected location, it has been compressed into psychic space, and even that is permeable.

An additional, often overlooked, dimension of the private/public distinction arises out of the seventeenth-century discovery by European philosophers of consciousness. Represented as an individual's awareness of "ideas" or occurrent mental events (sensations, images, thoughts, dreams, and reflections), consciousness imposes a gulf between a private and certain world within and a public and possible one without. These two realms stand in a problematic relation to one another, for we cannot assume their causal connection, their similarity, or even the existence in fact of something that is merely possible. By what right do we say that an idea is a sign or symptom of something external to the consciousness that experiences it? What warrants my belief that whatever might be "out there" corresponds in some way to my idea of it—much less to yours, which to me is even more opaque than the presumed object?[18] What justifies our faith that private thoughts are evidence of public events? Concern regarding the exclusivity of ideas led to the extreme solipsism of Bishop Berkeley, the eighteenth-century philosopher who argued that only the benign presence of an all-containing mind of God conserved the ideas of multiple minds in an arguably public order. Note that Berkeley's solution to the problem dispenses with the external world altogether. It is diminished to no more than a congregation of private beliefs. That does not resolve the question whether anything (except for God) exists apart from private experiences, but it no longer matters as long as we agree about them. But what if we don't? Why should your experience influence mine? How can I be sure that you are not merely one of my mental constructions?

Western philosophers have never fully overcome their uncertainty whether private thoughts are evidence of a public world, although most of us are prepared to accept some kind of conventional connection between our experience and a world beyond it. Other thinkers, less extreme than Berkeley, have contrived ingenious gambits to warrant our confidence in knowledge gained through private ideas, but the possibility that each of us is forever locked in a world purely of our own devising has never quite gone away. At least it has contributed to a vast literature and funded untold therapies to salve the loneliness and anomie (or megalomania) that might follow in the wake of such isolation. With only one's ideas for companionship, one would indeed live in a private world. However, one could not know it to be different from the public world we believe we inhabit, since it would include the interactions that typically are found there. The public would be a myth but no more so than the private since, just as at present, their polarity is rendered meaningless by the removal of either pole. Public and private are codependent.

The gulf between private experience and public knowledge, or its possibility, has haunted Western philosophy and is responsible for the experiential and social character of modern science. We do not rely on the subjective observations and judgments of single individuals but demand that they be repeatedly confirmed, tested, and reinforced within a framework of conventional rules and practices. Science's claim to respectability and trust derives from its public character: by contrast, the art engendered in consequence of the same discovery of consciousness offers a singular and very private solace. Art genres that reflect the new subjectivity, such as the novel,[19] express a unique sensibility, meant to be recognized in solitary resonance.[20] Insofar as science has gained preeminence in the modern world, it has set the parameters of the public/private distinction and rigorously patrolled the boundaries of public legitimacy.

In consequence, the prevalent notion of art in modern times associates it with private enjoyment, although nonprivate art forms have existed continuously since the beginning of mankind. It all depends on what we mean by "art." In line with today's perceptions, I think the Lascaux and Altamira cave paintings, made more than 30,000 and 15,000 years ago, respectively, would count as public art, but we cannot be sure what their contemporaries thought about them. They are certainly nonprivate. Were they aspects of religious ritual? Instruments of invocation or magic? Were they lamentations of cosmic insecurity or expressions of joyful harmony with the universe? Were they methodical census tabulations? Playful decoration? News reports? We do not know, but I consider it doubtful that they could have been the ruminative self-exploration of a solitary genius.

What we call their art—assuming a collective origin—is all that remains to us of most ancient civilizations. From these remnants information is reconstructed about the culture and history of bygone civilizations. This is a task for archaeologists and anthropologists, not art critics or aestheticians. We can marvel at the skill and industry of these people and admire their aesthetic sensibility. We are thrilled by their ability to animate matter with (apparent) spiritual value, but we cannot claim to understand their motivation. The ancient artifacts undoubtedly qualify as nonprivate art, but we should not attribute the same incentives to their makers that would inspire a modern (private) artist, not even where there are visual resemblances. Severed from their historic origin, the objects we admire bear the aura of antiquity but lack the currency of private art. To become that, they must be reborn and endowed with subjectivity that neither beauty nor endurance can guarantee. Effectively, museums have enabled that rebirth.

The designation "art" is generic insofar as it encompasses all aesthetic production and justifies our preservation of such objects as might otherwise be destroyed or discarded, but it also causes confusion. Art and artists belong to a modern construction and to a sensibility that we ascribe to ancient times by extension. Art problematizes the reality of self and other, of public act and private experience, and the necessity of reconciling them. It affirms and denies the self and affirms and denies the other. Art seeks to surpass the limit of privacy but not its intimacy. It aspires to universality but rejects its impersonality. It has need of these contrary concepts, for they are its source and sustenance.

Private and Nonprivate Art

I have reached the subject of art indirectly, by way of exploring the concepts of public and private. I employed the expression "nonprivate art" somewhat evasively with reference to the cave paintings for want of an adequate categorical description of them. The commonly used, unmodified term "art" is ordinarily reserved to designate creations produced by an individual (or identifiable small group of individuals) for limited display / performance to be experienced by other individuals, not excluding oneself. In the philosophical sense discussed above, all art would correctly be classified as public insofar as it is projected to be experienced by others.[21] Hannah Arendt goes farther to declare culture a phenomenon of the public world. The permanence of art, she says, is of a "higher order" than that needed for things that pertain to the private survival use of human creatures. The artifice of culture, i.e., the creation of works of art, is preservative, transforming the life of what it prolongs from private to public. While nothing wholly escapes the corrosion of natural processes, art enters the public realm and thereby evades the absolute evanescence of private temporality.[22] The escape is qualified, however, for to be fulfilled, art must re-enter the cycle of private experience. Thus, even private art has a public dimension and public art a private one. I will return to this liminality, which I take to be a critical feature of all art. Here I mention it to introduce my use of the adjectives "private" and "nonprivate" to distinguish among species of the generic concept—art. I take nonprivate art to be the ancestral, uncatalogued form of human production, while private art is a newly minted variety of aesthetic expression that enters history with the advent of self-conscious self-alienation.

"Private art" is thus a retronym, a word invented after the fact of a newly contrived distinction. By analogy, the verb "to parent" is a retronym devised to identify a neutralized function that traditional practice and linguistic usage did not require (although people of both sexes have been parents and carried out the relevant activities for centuries).[23] In retrospect, nonprivate art is likewise a very old phenomenon, repeatedly reincarnated and revitalized. There can be little doubt that it preceded private art historically, and it is therefore puzzling that it is the older art form, rather than the more recent cultural phenomenon, to which the qualifying marker—"public"—was assigned.[24] Unmarked terms generally imply greater respectability, and so it is that (private) art (normally left unmarked) has captured the higher ground and serves as the definitive referent.[25] Private art is sometimes called "museum art," even though much of it preceded the existence of museums and most of it will never be found in one. Nonetheless, private art, associated with individual artistry, has come to be the standard against which all art is measured.[26]

Art history and aesthetics are no longer invincibly wedded to the idealistic doctrine that (private) art stands radically apart from social history, but that connection is affirmed only cautiously with the admission that artists are not immune from the temper of their times. The greatest art is still celebrated as transcendent and valid universally. In practice, however, (private) art has drawn ever closer to the condition of public art, declaring its social affinity and repudiating the isolation of both artist and artwork.

Critics and historians now situate art within a substantive social history and environment. Nonetheless, the popular ideal persists that art is produced by a solitary individual (possibly with a few collaborators) and results from purely aesthetic inspiration. Exhibitions of art in museums are becoming more contextualized, but the institution's typical taxonomic segregation and internal departmental organization are a structural constraint that interferes with the scope of exhibition potential.

The presentation of private art in art museums, for example, tends to discourage questions about its material sources. We know that most religious works once adorned holy places and were part of their public ritual. We know far less about their production and how they came to be privatized in the museum. How much of the "high art" of the Renaissance was commissioned for ducal and pontifical palaces not only for private enjoyment but to publicly impress visiting subjects and ambassadors with the authority and power of their owner? Cooling one's heels as one awaited an audience in the vestibule, one might ponder these worldly concerns, but one's compliments to the great lord would be confined to his exquisite taste and the sublime qualities of the work. Neither etiquette nor good sense would countenance drawing attention to ulterior political motives and pressures. Considering the "pure" aesthetic product, one is easily seduced by formal and representational properties. Yet there usually were explicit practical instructions to impart a message sustained by a normative iconology. Fuller disclosure of the art's function would qualify the romance that insulates fine art from its worldly sources and keeps it private.

Somehow the grubby politicking and money-raising that tend to accompany the production and installation of openly public art reduce its mystery and diminish its aura.[27] The aesthetic dimension that sanctifies private art is pushed to the background by the social and other short-term factors involved in creating and protecting public art. Although they are not irrelevant to its judgment, the features that attract critical attention to private art receive comparatively little notice in discussions of public art. Beauty and ugliness, while not ignored, are secondary to what the work signifies, where it is sited, and who pays for it. Tellingly too, the creators of public artworks are frequently left unidentified unless they happen also to be well-known artists of the private sort.[28] In contrast to private portraiture, where the sitter may be of little interest to subsequent viewers while the name of the artist is featured, public art is more likely to be remembered for what or whom it commemorates or for its local significance than for its creator(s). Few people today know much about La

Gioconda, the subject known as Mona Lisa, but most Americans know the four men whose faces adorn Mount Rushmore. On the other hand, Leonardo Da Vinci's name is universally known as the painter of *Mona Lisa*, and almost no one can identify the sculptor Gutzon Borglum, who carved Mount Rushmore's *Shrine of Democracy*.[29]

Varieties of Nonprivate Art

Anonymity was the norm rather than the exception before there was private art. There were skilled human fabricators who exercised the power of practical intellect, but that was neither remarkable, nor was it accorded special moral significance. The maker applied nature to human needs, a necessity given human fallibility. Medieval theologians wrote worried treatises about the risk of seduction by beauty that "turns the shadow of things into things and changes every lie to truth,"[30] but ultimately that seduction could be reconciled with reverence toward the Holy Spirit. The glory of God overflows in the splendor of the chalices, censers, surplices, and altar pieces that now fill the private spaces of modern museums. They were produced by common laborers in the service of their faith, and they once adorned houses of public worship. Only in museums do they exist as private art. The epic fables and sagas of early civilizations are likewise works of anonymous public artistry. We know the names of some of their compilers and adapters who turned them into private art—they include Shakespeare, Wagner, and the Brothers Grimm—but the original storytellers are unknown. Their tales were circulated and, no doubt, embellished by wandering traders, soldiers, holy men, and minstrels. Whether received as history or news or entertainment, they reinforced cultural bonds and in time were reborn as art.

Every culture possesses "folk art," produced by people who did not go to art school and never identified themselves as artists. It does not follow that they were untrained, for many served apprenticeships or learned their skill informally at the hands of family or local masters. Their work was not intended for display only, though presumably it was enjoyed by their community and sometimes transported abroad.[31] Folk art often has ceremonial or religious functions; sometimes it decorates utilitarian objects; and some of it has an irreducibly idiosyncratic quality. Significantly, the appearance of irregularities in such work, while prized by collectors, may be taken to be a byproduct of the imprecision of folk techniques rather than as the result of aesthetic decisions. Comparable deviations from machine standardization in private art are not considered flaws but are viewed as the mark of personal inspiration or even genius. Curiously, modern art critics deprecate "imperfections" in folk art as externally determined rather than qualities willed by their makers. Recognizing them does not preclude personal preferences but is thought a matter of cognitive expertise rather than of aesthetic sensibility by connoisseurs. As a result, the assumption that folk art is produced anonymously by simple, uneducated people remains with us—notwithstanding the widespread plunder of its themes and techniques by sophisticated private and public artists.

Modern museums collect and display decorative arts and crafts products involved principally in the design of furniture, fabrics, household items, and jewelry. Notably produced by women and unnamed artisans, these objects are considered secondary art forms and less distinguished than the "fine" arts of easel painting and sculpture.[32] They are made for use and rank neither as public nor private art, although they figure widely and prominently in domestic life, where they become emblems of distinct social classes.[33] In the twentieth century they were "uplifted" from base utilitarianism by the pioneers of abstract art, who, in the words of Kandinsky, saw in them "vibrations of the spirit."[34]

Similar vibrations resound in popular art, which, unlike folk art (and more like private art), is associated with the names of specific artists (Elvis Presley, the Beatles, Madonna, and Charles Schulz). The social historian Arnold Hauser maintains that, while folk art emerges from the ranks of the nonelite country folk who enjoy it, popular art, which emerged with urbanization and the rise of a middle class, is produced commercially by professionals to entertain a moderately educated public.[35] In both types of art, Hauser holds, the artist is addressing a public distinguished by a lack of any uniquely personal taste. This, he says, is not because there is some mysterious collective spirit or common human psyche; the uniformity is a result of class, environmental, and educational standardization. Popular art, unlike folk art, pretends to a degree of cultural and political independence, but unlike private art, its success is measured by the magnitude of public response.

All art, private or not, involves a degree of adherence to conventions. These distinguish it from non-art. Invariably, there are deviations, but while conventional practices are the bedrock of traditional folk and popular art forms, they challenge the originality of private artists to transcend them competitively. Private art is effectively driven to obscurity by such competition and the need to distance itself from popular norms. Popular culture, in turn, can assume a stance of indifference to domination by high culture, mocking its values even as it adapts them to its own ends.[36] America lacks a single popular art form, but the diverse cultures come together even while resisting homogenization.[37] Uprooted from their origin, they are linked by otherness. One rather Tolstoyan analysis of popular art holds, against Hauser, that it does stem from a spiritual core at the heart of all humanity that is betrayed by the private art of "high" culture. According to this view, popular art seeks a return to universal roots, and its popularity testifies to its success. A less sympathetic account accuses popular art of catering to lowbrow taste and deplores it as banal and mindless escapist entertainment. The most severe condemnation of popular art is moral and comes from those who consider it malevolently subversive, crassly designed by elites to stupefy and exploit the public.

The formalist art critic Clement Greenberg proclaimed, "Kitsch is the culture of the masses."[38] Like C. Wright Mills, he believed that totalitarian regimes seek to ingratiate themselves with their subjects through its encouragement. The credulous public hungers for predigested art that gives immediate satisfaction without effort. "Mass art" is an outgrowth of popular art that derives from industrialized regimentation. It is also claimed that the "democratization" of society is a source, but mass art seems to flourish under every political system. If the public for popular art retains some vestiges of the harmonized interest and rational agreement that Habermas traced to Enlightenment origins, the mass that descended from that public has lost its deliberative power. It is reduced to selecting from an array of predetermined options that are the product of technological capability and the manufacture of aspiration—teeth whitened in only an hour. Choice is illusory, however, for it is divorced from genuine historic interest.[39] The mass media, functioning on a worldwide scale, construct abstract individuals, pried loose from the formative cultures that engendered them. They gratefully succumb to the stylization of their feelings and desires—in language fashioned by "experts"—and exult in the variety of means available to satisfy them.[40] Mass art delivers diversion in capsules unrelated to the specificity of anyone's actual character or environment but sufficiently neutralized and aestheticized to be swallowed painlessly and with pleasure.

Ironically, the public reached by mass art today is more "privatized" than ever. So-called personal opinions are solicited from "the man in the street," and "public" figures are reduced to bite-sized television personalities, their foibles and fables on display. Villainy is on a par with heroism and virtue, since all stories are equally fascinating, each a detached nugget of endlessly replicated self-expression.[41] Public issues are determined by polling, as are the policies of public leaders. Politics is a popularity contest; elections a form of dramatic entertainment. Like other aspects of this culture, art is also penetrated by the market, which determines not only what is produced and how it is distributed but, most importantly, how it is to be loved and wanted—for criticism is guided by the same system. The public consists of an aggregate of private interests, its unity manufactured and measured by consumer approval. This public craves diversion and willingly adopts the next upgrade. Where folk art resounds with the pulse of its people and popular art plays it back, mass art prescribes the tune, sets the metronome, and synthesizes a public chorus.

Moving from the conformist center to the social periphery, a recently minted art category may be listed among the nonprivate varieties. The expression "outsider art" originally designated the artistic productions of persons outside established society but inside such institutions as prisons and hospitals for the insane.[42] It has since then come to be applied collectively to visionary art, i.e., the art of children, untrained or self-taught adults, lucid dreamers, isolated religious enthusiasts, and other yet-unclassified individuals, possibly including chimpanzees. Their works may be viewed along rural railroad tracks, in city parks, on the temporary barriers of building or demolition sites, on abandoned trolley cars, on the backs of billboards and fences, and in basements and backyards everywhere. Psychiatrists collect examples from their patients—and not only for diagnostic purposes. They have an uncanny aesthetic appeal and are currently selling at high prices in big-city galleries. The Baltimore Museum of Visionary Art, housed in a former whiskey warehouse, is devoted to outsider art. Its content, though attracting art world interest, is not officially recognized as what I am calling "private" or "museum art." It is too far out—or too private.[43] Outsider art does not have the collective anonymity of folk art, for its producers are often highly visible and their style unique. Simon Rodia spent thirty-three years building *Nuestro Pueblo*, Watts Towers, in Los Angeles and became a national celebrity, attracting millions of admirers to his construction. But few called it art. A catalogue for a 1967 exhibition of what was then known as *Art Brut* refers to "works that . . . escape cultural conditioning and proceed from truly original mental attitudes." Since marginality is a sometime thing, the sobriquet may be self-limiting. For the present, it points to an absence of community or political affiliation or even a common audience. By definition, outsider art is bound

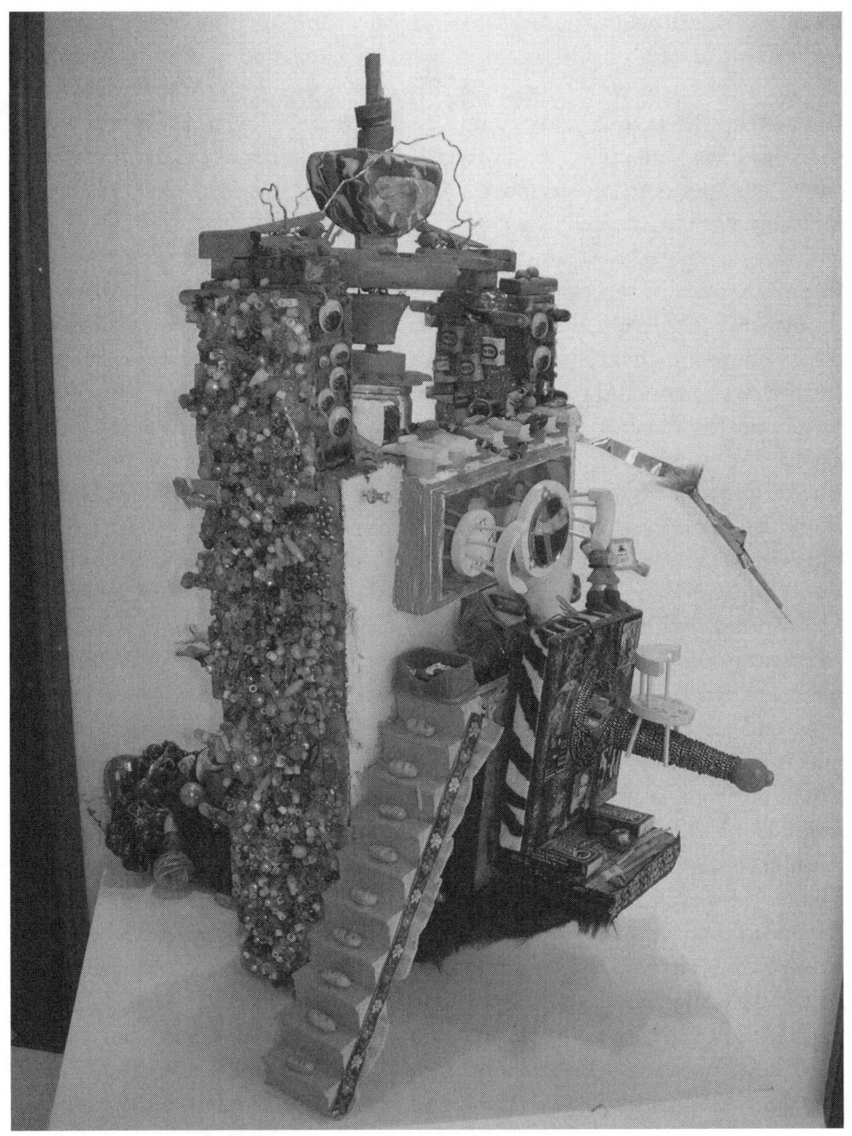

It Takes a Village. Outsider Art sculpture by Korie Seagull (2004). Courtesy of Gateway Arts, Brookline, Mass. (Photo by Hilde Hein.)

by no conventions or theories. Strictly speaking, it cannot be counted as private art, though nothing could be more exclusive; neither is it public, though nothing is less exclusive. Perhaps "esoteric" is the appropriate qualifier, except this conveys the intentional transmission to a select few and deliberate mystification of all others. There is no reason to attribute such ulterior motives to outsider artists, although many of them do claim to answer to private voices.

Every type of aesthetic practice generates its own community and inspires a range of reactions appropriate to it—boisterous or polite applause, foot-stomping, silent contemplation, active collaboration, or sometimes defiance. There are characteristic styles of expressive behavior appropriate to distinct art forms, and these are acquired along with the appreciative skills. Rock-and-roll fans tone down their display of enthusiasm when attending a chamber music performance. Privileged individuals can pass easily from one to another public, partaking briefly and for a price. It is not by their difficulty or comparative accessibility that nonprivate art forms are distinguished—no more than inaccessibility defines private art, but these differences suggest a conceptual handle for exploring art that is nonprivate and a vocabulary with which to approach public art.[44] I will pursue that topic in greater detail in the next chapter. Here I observe only that technology has privatized accessibility and made it a matter of means. Books, television, and the computer enable access to events that once required personal admission to a place that was at least quasipublic.[45] The access, now possible in private to anyone with appropriate equipment, was formerly available to only a few—and in the company of others. Today, "public" often implies government administration or ownership. While this does not guarantee access—and frequently denies it—the designation suggests trusteeship or stewardship, the agency acting protectively or on behalf of a public that may no longer exist or not yet be born. In that case, access is hardly an option.

"The public" exists today in fractionated form, dissociated as countless individuals. It is a fiction that has survived through centuries of redefinition. From "public" and its antonym "private," we derive the contrary concepts of public art and private art, which must likewise be elastic. The terms must extend even to some things that were not deliberately produced as art at all.[46] According to the system of classification that I have introduced here, private and nonprivate are true contradictories, while public is a subset of nonprivate. But the career of art does not follow the sharp divisions of formal logic. I have discussed several varieties of art that

I call nonprivate, which are not public art. I turn next to the category of public art. My aim, ultimately, is to consider museums under the rubric of public art, but this requires a closer look at what that term entails and to what it has been applied.

Notes

1. Hannah Arendt, *The Human Condition* (Chicago: University of Chicago Press, 1958).

2. Jurgen Habermas, *The Structural Transformation of the Public Sphere* (Cambridge, Mass.: MIT Press, 1962, 1989).

3. Rene Descartes, *Discourse on the Method of Rightly Conducting the Reason and Seeking Truth in the Sciences* (Paris, 1637).

4. Both Mill and de Tocqueville opted for representative government in order to avoid direct rule by the uninformed masses. They advocated a meritocracy of the educated in place of property ownership but thereby inevitably favored a social hierarchy.

5. Louis Brandeis and Charles Warren, "The Right to Privacy," *Harvard Law Review* 4 (1890).

6. John Dewey, *The Public and Its Problems* (New York: Holt, 1927).

7. Of course there were indirect benefits to donors as well. Public beneficence does not demand personal misery but only that private advantage not be its sole reward. It merits observation, however, that the "public" targeted by nineteenth-century "democratizers" included skilled workers, tradesmen, and a few immigrants but not blacks and Indians, who might be deemed incorrigible and beyond salvation even by culture. viz. Vera Zolberg, *The Happy Few—En Masse: Franco-American Comparisons in Cultural Democratization* (Washington, D.C.: Woodrow Wilson Center Press, 1997).

8. C. Wright Mills, *The Power Elite* (Oxford, United Kingdom: Oxford University Press, 1956).

9. Siegfried Kracauer, *The Mass Ornament: Weimar Essays* (Cambridge, Mass.: Harvard University Press, 1995).

10. Noel Carroll, *A Philosophy of Mass Art* (Oxford, United Kingdom: Oxford University Press, 1998).

11. To publish (German): *veroffentlich bekanntmachen*; publication (French): *ouvrage*.

12. In between the private and the public institutions is the hybrid not-for-profit sector, which in fact is where most museums are to be found. A specific set of privileges and responsibilities applies to them and an increasingly complex set of laws. Marie Malaro, *Museum Governance* (Washington, D.C.: Smithsonian Institution Press, 1994).

13. The converse argument is also made that government support can enable minority enterprises and unconventional art forms to survive where private funds are not sufficient. The philosophy and policies of government arts agencies are beyond the reach of this book.

14. Not all audiences constitute a public. Guests at a private musical soiree, judges at an audition, or classmates critiquing a presentation are an audience but not a public. It is possible to have an audience of one but not a public composed of one person.

15. This is not to deny that we may resent the communities that claim us and find them restrictive. Family, church, and nation impose their identity on us, sometimes against our will.

16. "The individual" may be the correct antonym.

17. It is, moreover, preposterous to pretend that people's sexual and family lives are beyond the scope of public regulation. Among early challengers to the public/private dichotomy were Kate Millett, *Sexual Politics* (New York, 1970); Jean Elshtain, "Moral Woman and Immoral Man: A Consideration of the Public-Private Split and Its Political Ramifications," *Politics and Society* 4 (1974); and Catharine MacKinnon, "Feminism, Marxism, Method, and the State: An Agenda for Theory," *Signs* 7 (1982) and *Feminism Unmodified: Discourses on Life and Law* (Cambridge, Mass.: Harvard University Press, 1987). These references to Second Wave feminism explicitly employ the public/private language, but its disputed gender specificity is clear throughout feminist history, traceable in Mary Wollstonecraft, Christine de Pisan, and even Aristophanes' *Lysistrata*.

18. The tree outside my window is present to me through my visual tree-experience, but only your words or other indirect expression convey your experience to me, and these offer little to convince me that yours is the same as my experience.

19. Contrasted with other prose fiction such as the romance, which dealt with heroic and epic subjects, the novel concerned commonplace topics and odd but not extraordinary events close to ordinary human experience to which readers could respond empathically.

20. Philosophers hoped to develop a science of taste that would assimilate the apprehension of beauty and the judgment of art to cognitive science, but that endeavor drifted quickly toward an analysis of sentiment as the basis of aesthetic apprehension. Where science sought connection and systems, art was the domain of things in isolation and exposed them in their immediacy.

21. Were the connotation not so negative, I would say that art is ultimately an *alienation* of self, for as an externalization or projection, it objectifies the self, a small suicide that wins entry to the public world of the not-self, which is the world of culture that Arendt celebrates.

22. Hannah Arendt, *The Human Condition* (New York: Harcourt, Brace & World, 1954) and *Between Past and Future: Eight Exercises in Political Thought* (New York: Harcourt, Brace & World, 1968).

23. "To father" was to beget, while "to mother" was uniquely nurturing; "to parent" implies the neutral, nonbiologically related routine of raising children. The phenomenon merited linguistic notice only after men and women began taking part interchangeably in the rearing of children.

24. A similar puzzle arises with the current expression "performance art," which also precedes what I am calling private art by eons. In its present manifestation it is understood to be subversive of and pose a challenge to private art and the institutions that perpetuate it, such as museums. Ironically, however, museums have themselves become sites for public performances.

25. "Male nurse" and "child actor" still suggest deviation from a norm of, respectively, female and adult that requires no specification.

26. This is the case in the Western world and as far as its hegemony extends.

27. This is the point made by Christo and a growing cadre of artists who choose to display the process of negotiation and fundraising, as well as the collective fabrication of their work. Walter Benjamin would affirm that such divulgence undermines the work's cultic aura and thereby politicizes it. And so it does, but to withhold that portion of the work's history is no less a distortion (*The Work of Art in the Age of Mechanical Reproduction*). If we include Michelangelo's conflicts with popes and patrons as elements of his art, its sublime untouchability might also be compromised.

28. Chicago's civic center boasts a sculpture by Pablo Picasso because its sponsor wanted a work by "the greatest artist alive" as a matter of civic pride, but neither the artist nor the work has any other connection with the city. The same is true of Alexander Calder's sculpture *La Grande Vitesse*, which is in Grand Rapids. I have often walked around the base of a public sculpture, searching in vain for the name of its creator. Similarly, the artist/producer is commonly left out of dedication ceremonies for statues commemorating important persons or events.

29. A good thing, perhaps, since according to James Loewen's account, he was a rabid Klansman. viz. *Lies across America: What Our Historic Sites Get Wrong* (New York: The New Press, 1999).

30. A very Platonic sentiment, cited in Umberto Eco, *Art and Beauty in the Middle Ages* (New Haven, Conn.: Yale University Press, 1986), 101.

31. "Ethnic" or "tribal" art is still exported informally through tourism. American folk festivals for nearly a century have proudly preserved the genuine art of all the hyphenated Americans, and record-breaking crowds flock to craft and antique fairs, their zeal enhanced by the popular television production "Antiques Road Show," which adds the allure of stumbling upon unsuspected treasure.

32. In a recent exhibition, "Art Deco: 1910–1939," the Boston Museum of Fine Arts did identify many of the designers of the objects displayed, but most were not familiar names. The names of Cubist and Constructivist artists, whose painting sometimes inspired the Deco pieces and were shown along with them, were far better known. Their placement among the lesser-known utilitarian items was disturbing to some visitors.

33. Arguably, they are simply nonprivate since they are not associated with individual inspiration or constructive of a public.

34. Wassily Kandinsky, *Concerning the Spiritual in Art* (New York, 1947), 67. It required the effort of feminist women artists to restore the element of creativity to its original source in the previously despised handicraft tradition itself. viz. Miriam Schapiro, "Notes from a Conversation on Art, Feminism and Work," in *Working It Out*, eds. Sara Ruddick and Pamela Daniels (New York: Pantheon Press, 1977).

35. Hauser admits that the boundaries between the several levels of art are hard to draw and that even the most sublime work is likely to include elements of the "lower" sort. "Even with Shakespeare, the boundary between his poetry and his clowning, between his tidbits for the boxes and his strong meat for the pit" (from *The Philosophy of Art History* [New York: World Publishing Company, 1958], 283).

36. The reverse is also the case. Currently fashionable private art appropriates the images and language of popular art, bending them to its purposes.

37. As with ethnic restaurant cuisine, survival demands some calibration to a median "American" taste.

38. Clement Greenberg, "Avant-Garde and Kitsch," *Art and Culture: Critical Essays* (Boston: Beacon Press, 1961).

39. The illusion synchronizes with the capitalist promotion of boundless gratification of individual choice. Satisfaction is never achieved, since the system is rigged to stir new hungers, always perceived to be plausible personal needs.

40. The concept of the mass, popularized in the 1950s by Ortega y Gasset's *The Revolt of the Masses*, derives from the psychological study of Gustave Le Bon (1910). He believed in a psychic unity or "mass psyche" that emerges from individuals in crowd circumstances, freeing them without the usual constraints to revert to their original irrational instincts. Propagandists of all types, working from this premise, have studied the art of shaping the opinion of the mass by every means possible. A contemporary view of the mass manages to be more pluralistic but no less manipulative.

41. Public figures, from Tom De Lay to Paul Farmer, from Martha Stewart to Jane Fonda, are heralded for their celebrity, not for the merit of their origin.

42. Roger Cardinal, *Outsider Art* (New York: Praeger Publishers, 1972).

43. The strangely sinister art of Henry Darger is an example that has now made its way into museums and film.

44. The entry of folk and popular art into museums and a growing interest in their collection confuse these categorical distinctions in practice. There is relatively little intellectual confusion, however, among the concepts. Dr. Barnes was pleased to mystify visitors by interspersing door hinges and weather vanes among the Impressionist paintings in the galleries of his foundation, but he did not hang Renoirs atop the roof of his stable. He was making political as well as aesthetic statements. Consider, however, such ancient folk symbols as the swastika, which

has arguably become the most potent instance of public art ever devised. Its appropriation by the Nazis has effectively preempted its meaning for any usage in the foreseeable future.

45. This includes "private" showings, salons, artist studios, and practice sites.

46. A case in point is the FAO Schwarz trademark teddy bear, which was removed from its Boston site after the bankrupt toy store was forced to close. Dearly beloved by local children, it was compared by residents to the Eiffel Tower and the Statue of Liberty. A contest to decide its new location elicited thousands of proposals, including the Children's Hospital lobby and Franklin Park Zoo. *Boston Globe* (19 August 2004). A similar fate befell a milk bottle–shaped ice cream stand that was refurbished by the Hood Milk Company and now occupies the plaza in front of the Boston Children's Museum. The utilitarian elevated bridge of a Boston subway line that was torn down to make way for the new underground artery was mourned by a state legislator, who said of it: "The El was the Eiffel Tower on its side. It was a wonderful thing. . . . a kind of linear piece of public art." *Boston Globe Magazine* (15 August 2004). None of these edifices were initially intended as art. One was a symbol, another an advertisement, the third an urban conveyance. Their outdoor situation made them accessible to the public, which has since claimed and anointed them as public art.

Public Art: History and Meaning

Inevitably, in the path of our advance will be found historical monuments and cultural centers which symbolize to the world all that we are fighting to preserve. It is the responsibility of every commander to protect and respect these symbols whenever possible.

—DWIGHT D. EISENHOWER

The statesman is an artist too. For him the people is neither more nor less than what stone is for the sculptor.

—JOSEPH GOEBBELS

Public Art Constructs a Public

If private art suggests an intimate exchange, public art gathers a congregation. While I have observed that all art is to some degree public, public art merits its name in virtue of the fact that the creation of a public is its point of departure. Public art presupposes the public sphere and produces a public in relation to that concept. Unlike popular or mass art, it does not assume a preexistent generic audience to be entertained or instructed but sets out to forge a specific public by means of an aesthetic interaction. The constructed public's response need not be unanimous or favorable, but a reaction is crucial to the work's actualization. The art-making is implicitly a social process: it can be exhortative, commemorative, triumphal, perhaps expressive of collective grief, anger, celebration—or occasionally aggressively provocative. The public may be enlisted to join a movement or antagonized, incited to protest or exhilarated. Personal expression is not the central motivator of public art, and originality is less imperative for public than for private art, where the individual artist's psyche initiates the work.

Public art preceded "art world" institutions such as critical journals and museums that came into being with private art and is not dependent upon them. Arguably descended from antiquity, public art thrives in the real world of bird droppings and vandalism. It is so commonplace as to be easily overlooked, yet the powerful feelings it sometimes evokes, principally toward what it represents, can explode into bloody violence. There are fabled histories of public art that no longer exists but remains in memory or imagination. Among them is the golden calf built by the Israelites, impatient in the absence of Moses, who, upon descending from Mount Sinai with the tablets of the Ten Commandments, ordered the idol destroyed. Another example of persistent public art is the Bamiyan Buddhas, erected in the second century C.E. during the reign of the emperor Kouchin Kanichka, sovereign of Bactria, along the "silk road" that conveyed Buddhism from India. The Buddha statues were demolished by Taliban Islamists in 2001, but their exact replication is under consideration. Both of these razings were carried out in a spirit of righteous repression of idolatry. Attacking the "idols" is also a displaced assault on the people that worship them, and their replacement would be a political declaration.[1]

Hybrid in many respects, public art cuts across a variety of polarities. It is not addressed to a specific sensory receptor or limited by medium but appears in every mode of aesthetic expression and some that have never been considered that.[2] Remarkably, public art is able to transgress temporal and spatial constraints to achieve such feats as the simultaneous, worldwide millennial choral performance of Beethoven's *Ode to Joy*. A comparably synchronized global event was the "Lysistrata Project," coordinated with telekinetic synergy by feminist and peace organizations and consisting of independent performances of Aristophanes' antiwar classic. Note that conventional performances of these well-known works in theaters and concert halls are not perceived as public art, but the scale of their "orchestrated" worldwide production introduces a new dimension that

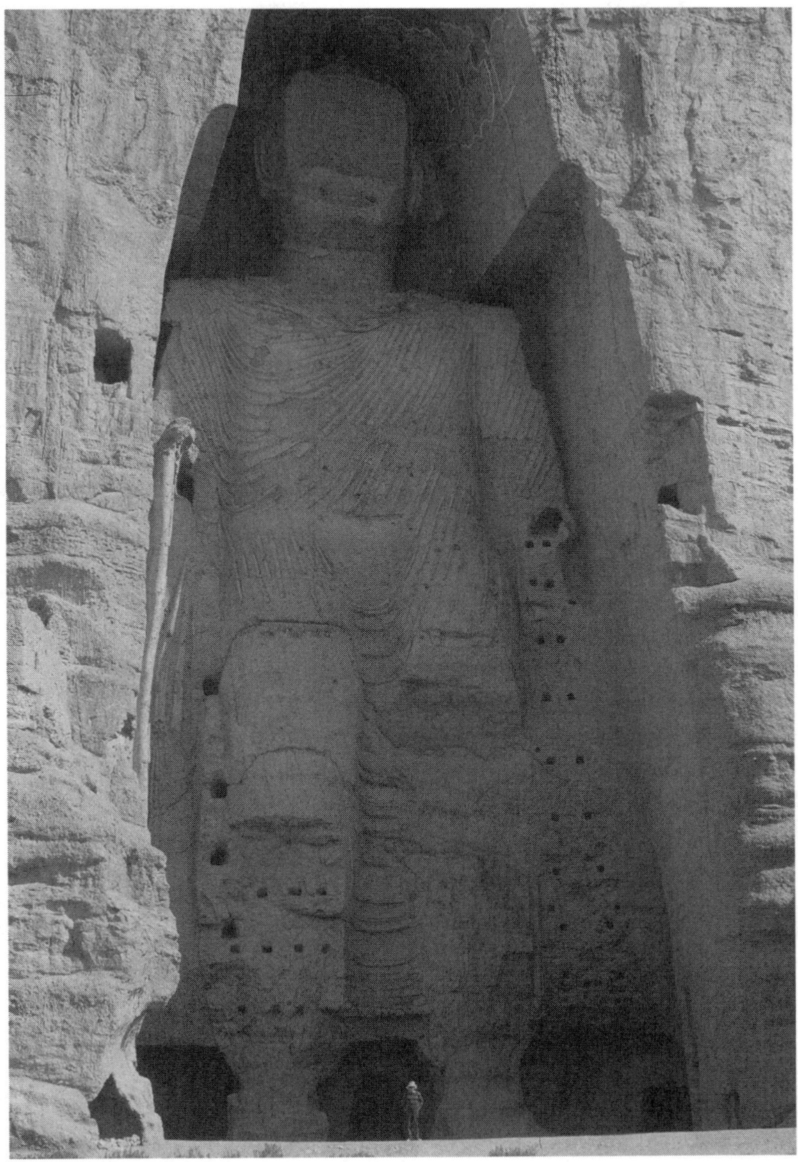

Bamiyan Buddha with statue. (Photo by Fabio Remondino, ETH, Swiss Federal Institute of Technology, Institute of Geodesy and Photogrammetry, Zurich, Switzerland.)

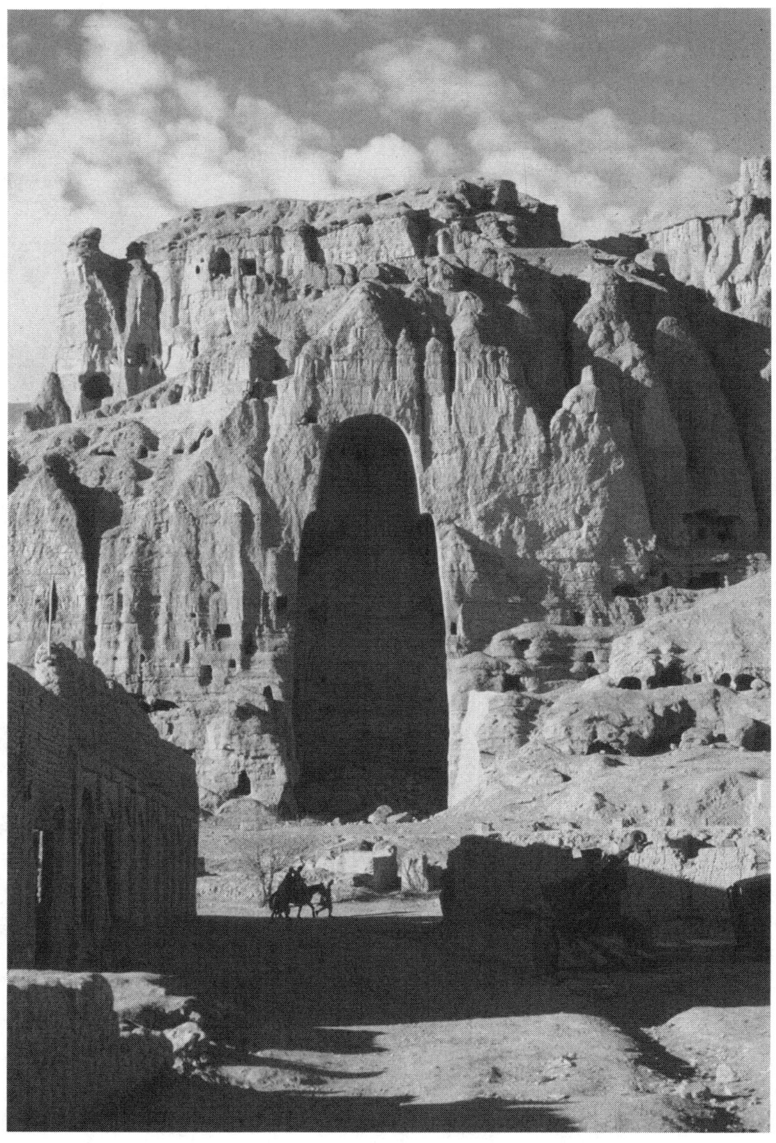

Enclave of destroyed Bamiyan Buddha. (Photo by Luke Powell.)

rendered the art public. However, scale alone is not a defining parameter of public art.

Like other contemporary theorists, I distinguish between "public art," which, I hold, constructs a public, and "art in public places," which, while it may have public value, is characterized chiefly in virtue of its location and bureaucratic legitimization.[3] The geography of the public sphere is not reducible to either site or function. The extremes are clear enough, but the distinction between public art and art that is publicly accessible is not rigid. Neighborhoods are well served, for example, by art sited to conceal the sights and sounds of highways or to relieve road-weary automobile passengers with pleasant diversions along the way. The art that decorates town plazas, shopping malls, and the lobbies of public buildings also provides physical comfort and gathering places for socializing elders and workers on lunch break. Urban (or suburban) design features such as these are designated "real estate architecture," and the public, often unaware that they are commissioned projects by professional artists, accepts the landscaped sites and benches as a species of background music. Formally this is designated public art.

Known also as "corporate baubles," some publicly situated decorations contribute aesthetic value to office buildings and industrial parks, but they are public art only by linguistic courtesy. They advertise the (semi)-public character of the space they occupy insofar as their aesthetic presence invites public entry.[4] They pacify, but they do not promote affinity among the patrons. Fellow elevator passengers or occupants of the lobbies of commercial centers are linked spatially, but they do not constitute a public. They have little to say to one another unless the lights go out. A shaping event is necessary to make a public of them. Like the law, public art aims both to express and to affect its culture. If too extreme, it will be rejected or destroyed; if too banal, it will be ignored.[5] Like legislators and judges, public artists are absorbed into the historic process of cultural transformation, of which their art is a manifestation. It is measured against the double and sometimes contradictory standards of aesthetic merit and social or political acceptability. Public artists thus incur the risk of both artistic and social failure. Their achievement in one dimension can be injurious in the other and may not survive the conflict.[6]

Obscurity sometimes provides political sanctuary. In the 1980s, for example, the masked Guerrilla Girls startled art establishments with a barrage of brilliantly executed assaults designed to expose the unequal and exploitative treatment of women by the art world. The gorilla disguises and anonymity adopted by these women, all of whom were, to some degree, members of the art world, attracted attention and lent them authority they could not otherwise have achieved. That was part of their message—who would listen to them without the novelty of their masks? The gorilla masks they donned and *noms de guerre* borrowed from historical women artists were also a protective device, necessary to preserve careers and personal safety as these public artists broadcast their exposé of sexism in the art world.

Intentional anonymity is also a means to express solidarity with a similarly unidentified public. The workers who sculpted the "Elgin" marbles on the Acropolis or constructed the medieval cathedrals were artisans neglected by official art history. We do not know their names and can only hope that their labor was adequately rewarded by the public of their day. But in 1979, an association of young artists assigned themselves the impersonal title "Group Material" in order to challenge the individualistic premises of modern private art-making. Working collaboratively and anonymously, deliberately eschewing fame, they sought to imitate their ideal of the obscure medieval artisan by foregrounding the social activism of their art instead of their own personalities. While the collectivism of their art-making is not to be confused with collectivism as a political doctrine or with tribal communitarianism, these artists were seeking a new aesthetic idiom in a society indifferent to collective ideals and interests. Other artists, similarly motivated to reject the cult of the isolated genius, have also been working with and deferring to the public served by art. This public is not enticed by commodities destined for idiosyncratic collectors or connoisseurs. Found conceptually between the privatized consumer and an impersonal state structure, the public persona comes together and grows through its encounter with art.

The Public Construction of Public Art

Public reaction to public art takes a variety of forms including, but not restricted to, the aesthetic evaluation typically applied to private art. Since the public is differently situated relative to the varieties of art, its judgment when confronting public art departs from gallery expectations. Alternative standards apply, and the criteria used to judge private artwork aesthetically are inadequate to public art. Conditions of scale and proportion change in different environments, and entirely new aesthetic features come into play in the public domain, so that excellent private art can fail as public art and vice versa. A wonderful work of public art can disappoint as private art—and not simply because *Liberty Enlightening the World* would be a formidable presence in your living room.

No less important a distinction between public art and private art is the fact that encountering public art is not entirely elective. We enter museums voluntarily, but crossing city streets and using public facilities are not easily avoided. We go to private art, but public art is come upon. Feeling oneself a captive audience, one may well resent not only the intrusion of unwanted art but also the "waste" of resources, including one's own tax dollars that might be better spent otherwise. Where real-world accountability is a factor, cost, maintenance, security, accessibility, and site appropriateness, alongside more partisan social and political considerations, are criteria for judging artworks no less legitimate than their sheer beauty.[7] Public art need not be ugly to be plausibly disapproved, and its approval may have little to do with aesthetic merit.

Judgments of public art involve a moral dimension considered nonessential in judging private art. Contrary to idealists who argue that great art is necessarily both good *and* beautiful, I hold that moral merit and aesthetic merit are independent of one another. Beautiful art can be morally repulsive. Its aesthetic seduction is then a double affront. Conversely, the miserable expression of nobly inspired ideas is only partially salvaged by the grace that their moral quality bestows. Public art, however, is inescapably ethical because of its social reference. It necessarily overflows into the world. This is why the toppling of statues (e.g., of Lenin and Saddam Hussein) is not equivalent to the mere removal of an object but is an act of desacralization, a form of public denunciation.[8] No lessons in art appreciation are needed to understand the message; it is an aestheticized moral pronouncement that does not require media sophistication. The public grasps the meaning of the gesture intuitively and responds with acute discrimination.[9]

Obscurity that is indulged in private art where it does not conflict with aesthetic merit can defeat the purpose of public art, however. If people are made to feel stupid or ridiculous, they react resentfully toward the incomprehensible source that excludes them. Public art compels both artists and public to refine communicative skills, and the endeavor cements their affinity. Using familiar commercial techniques and vehicles of mass media, public artists interweave art with common activities of life to enlist it readily in social and political causes. This interpenetration of art with contemporary lived experience is characterized as "democratization," but it does not always refer to real-world populism. It repudiates art world exclusivism. Public art is not invariably progressive socially or politically, although it must be socially referenced. Political advocacy of fascism or any form of demagoguery is as possible as liberal or left radicalism. However, public art need not be political at all and is often naively apolitical.[10] It constructs a public—a social, not necessarily a political, body. It must also be emphasized that public art is not simply a *use* of art for social purposes; it *is* art *and* it is social, a point often overlooked by critical activists of all persuasions.

Technological innovations bring about not only new modes of expression and means of making art but also new ways of thinking that affect our perception of earlier art retrospectively. We reanimate old objects by importing new meanings into them. What one generation perceived as right and proper seems downright incomprehensible to the next. We wonder: how could our ancestors have been so insensitive? How could they have failed to see what they were doing? The invention of new categories of thought and words to express them reinscribes history and interprets it anew. To illustrate this point, consider the concept of sexism. Fifty years ago no such concept existed, notwithstanding its prevalent exemplification. We did not have a word to speak of it, yet only the language that clusters its practices was missing—that required the invention of a retronym. Once named, sexism could easily be recognized where before it had been unidentifiable, if everywhere endured.[11] Artworks also are recast perceptually when their conceptual foundation is displaced. We see, hear, and think of them differently. Aesthetic devices, such as the appropriation of earlier artworks to new frameworks, effectively recharge the conceptual order, just as retronyms do.[12] They cause us to revise our apprehension of the world. If the new work is to make its point, however, the initial artwork from which it derives must be known by the perceiver, a condition not always fulfilled. The use of the appropriation as a technique in public art is therefore risky, and it is more prevalent in private art, where historical sophistication is (rightly or wrongly) presupposed.[13]

All art risks losing its impact as conceptual and stylistic fashions pass, but public art is especially vulnerable due to the centrality and multitude of temporal social factors that affect its identity. It is subject to physical damage and relocation, but even when permanently placed and protected, its neighborhood changes. Populations come and go; buildings are razed and new constructions take their place. Surrounding flora and fauna are altered, sometimes by neglectful overgrowth and sometimes by incidental migrations. Transportation and commercial development, business trends,

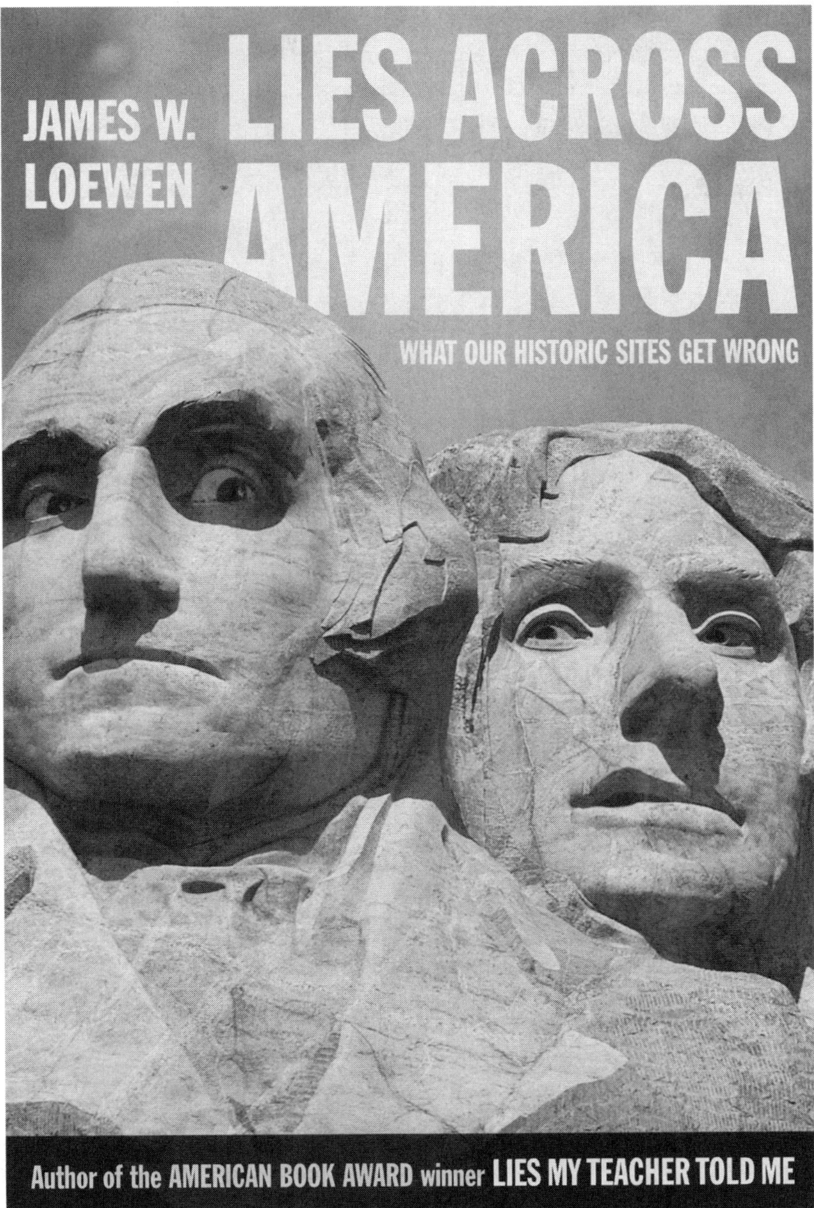

Mount Rushmore, book cover of James Loewen, *Lies across America* (New York: The New Press): Altered public art is public art. (Jacket design and photo by Hall Smyth.)

recreational fashions—all leave their mark on public artworks, often diminishing them in consequence of environmental competition. At least as significant as these external factors are transformations in public consciousness and perception. We do not live in the world of our grandparents, and our grandchildren will not inhabit ours.

Forgetfulness is a primary actor: memory is short, and most of us simply do not remember, or care little about public figures and events honored by our ancestors. For many people the civic history recorded in public places is not their history, and what they bring to it is a different memory (e.g., that of victim rather than victor). Art that stirs unmediated emotive resonance in witnesses of a memorialized event holds only mediated symbolic meaning to those not originally present and becomes an occasion for ideological history learning to the next generation.

A striking example of this sequential distancing is given by the historian Martha Kendall Winnacker, who describes her 1977 pilgrimage accompanying a shipment of hospital supplies to the Vietnamese village of Son My, site of the notorious My Lai massacre by U.S. soldiers in 1968. The ravaged site had been made into a monument dominated by the double-life-sized statue of a woman "with one fist raised to the sky and a stare fixed eternally on the horizon. Her other arm cradled a dead or dying child and at her feet an old man supported a mortally wounded younger one." The statue "stood alone in a barren landscape that had not recovered from being bulldozed and evacuated and did not appear to be inhabited." A small, cinderblock museum nearby held U.S. Army memorabilia, a list of the 504 Vietnamese victims killed at the village, and horrifying photographs torn from *Life* magazine. It was tended by stern-faced women whose families had been killed and who now had no one to care for them. They would never forget.

Fifteen years later, Winnacker revisited the same site, which had now become a destination for tourists. A marker indicated the turnoff, and children shouting "hello" and "okay" guided the way. A manicured park surrounded the statue, where a mosaic mural and wooden bas-reliefs depicted battle against a background of stylized tears. The young curator, a graduate in museum studies from Hanoi University, greeted the delegation and pointed out the U.S. Army movements to visitors on a map. Visitors were asked to make donations and an offering of incense, a symbolic but unfamiliar gesture of reconciliation made by people unhaunted by ghosts.[14]

Few people remember what happened there; for them the statue and museum are only a memorial. For their children, the powerful story will

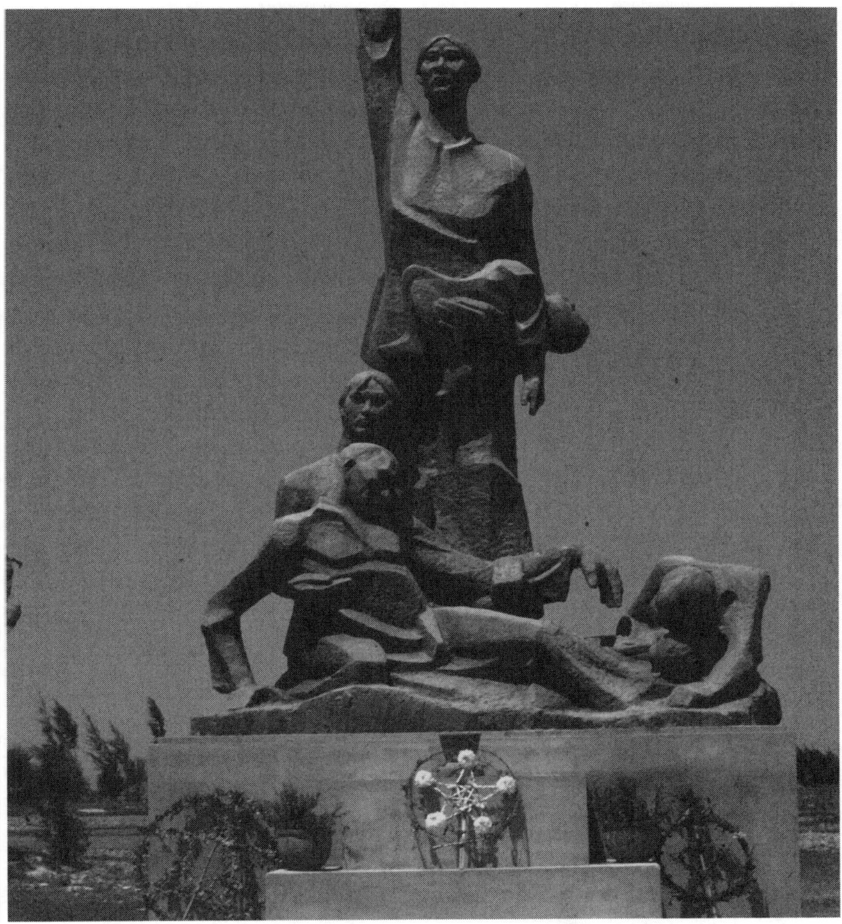

My Lai (Son My) memorial statue (1977). (Photo by Martha Winnacker.)

become legend; for some, a lesson. But for the Peers Commission, charged by the U.S. Army in 1969 to investigate reports of the massacre, the stories and images taken by an army photographer were evidence of events, dutifully analyzed and now stored in various U.S. government archives.[15] For the rest of us, whose investment may be less personal, the witness testaments to memory become history and the matter of political dispute. The My Lai site is now a Peace Park annually revisited by pacifists and occasionally by tourists.

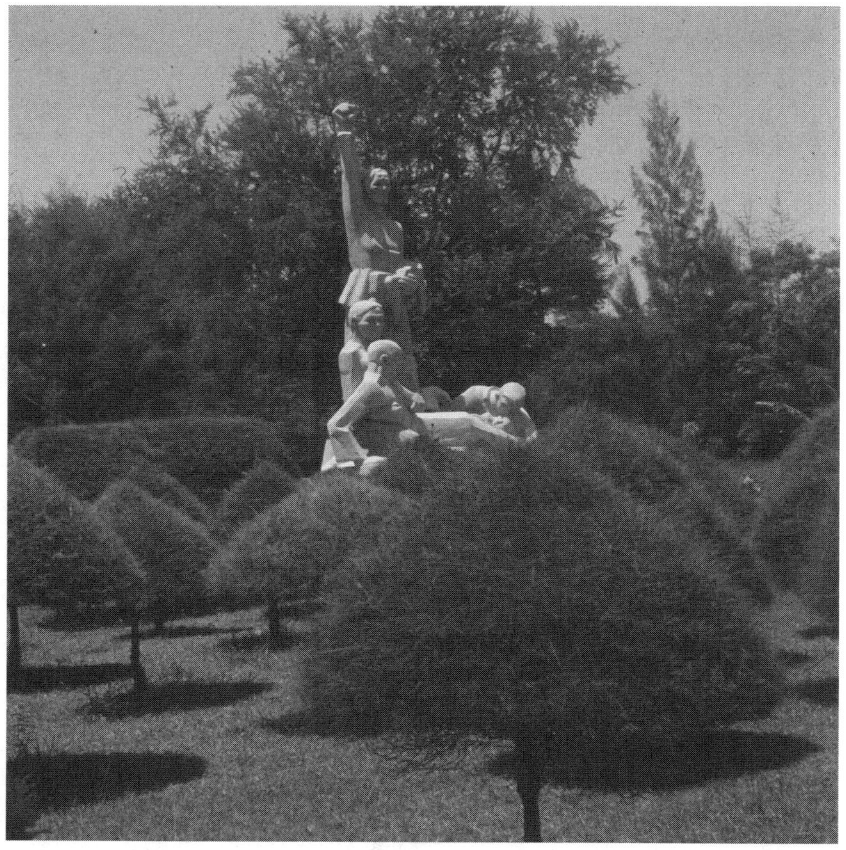

My Lai (Son My) memorial statue (1992). (Photo by Martha Winnacker.)

A similar advance toward oblivion befalls the many Holocaust memorials throughout Europe and America, as the number of those who survived the Nazi experience is rapidly declining. And as they decline, a torrent of memorializations in the form of books, TV series, films, dramas, and other representations is increasing to the point that some complain of "Holocaust overload" and "Holocaust burnout," while others wear Nazi uniforms to Halloween parties. The resulting trivialization of the historic event displaces memory, leaving moral complacency to confront the rancor of survivors.[16] The Holocaust has become a genre whose symbols serve new tribes as heraldic standards. Their clash is contemporary, though born of history, and the memorials speak a language that does not parse the past.

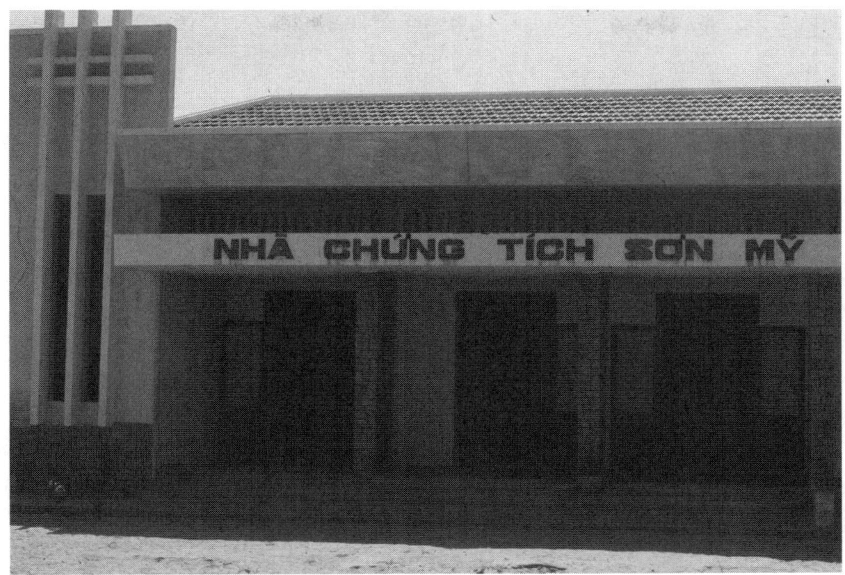

My Lai (Son My) Museum entrance (1977). (Photo by Martha Winnacker.)

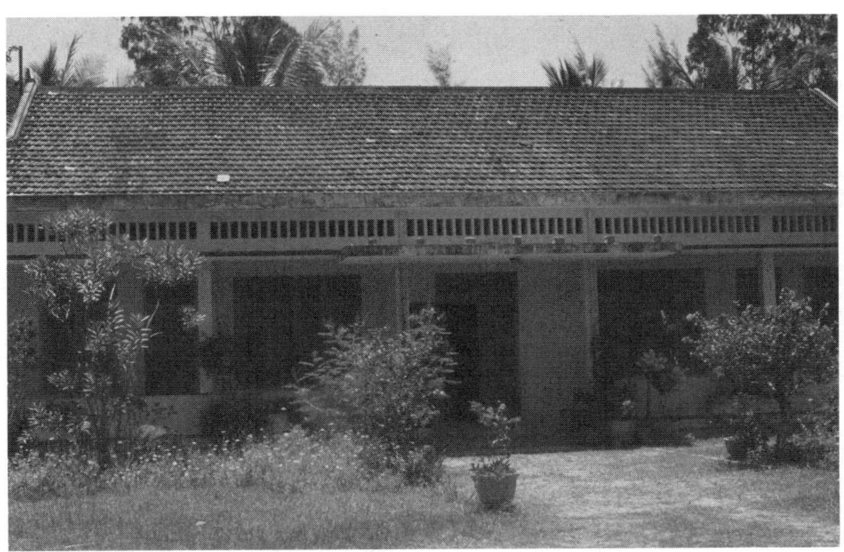

My Lai (Son My) Museum entrance (1992). (Photo by Martha Winnacker.)

Public art that memorializes historic events cannot help but aestheticize them according to imagery and an idiom in fashion at the time of the art's construction. In so doing, it revises the history recollected by those who underwent the experience, but their memory, too, is charged with intervening influences, desire, and forgetfulness. Memorials cannot preserve truth, but they do construct communities of interest, binding them where memory fails and mere scholarship survives. Peter Eisenman, the architect who designed the most recent Holocaust Memorial in Berlin, acknowledging that he could not expect to "please everyone," admitted to an interviewer that skateboarders and children playing hide and seek among the stone slabs would not demean the memorial. Even someone scratching Nazi symbols on it might "add to it," he said.[17] That remark expresses a very contemporary sentiment.

Structures carved in stone do not easily accommodate divergent mindsets. Yet they support new and startling ideas that rise to the surface, occasionally overcoming the world's inattention and forcing it to reassess received opinion.[18] Moreover, the receivers of opinion talk back in unexpected ways that vary from vengeful defacement or the destruction of offending art to its enthusiastic embrace and embellishment.[19] Incidental circumstances can also redefine artworks, for example, when pranksters temporarily make off with a sculpture, thereby endowing it with totemic status that is henceforth ritually honored by the sculpture's ceremonial abduction and return.[20] No aesthetic reevaluation or esoteric interpretation of the art need be inferred from this gesture, but the work of art acquires a cultic meaning as a result of its displacement and the implicit challenge to its ownership. It may have been both private property and private art, but the kidnapping renders it public art.[21] Thus, neither creation nor ownership legislates the public identity of art. Ultimately, that privilege rests with the public.

Publics—not one, but many—while not directly responsible for the production of art, have a sense of entitlement toward what is done in their name. No longer content to be merely spoken to or for, they are emboldened by art and wish to be heard. Public art broadcasts to a populace, but increasingly, people are part of the art-making process, enlisted at an early phase of its enunciation. Especially where public funding is involved, tax payers claim the right to its allocation.[22] They take possession by word and deed, assuming territorial rights. And in this, as many public artists have come to understand, they are right—for, like the streets, public art belongs to the people.[23]

A Short History of Public Art in America

There is no single evolutionary thread that defines the history of public art in America, but there are pivotal nodes. Since private individuals rarely have the resources to produce public art unassisted, support normally emanates from leaders or governments or associations of civic-minded people who commission art. This, at least, is true of the art that stays in one place for a long time; someone must be responsible for it. Yet there have always been countercurrents of resistance, some of them preserved in the anonymous music and imagery we know as folk art.

America began honoring its war dead with statuary when it had barely come together as a nation and decorated its public buildings with heroic murals as soon as they were constructed. Notwithstanding limited resources, the Founding Fathers promoted science and the arts as elements of the public good. They were influenced by the eighteenth-century ideal of civic republicanism, which militated against monarchical extravagance, tending instead toward the more severe example of Roman virtue.[24] John Adams famously affirmed his need to study politics and war so that his sons could study philosophy and science and his grandchildren painting, poetry, music, and architecture. And in fact, John Quincy Adams overcame powerful opponents to realize James Smithson's bequest to the nation to found the cultural institution that bears his name. Puritanical opposition to the arts as unnecessary luxury, reinforced with the belief that government subsidy interferes with popular self-governance and economic autonomy, divided republicans from federalists centuries ago and still fuels arguments against public arts funding.[25] As a result, American patrons of the arts and would-be artists turned to Europe for inspiration and education.

Artists from Europe had to be imported to fill American commissions, while Americans traveled and studied in European schools of art and architecture throughout much of the nineteenth century, returning at last to develop their own iconography based on classical models. Their legacy is everywhere evident today in civic centers and state capitol domes. Probably the best-known and—until the overwhelming impact of Maya Lin's Vietnam Veterans Memorial—most beloved work of public art in America is the Statue of Liberty. Called by its sculptor Frederic-Auguste Bartholdi *Liberty Enlightening the World*, the statue was a centennial gift to the people of the United States, paid for by ordinary French citizens through a lottery. It was rather ungraciously received by a nation (even then) obsessed with security and not at all unanimous in welcoming "your huddled masses

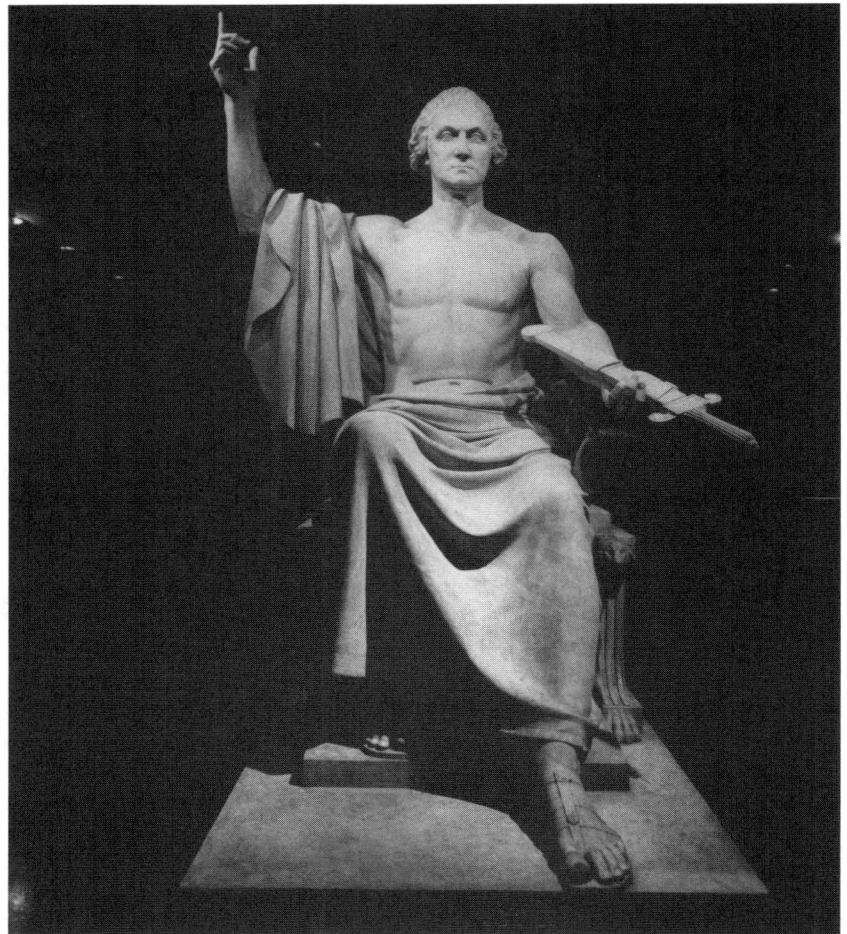

Horatio Greenough, statue of George Washington. (Courtesy of Smithsonian American Art Museum, transfer from the U.S. Capitol.)

yearning to breathe free." Nonetheless, "Lady Liberty" was positioned, as Bartholdi intended, across from Ellis Island, the Atlantic entry point to America, a symbol of hope where hope was sometimes abandoned and sometimes renewed.

Monumental construction and mural decoration began in earnest after the Civil War, when every city and village acted on the compulsion to memorialize its victors and its dead. Images of generals on horseback and

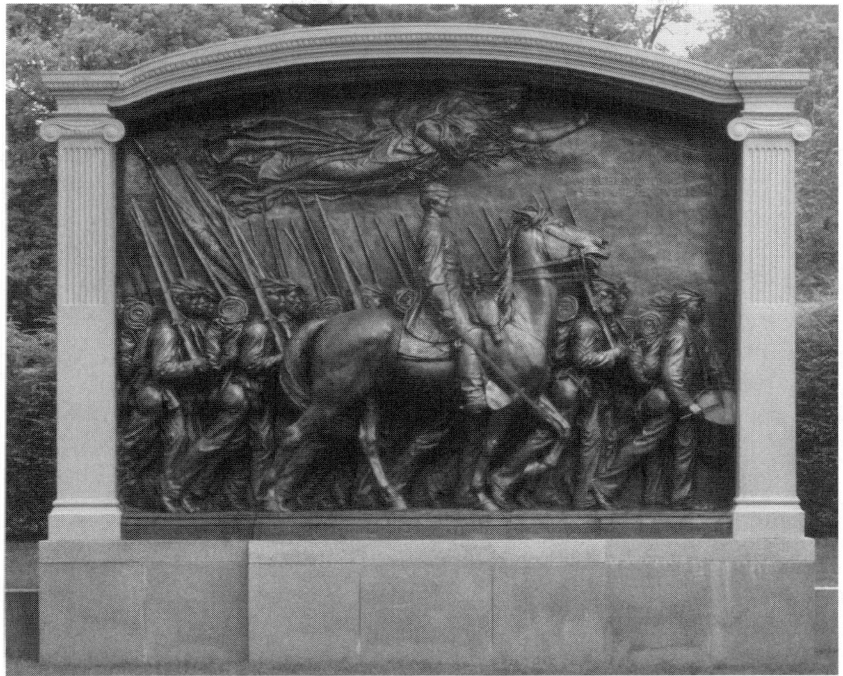

Augustus Saint-Gaudens, Shaw Memorial, Massachusetts 54th Regiment, (1897/1900). (Courtesy of U.S. Department of Interior, National Park Service, Saint-Gaudens National Historic Site, Cornish, N.H.)

soldiers in uniform, on pedestals in parks or bas-reliefs on courthouse walls, continue to be the standard model that most people think of when asked for examples of public art. Most were commissioned through private subscription and with public encouragement. One that stands apart, both for its content and its unprecedented style of realization, is Augustus Saint-Gaudens's *Memorial to Robert Gould Shaw and the Massachusetts Fifty-Fourth Regiment*.

The artist, conventionally trained both in Europe and the United States, had previously executed an idealized memorial to Admiral Farragut, hero of the battles of New Orleans and Mobile Bay, and had worked with the architect H. H. Richardson on the decoration of Boston's Trinity Church. The Fifty-Fourth Regiment was a unit of African-American soldiers, most of them free blacks, commanded by Colonel Shaw, the son of an illustrious abolitionist Boston family. On May 18, 1863, Shaw led his troops in a charge against Fort Wagner, a key to the Confederate defense of Charleston. Shaw and nearly half of his vastly outnumbered men were killed in that battle, but the fort was ultimately won, and the valor of the regiment inspired many additional blacks to fight for the Union. After the war's end, an African-American businessman led an effort to raise a monument to Colonel Shaw. A biracial committee was eventually formed to mark the public's gratitude to the fallen hero and to commemorate the "colored men as citizen soldiers." It was the artist's unusual idea to integrate the leader directly with his troops in a bas-relief, rather than as a free-standing equestrian figure. Sixteen visible soldiers were carefully and individually modeled and incorporated into a complex, rhythmic, yet realistic scene suggesting many marching men with their leader in the foreground.[26] In her descriptive essay for a National Gallery exhibition of the sculpture in 1997, assistant curator Deborah Chotner underlines the socially inspired aesthetic device: "No European monument . . . whether ancient or modern, could act as a prototype for such an American subject as that of the Shaw Memorial. Saint-Gaudens reinterpreted his sources to create a new and totally original public monument that democratically united a commander with his troops."

A century after the Saint-Gaudens dedication, another sculpture was erected in a predominately black neighborhood of Washington, D.C., to commemorate the same event. This one, called *The Spirit of Freedom*, also celebrates the African-American soldiers (and sailors) who fought for the Union. The sculptor, Ed Hamilton, won a competition proposed by Congresswoman Eleanor Holmes Norton and funded by the District of Columbia Arts Commission. The life-sized figures that emerge out of a rectangular stone block are clearly derived from those modeled by Augustus Saint-Gaudens, but they are freed from the regimental confinement of the bas-relief. Hamilton renders them in the round, without a pedestal or classical embellishment. They carry out their variously oriented tasks with no visible sign of a leader. The back of the sculpture depicts an agricultural family scene, implying the men's humble origin. The sculpture honors the ordinary men and women who suffered and gave no less than their commander. Each of the two historical monuments advances a tradition that presumes to illustrate the spirit of a nation and to rally public sentiment. Inevitably there would be disunity, but the art conveys a message of singular commitment and individual sacrifice to a cause.[27] Both memorials endeavor to find an aesthetic mode of expression appropriate to their own historic moment that fits an evolving and pluralistic social ideal.

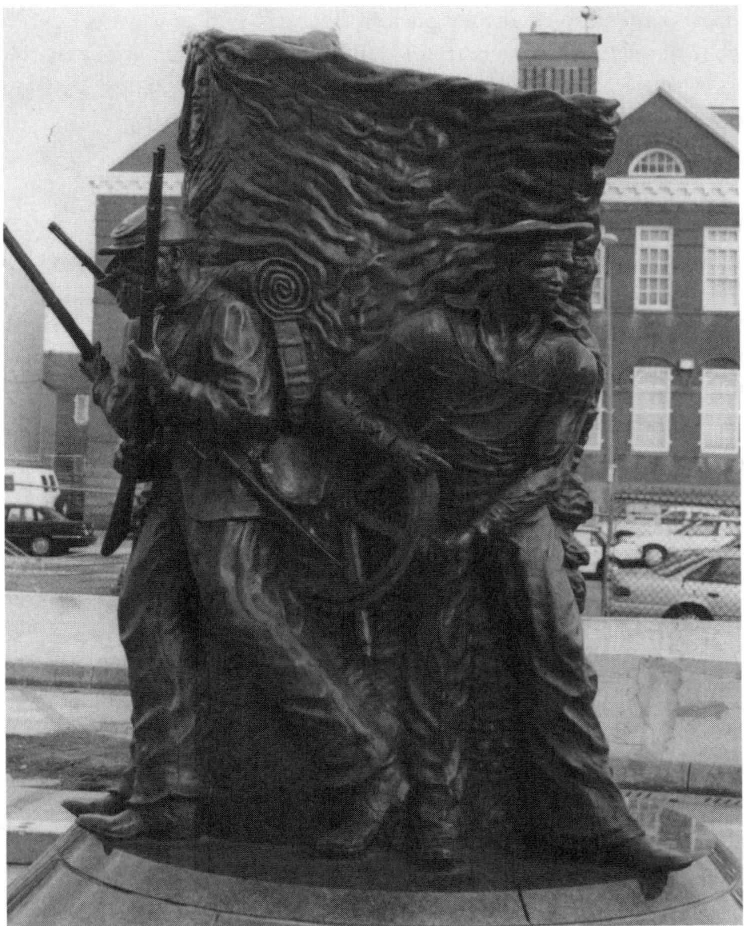

Ed Hamilton, *The Spirit of Freedom* (1998) bronze sculpture, African-American Civil War Memorial, Washington, D.C. (Photo by Hilde Hein.)

There would be more public art but less unanimity in the decades that followed.[28] It was a period of discord marked by westward expansion, imperialism, racial and labor violence, flourishing industry, rapacious commercialism, and the accumulation of wealth. It culminated with the official Columbian Exposition in Chicago in 1893 that celebrated four centuries of American triumphalism. The Chicago Museum of Science and Industry stands as a remnant of Daniel Burnham's Great White City, an idealized confection of snowy plaster that spawned a (counter)revolution of sober neoclassical government buildings and public parks constructed across America. The fashion took hold in shopping arcades, amusement parks, museums, and fin-de-siècle resort hotels, inspiring optimism and civic pride amid an explosion of commercial development.

Shortly thereafter, in San Francisco, devastated by the earthquake and fire of 1906, local businessmen set about rebuilding the city, not as the rough frontier town it had been but according to an image that displayed the rising prominence of commerce. This project was combined with a plan to celebrate the 1915 opening of the Panama Canal that would join the Atlantic and Pacific oceans, signifying America's achievement of world eminence. A yearlong festival, the Panama Pacific International Exposition (PPIE) would glorify industry and technology, promote tourism, and symbolize human betterment.

A part of the reconstruction effort was a program of public wall painting. Spurred by the organizers and patrons of the affair, local artists and others from farther afield were recruited to create more than thirty "official" allegorical murals linking the rebirth of the city with a utopian vision of mankind. One commentator declared that investment in the murals on the part of the fair's organizers was a substitute for much-needed political reform.[29] Grand pronouncements were made about the public good, but the chief beneficiaries of the fair were San Francisco's business "aristocrats," who shrewdly applied the wealth they had accumulated in the California gold rush toward gaining political control of the city.

The PPIE put in place a paternalistic business climate with a compliant public and a generous appetite for culture. This was the opening wedge for a new consciousness that would transform public art, imbuing it with explicit political content and a revolutionary aesthetic. It arrived in the person of Diego Rivera, who was to leave an indelible mark on contemporary mural art. Rivera swept into North America on a wave of interest in decorative art and his own bravado: he was compared to the "carnivalesque" circus and museum director P. T. Barnum.[30] Though tainted with Communist affiliation, Rivera was perceived as a solidifying element in relation to American investment interests in Mexico. Having studied with the currently fashionable European masters, Rivera had the right credentials. He managed to convey his faith in a modernist aesthetic, while also appearing to his industrialist sponsors to be a simple man of the people. They labeled him a "paisano," eminently suited, it seemed, to adorn the wall of what was, in the end, the private space of an exclusive club whose members included all the first families of San Francisco finance and business.[31]

The iconography of Rivera's painting *Allegory of California* was puzzling to critics, and so was its fragmented style. The mural featured a vast, hovering female figure that glorified the bounty of the earth and the labor that transforms it. Though decorative, the painting made viewers uneasy, for it suggested a disrupted relationship among the land, its economy, and

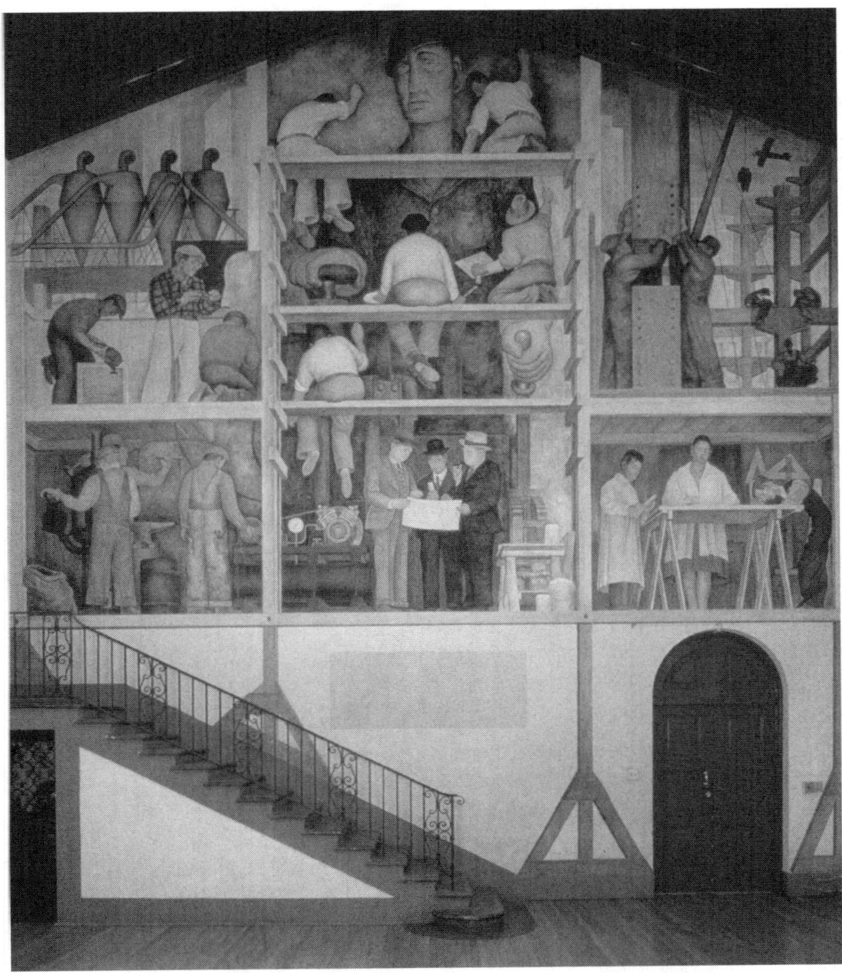

Diego Rivera, *The Making of a Fresco Showing the Building of a City* (1931), fresco, San Francisco Art Institute, gift of William Gerstle. (Photo by David Wakely.)

its laboring forces. In fact, most of the land was owned by wealthy absentee landlords and cultivated by unskilled immigrants. Far from celebrating an Edenic paradise, Rivera signaled the exploitation that was well under way in California. A later, more publicly placed mural at the California School of Fine Arts, *Making a Fresco,* merges the building of a skyscraper with the heroic figure of the worker, again posing questions about their relationship.[32] During his years spent painting and teaching in the United States, Rivera influenced a number of radical young, political artists, who worked with him and sought to create a visual vocabulary that would appeal to working people instinctively.

If the course of empire is westward, its countercurrent flowed eastward, as Rivera was invited to create murals in Detroit and New York. Although reviled by detractors as a "half-breed Mexican Bolshevist," he nevertheless drew hordes composed of both art lovers and laborers who came not only to admire the finished paintings but to watch their hero at work. They were excluded from witnessing the demolition of Rivera's provocative mural *Man at the Crossroads* in Rockefeller's Radio City Center when the owners, confronted with the realization that prominent businessmen would not rent space alongside a portrait of Lenin, were compelled to destroy the painting they had commissioned. Recording the event and the artist's refusal to erase the offending image, *The Nation*'s art critic pointed out that Rivera had "violated the second-rate architects' creed that decoration, to be 'harmonious,' must be practically invisible; that neither in color, idea, nor style should it be anything that you stop to look at."[33] To replace Rivera's panoramic scene, the Rockefeller Center owners engaged the English artist Frank Brangwyn to paint a mural of the Sermon on the Mount. The artist was required to omit representation of the Christ—depicting instead a light descending from heaven—since no likeness could adequately portray this exalted subject.

Meanwhile, in California, in the wake of *Making a Fresco*, Rivera's politicized disciples labored on, experimenting with new artistic styles to create a public art form that would incorporate the public. A new populist spirit was afoot throughout the country, as thousands of artists were turned loose and commissioned to decorate public buildings at government expense under the newly announced Public Works of Art Project. PWAP (1933) was the forerunner of Franklin Delano Roosevelt's New Deal WPA (Works Progress Administration) program (1935) that subsidized jobs for unemployed artists. This program, together with the Federal Art Project, the Treasury Department's Relief Art Project and its Section of

Painting and Sculpture (later designated the Section of Fine Arts), and corresponding theater and writers' projects, represents the closest approach ever made in the United States to federal support of the arts on a scale comparable to the British Arts Council or the state cultural ministries of France and Germany. Most of the New Deal agencies provided only temporary relief through employment of artists, and the entire program was scuttled in 1943, as the nation turned its resources to fighting World War II. But, throughout the decade of their existence, administration of the agencies cast the government in the unfamiliar role of patron of the arts. Not everyone was pleased with that legacy.

Roosevelt's declaration that "government has a final responsibility for the well-being of its citizens" translated into a degree of paternalism, a trickling down of "elite" cultural benefits intended to alleviate the burdensome ugliness of the lives of the masses. There was also a measure of idealism and a new national pride in homegrown, regional art, which was cautiously and conservatively promoted. Consistent with other New Deal provisions—the right to unionize, rural electrification, regulation of banks and the stock exchange, conservation, Social Security, and agricultural reform—the arts programs endorsed an attitude favoring "the common man" and an idealized balance between individualism and collectivism. New Deal art, much of it created by what were then young and unknown artists, tended to romanticize the merits of community, family, hard work, and the day-to-day routine of ordinary life. It did not feature classical allegory or the grand historical references that had prevailed at the turn of the century. To a considerable degree, commissions were awarded to traditionally excluded artists—women, people of color, and self-taught artists—thus implicitly endorsing a modern style that was meant to be popularly accessible.

There were links to left-leaning causes, and certainly some of the recipients of grants were Communist sympathizers. Some of them took part in creating the murals for San Francisco's Coit Tower, the largest collective project funded by the federal programs. Occurring in the midst of a major strike of the International Longshoremen's Association, whose picket lines were visible from the site, that project polarized its sponsors and participants. Openly polemical, the paintings elicited protest and ultimately provoked the withdrawal of government support. Intermingled with widening labor unrest that led to a Bay Area general strike, the Coit Tower artists' project met with the same defeat that broke the labor struggle. A few of the paintings were destroyed, but more important, the remaining ones were subjected to a new, conservatively initiated, aesthetic critique that debunked rhetorical content, discounted the Riveraesque fractionation, and called for a return to compositional unity and grandeur of design.[34] Together with the termination of the PWAP program and the end of the project's support, Coit Tower was closed, the murals covered and the windows blackened—not to be reopened for decades. Although immediately demoralizing, this suppression clearly testified to the wide legibility of the art and to its power to mobilize popular opinion. That lesson was not lost on artists and activists, but neither did it escape the notice of officialdom and the corporate patrons of public art. They grew more cautious in their support of projects and more censorious in their judgment.

The critical tide swung toward modernism and to the abstract easel art by European painters that was making its way into American galleries just prior to and during World War II. Mural art suffered a corresponding demotion; it was reined in to apolitical design elements that were tinged by commercial advertising. Where, for a moment, radical artists, in rare unity with a perceptive public, had explored ambiguous meanings and found a medium for their expression, convergent business and governmental interests now reasserted control. They held the purse strings and were not to be bamboozled by clever allusions and parodies. Striking a middle road, the enfeebled WPA programs avoided the extremes of both elite avant-gardism and direct advocacy for social change. Briefly, all seemed to be sweetness and light—in a country of happy, industrious families, at peace, and untouched by economic insecurity or unmanageable racial and ethnic strife. But this was an illusion that could not endure. People turned inward, immured in solitary anguish and private indulgence—as their art was soon to express.

Some artists resisted the introverted individualism characteristic of the period while appearing to capitulate to it. Meyer Schapiro, a leading art historian and social critic of that time, explained the artists' tormented forms as part of an evolving (a)sociality. This, he said, was the product of modern democratic institutions and juridical relationships that sanction unheralded freedom of expression, transcending traditional bounds of order and decency.[35] If the critical discovery of revolutionary art in the first half of the nineteenth century was the historicist (impersonal) nature of social humanity, its revised creed of the twentieth century may have been the paradoxical interiority of freedom. The art that emanates, painfully, from this contradiction can be cruel, antic, surrealistic, obscene, or violent. It does not conform to conventional standards but rebelliously seeks new media and means of expression. Forever discontented, it is affirmed only in the excitement of constant change. The media best suited to convey such idiosyncratic, asocial sentiments were film and later television, which, paradoxically, reaches the public through privately segregated spaces.

In the post-World War II climate in which modern art as a whole could be denounced as "a weapon of the Kremlin," a coherent public was not easily identified.[36] Though governed largely by individual self-interest, people followed the herd. Swept along by Cold War hysteria, conservative "patriots," including some artists, nearly succeeded in bringing about the destruction of a series of murals in a San Francisco post office. One of the last commissions awarded under the New Deal programs, the paintings by Anton Refregier chronicled the century-long history of California from the gold rush to the founding of the United Nations in 1945. Antagonists purported to decipher the left-wing populism of the artist in the iconographical detail of these premodernist murals and saw there a Communist conspiracy. Large-scale public representations—too much akin to socialist realism—were now suspect. [37] But the triumph of abstraction did not bespeak the absence of political meaning; it signaled only an end to a manner of expression. Commenting on art in general, Schapiro noted that its inevitable interrogation of the human condition is fundamentally social. However, at any given historic moment it takes place within a network of constraints that limit its conceptual and aesthetic possibilities. Like private art, public art was at an aesthetic crossroad that would eventually lead to unprecedented liberation.

Expanding the Field

New Deal artists, though unemployed, were conventionally trained professionals. They sought commissions in standard fashion, by submitting proposals—sketches and maquettes—to panels of art-trained judges who criticized and sometimes modified them. Many of the artists believed in a populist ideology and expressed it in art meant to be legible to an audience that was awakening to its own power. The artists of the next generation expanded their own consciousness and reached out to the public in unexpected ways, culminating in the breakdown of barriers even beyond status and class. Conceptual distinctions and hierarchical orders of every type were cast in review, among them the gulf between art and life.[38] "Happenings," an art form that flourished briefly in the early 1960s, gave the lie to the adage *Ars longa, vita brevis*.[39] Repudiating both genius and claims to immortality, happenings emphasized the immediate, spontaneous, unrehearsed accident. Far from the studied distance of classical aesthetic judgment but also from the egocentrism of modernism, happenings were participatory—demanding engagement. Decades later, they persist only in memory and in their aura-less documentation, but happenings democratized art. Scorning "art-like" art's contrivance of detached aesthetic experience, happenings disclosed a Zen-like quality in commonplace trivia. Creation of art-without-objects became a "do-it-yourself" activity, like home improvement, that affirmed everyone. We could do it, and it was liberating.

Happenings brought art into the streets and shifted attention—as the more theoretically loaded action painting had failed to do—away from completed objects to the collective process of art-making. Moreover, in elevating the technology of its documentation to partnership in the creative process, happenings opened the door to a reconceptualization of art's ontology from which no turning back now seems possible. Performativity, which had long been sidelined as a necessary condition of realizing art or treated as mechanically following upon a prior creative mental act, now emerged as a fundamental element of all creativity. Performance had become a philosophical category.[40]

Coming from a very different origin but with comparable effect were the hundreds of art projects facilitated by the National Endowment for the Arts (NEA) 1967 Art in Public Places Program. Intended to disseminate the experience and enjoyment of the arts beyond the museum to the widest possible audience, the program initially retained the paternalistic aspect of the New Deal. It was *for* the public but not *of* it. The purpose was to assimilate more people into the American melting pot, not to glorify their diversity. However, the greater its nominal success, the greater the challenges to the premises of the program, for the myth of the generic (amalgamated) American could not withstand confrontation with actual multiplicity. Appeals to an "atypical" public and to artists seasoned outside the established academies undermined the canons established for an earlier generation of art connoisseurs. Demographically, the United States population no longer traced its ancestry to predominantly European roots, and the public that clamored for recognition in the mid-twentieth century included people who were not white, not male, not middle class, and not heterosexual. Above all, they had lost their reverence toward traditional authority and its narrow value structure.

They wanted more than tolerance or recognition; they claimed validation and they demanded to be heard. They did not stop with protest against the imposition of art that misrepresented or humiliated or ignored them. They did not confine themselves to complaints about the misuse of public funds or ethical or aesthetic outrages: they insisted loudly on having a voice in the selection and decision-making process. Finally, they seized the initiative to make their own art, finding alternative support structures and spaces to do so, while perfecting forms of expression that translated and mediated between cultures. Feminists, homosexuals, Marxists, environmentalists, ethnic artists, and community groups, separately and in collaboration, began to develop ways of making art that were self-generated, activist, and uncompromisingly didactic. Without giving up altogether on the individualism of modernism, they abandoned its apparatus of formalism along with the myth of disinterested aesthetic purity. They were engaged and so was their art. Suzanne Lacy, a feminist artist and disciple of Happening guru Allan Kaprow, introduced the term "new genre public art" to distinguish the new movement from the "top-down" old-style public art.[41]

Problematizing the vacuous universality of traditional connotations of "public," Lacy asks: is it "a qualifying description of place, ownership, or access? Is it a subject, or a characteristic of the particular audience?" There are several scripts that define the public differently, but they agree that the new art form is "not built on a typology of materials, spaces, or artistic media, but rather on concepts of audience, relationship, communication, and political intention."[42] In its adoption of the social as focal concept and its refusal to fix an identifying medium, new genre public art clearly descends from the old public art. Where it differs is in its analytic articulation of the public (or publics) and its collaborative inclusion of this public in the creation of art. The artwork may, in fact *be* the relationship between and among artists and publics—a process, not a thing. This process is social or even political at a grass-roots level. It is designed to build community, not to assume it. It is also meant to teach and to expose the conditions that separate communities as much as the communities link their members.

New genre public art projects generally involve complex negotiation—with local property owners; arts and building commissions; state, local, and federal government agencies; environmental organizations; funding sources; professional associations; trade unions; neighborhood and citizens' groups; purveyors of materials; immediate abutters of projects; and the actual performers and producers of the artwork. According to a traditional conception of art, all this is part of the auxiliary social infrastructure, tangential to the actual art product. Artists such as Christo and Jeanne-Claude, however, and the new genre collaborators hold that all these agents and procedures, collectively, *are* the art. The material product—if indeed there is one—is but one aspect of the whole and not necessarily the most important one. Instead, the work of art is a discontinuous temporal entity, defined by a loosely connected knot of relationships—physical, economic, personal, emotional, political, and aesthetic. Perhaps no one is in a position to appreciate the whole of the work, and no individual is solely responsible for it. The work creates its own authorship as it creates its public and comes to fruition in that synthetic process.

Thus, far from the classic horseman in the plaza or the cannon in the common, public art has become dematerialized, its molecules attenuated and mingled with those of its equally diffused makers. The history of a new genre work of public art may be momentary or prolonged by artificially memorializing devices such as documentation, reviews, films, and videos. Its continuity is atomized and reconfigured in multiple places and memories. It is absorbed in a narrative that acquires more excrescences with each retelling. In retrospect, its story infects the stories of older, conventional instances of public art so that they, in turn, acquire unanticipated dimensions.[43] We can no longer think them encapsulated according to the uncertain intention of an original designer, for other minds have encumbered them with additional meanings, some of them inspired by successor art. That, again, is why a toppled statue of Saddam Hussein remains and renews itself as art. It is also why a precisely "restored" Bamiyan Buddha would tell one story, while the "non-restored" damaged cavern that contained the "original" would tell another—both aesthetic extensions of the fifth-century work whose destruction the Taliban willed but could not achieve.

Reconsidered in retrospect, no art is confined by parameters of time and space. No museum has such power to incarcerate. Like private art, public art lives in a transient space of meaning. While public art typically addresses itself to a public sphere, it no longer claims to find that readymade and instead is dedicated to creating small public enclaves. The enterprise may be contentious: engagement can be disagreeable. It is often short-lived, and consensus is not invariably a happy state. Currently public art professes neither to command nor to seek unanimity but to interrogate and make room for doubt. In a world that hungers for answers and clings to certainty, this can be an unpopular ambition.

Today's public artists incline to replace answers with questions. They seek to advance debate and discussion. Their art is left open-ended and invites participation. Its orientation is toward process and change rather than material stability. Since its borders are indefinite, so is its authorship. Indeed the basic polarities that ground traditional thinking about all art—subject/object, artist/audience, art/non-art—have become fluid.

Notes

1. While their status as public art might be debatable, I cite these instances as particularly well-known examples of a practice, destroying the idols of one's enemy, that has been with us since the beginning of human history. A passage of the Bible (Jeremiah 10:3–5) clearly reviles the statues of wood and precious metals made by artisans and worshiped in Mesopotamia. See also Exodus 34:13. God exhorts Moses: "ye shall break down their altars, and dash in pieces their pillars, and ye shall cut down their Asherim." Christian conquerors destroyed the images of "pagan" civilizations throughout the world, just as Nazis desecrated the sacred objects of the Jews, and American settlers pillaged native artifacts. Vandalism toward public art, sacred and secular (and sometimes toward private art), continues to be one way in which both individuals and governments carry on (displaced) wars through assault on culture. See also "Life, Death, and Eternity of the Buddhas in Afghanistan" by Pierre Centlivres and "The Empty Niche of the Bamiyan Buddha" by Jean-Francois Clement in *Iconoclash: Beyond the Image Wars in Science, Religion, and Art*, eds. Bruno Latour and Peter Weibel (Cambridge, Mass.: MIT Press, 2002).

2. Consider, for example, Mierle Laderman Ukeles's *Barge Ballet*, part of a project undertaken as artist-in-residence with the New York Department of Sanitation. After shaking the hands of thousands of land-based garbagemen in the 1970s, Ukeles turned to the choreography of the tugboat-escorted barges that carry solid waste down the Hudson River to the Fresh Kills landfill on Staten Island. Handshaking is a well-established exchange of goodwill that Ukeles elevated to the status of art. Another unconventional adaptation of the commonplace was Peggy Diggs's *Milk Carton Project* (1991). The use of this most domestic item that crosses from the public marketplace into the privacy of virtually every household drew attention to domestic abuse by printing graphic images of common acts of violence on the containers and listing resource information for help.

3. Through its 1966 authorization of the Art in Public Places program, the National Endowment for the Arts commissioned projects that "were to be experienced and enjoyed by the widest possible audience." The assumption was that art for the public should be blandly generic and generally pleasing. The same premise underlies most of the agreeably inoffensive art funded by municipal and corporate agencies. Public art, proper, is more narrowly defined.

4. Aesthetic sensibility, symbolic and abstract, existed from the very beginnings of architecture. It is absurd to suggest that it came into being as a result of

modern legislation. However, government employment of artists under New Deal programs (1933–43) energized American consciousness of the public function of the arts and paved the way to the entry of artists into city planning projects of the 1960s and 1970s. Beginning with Philadelphia's 1% art allocation, incorporation of art into public structures was formalized in 1965 by the National Endowment for the Arts funding of the Art in Public Places Program (later renamed Visual Artists' Public Projects). These programs, initiated to employ artists, shifted their emphasis over time to encourage aesthetic embellishment.

5. viz. Barbara Melosh, *Engendering Culture* (Washington, D.C.: Smithsonian Institution Press, 1991).

6. viz. David Hammon's oversized image of a blond and blue-eyed Jesse Jackson, called *How Ya Like Me Now?*, which was torn down by angry neighbors before it was fully installed. On the recommendation of Jesse Jackson, it was partially reconstructed in the interior of the Washington Projects for the Arts (WPA) Gallery, together with its broken parts. This inclusion of its history in its presentation effectively reconstituted it as a more interesting, if more private, work of art.

7. This is the objection raised by Arthur Danto, among other critics, to the controversial sculpture *Tilted Arc*, by Richard Serra. In Danto's view, it would have been appropriately displayed among other works of art at the Storm King Sculpture Center, an open-air museum in Rockland County, New York, but it was unacceptable in the Federal Plaza in Manhattan. Serra, says Danto, "insisted that the esthetic override the political, which it cannot do when the art is public." *The State of the Art* (New York: Prentice Hall Press, 1987), 93.

8. This was clear in the staged "descent from the pedestal" performed in Baghdad by a few non-local Iraqis assisted by American troops and vehicles and hailed as the Liberation of Iraq by the U.S.

9. Long before the printing press made literacy widespread, people grasped the meaning of nonverbal symbols and were able to communicate social and political ideas subversively through their use.

10. In her essay "Group Material Timeline: Activism as a Work of Art," Jan Avgikos suggests that the group's earnest but unsuccessful endeavor to galvanize a new order of social relations by means of activist art might be interpreted as an act of colonization. See Nina Felshin, ed., *But Is It Art? The Spirit of Art as Activism* (Seattle: Bay Press, 1995). In practice, artists are frequently and unintentionally the vanguard of gentrification, as they move into inexpensive urban neighborhoods, soon to be followed by real estate developers. They then *become* a political cause to local inhabitants.

11. The subordination of women to men and their consignment to a separate sphere of child-rearing and domesticity seemed only a natural extension of the biological order. It was not perceived as a political artifact. That recognition spurred a new vocabulary that includes "gender" as well as "sexism."

12. I introduced the retronym "private art" in the previous chapter as a means of demarcating a form of art that has become the prototype of all art, although, in fact, it differs radically from the variety of older and more universal art forms, which I designated "nonprivate."

13. Cartoons, arguably a form of public art, frequently adapt well-known images to socially constructive purposes. The more famous the original work, the greater the impact of its renegotiation. One illustration shows a beloved work of public art used to this end. It is Bill Mauldin's cartoon after the assassination of President Kennedy: Lincoln, seated in the enclosure of his memorial, is depicted hunched over, head in hands, weeping. viz. James W. Loewen, *Lies across America* (New York: The New Press, 1999).

14. "War Crimes and Heroism in Vietnamese Commemorations of the U.S. War: Observations in 1977 and 1992," in *Bulletin of Concerned Asian Scholars* 27 (1995).

15. A commission headed by Major General William R. Peers completed a study made public in 1974 and later published commercially.

16. Andreas Huyssen cites Robert Musil's quip: "There is nothing in the world as invisible as monuments." (See "Monuments and Holocaust Memory in a Media Age," in *Twilight Memories* [New York: Routledge, 1995].) In a cynical frame of mind, one might think the cost of a memorial a small price to pay for the luxury of forgetting. The "burial" of history was confronted seriously in 1986 by two German artists, Jochem and Esther Shalev-Gertz, who constructed a Sinking Column in a suburb of Hamburg. Fellow citizens were invited to expose ongoing acts of prejudice and affirm their vigilance against it by adding their names to the column, which was gradually lowered into the pit over which it was suspended, finally disappearing altogether in 1990 (see James Young, "The Counter-Monument: Memory against Itself in Germany Today," in W. J. T. Mitchell, *Art and the Public Sphere* [Chicago, 1992]).

17. *The Boston Globe*, 11 May 2005.

18. To anyone who grew up listening to "fireside chats" by Franklin Delano Roosevelt on the radio and occasionally seeing his figure on film, the depiction of him in a wheelchair in the Washington, D.C., FDR Memorial is disconcerting. He was stricken with polio at the age of 39 in 1921 and was never again to walk unassisted. However, he painfully avoided any reference to or public representation of his disability, a decision politically necessitated at the time that now affronts a vocal community of handicapped people who celebrate him as an inspirational model.

19. Consider the accumulation of flowers, toys, and other memorabilia that visitors leave at the Vietnam Veterans Memorial, the popularly added "guests" to Judy Chicago's *Dinner Party*, and the inevitable children on the lap of Albert Einstein (formerly at the National Academy of Science).

20. Comparable purloinings have happened to private owners of lawn decorations, whose flamingos take flight on extended journeys, punctuated with postcards

from exotic places, to return "home" at last bedecked with new wardrobes and sunglasses.

21. The public has the power to declare art: as a symbol announcing a hamburger stand, the McDonald's golden arches are neither public nor private art. They are on private land and invite customers to enter it. From the perspective of the public, the arches have a public function; if they serve it with a certain élan, they become art by acclamation.

22. Hence the outrage over the disbursement of NEA grants for art that, if privately funded, would evoke little objection and probably would not be noticed.

23. Frederick Law Olmsted, who was to become an inspiration to Christo and Jeanne-Claude, thought of New York's Central Park as a work of art whose object and justification were to "produce a poetic influence on people and lift them out of the ordinary conditions of life in the city." Cited by Calvin Tomkins, "The Gates to the City: How the Christos Plan to Transform Central Park," *The New Yorker*, 29 March 2004.

24. Occasionally this led to moral collisions when statues of statesmen in Roman togas offended the sensibility of puritans who objected to seminudity. viz. Horatio Greenough's 1840 statue of George Washington, bare-chested with a laurel wreath. Banished from public display, it languished for years in the basement of the Smithsonian Institution. It has now been retrieved but continues to evoke as much ridicule as reverence.

25. Dispute over a Washington Memorial, its substance, support, and ideology began even before Washington's death in 1799 and was not concluded until the centennial anniversary of independence, when the two houses of Congress unanimously resolved to complete the obelisk. By then, it no longer mattered what Washington "stood for": the tide had turned in favor of "high culture" and an aesthetic of taste. The final design that was completed and dedicated in 1885 was by Lt. Col. Thomas Casey of the Army Corps of Engineers. viz. Kirk Savage, "The Self-Made Monument: George Washington and the Fight to Erect a National Monument," in *Critical Issues in Public Art*, eds. Harriet F. Senie and Sally Webster (Washington, D.C.: Smithsonian Institution Press, 1992). See also Douglas Stalker and Clark Glymour, "The Malignant Object: Thoughts on Public Sculpture," *The Public Interest* (1982): 66–9.

26. True to its classical influence, the sculpture also includes an allegorical figure flying overhead carrying an olive branch and the inscription *Omnia Relinquit Servare Republicam* ("He forsook all to preserve the public weal"). Saint-Gaudens worked on the sculpture at his own expense for many years before completing it, and it was not dedicated until 1897, when, with great fanfare, it was exhibited in the United States and abroad. It came to rest at the Saint-Gaudens National Historic Site in New Hampshire. After a complete overhaul jointly carried out by conservators from the National Park Service, the Boston Museum of Fine Arts, and the National Gallery of Art, it returned to the Boston Common facing the capitol dome.

27. The Negro soldier was mistrusted and treated with contempt by both the North and South, a story recorded in the 1989 film "Glory," which is based on the Fifty-Fourth Massachusetts Regiment.

28. Charles Griswold argues that a significant change in public art iconography took place after the Civil War, marking increasing ambiguity in national sentiment. "In a fight against one's brothers it is more difficult to feel without ambiguity that one is engaged in a battle between good and evil, a battle in which there can be a clear-cut winner and loser." (84) This leads him progressively to discussion of the Vietnam Veterans Memorial, which is completely abstract and symbolic and, as Griswold interprets it, interrogative. I find his argument substantively impressive, but I believe account must also be taken of a shift in aesthetic standards and styles favoring abstraction. No doubt, modern nonrepresentationalism lends itself more effectively than realism to the complexity and ambiguity that Maya Lin wanted to achieve. viz. "The Vietnam Veterans Memorial and the Washington Mall: Philosophical Thoughts on Political Iconography," in *Critical Issues in Public Art*, eds. Senie and Webster.

29. "The job of public art . . . was to help transform private interests into the general interest and to displace the issue of public services with that of public art. . . . Public mural painting was to be a sign of public consent to centralized control." Anthony W. Lee, *Painting on the Left: Diego Rivera, Radical Politics, and San Francisco's Public Murals* (Berkeley: University of California Press, 1999), 39. In modern dress, this language reiterates the Roman doctrine of "bread and circuses."

30. Lee, 46.

31. The mural *Allegory of California* was originally slated for the California School of Fine Arts but was diverted to the (more private) stairway of the Lunch Club of the Pacific Stock Exchange (Lee, 57).

32. *Making a Fresco. Showing the Building of a City* (San Francisco Art Institute, 1931). By depicting himself in the act of painting, Rivera identified himself as one among other workers, striving to build something as yet unfinished.

33. Anita Brenner, cited in Peter G. Meyer, ed., *Brushes with History: Writing on Art from* The Nation, *1865–2001* (New York: Thunder's Mouth Press, 2002).

34. Lee, 155–7.

35. Meyer Schapiro, *Worldview in Painting—Art and Society* (New York: George Braziller, 1999) (especially "The Social Bases of Art" and "The Value of Modern Art").

36. George A. Dondero, a Republican Congressman from Michigan and collaborator with Sen. Joseph McCarthy, also declared that "art which does not portray our beautiful country in plain, simple terms . . . is therefore opposed to our government, and those who create and promote it are our enemies." Cited by Weldon Kees (1 October 1949) in *Brushes with History.*

37. Ironically, a 1963 exhibition of German posters from the same period, 1919–61, entitled Weimar-Nüremberg-Bonn plainly showed that formal aesthetic

considerations are not inherently linked to any ideology, but may be put to the service of every political persuasion.

38. Race, gender, and ethnicity were at the political center, but intertwined with these were reassessments of thinking and doing, work and play, intellect and emotion, subject and object, high art and low art, and dozens of other dichotomies.

39. Allan Kaprow, the founder of the genre, developed it in the late 1950s as an extension of environmental art. Above all, it moved art out of the rarefied atmosphere of the studio and gallery, into the "real world," where it also abandoned the typical instruments of art to adopt those of ordinary living. More process than product oriented, it assimilated into itself performances and perceptions that previous art movements had merely observed and commented upon as a subject for art. A challenge on all fronts, the new art form contested the identity of art and the basis of its judgment as well as the political structures of society.

40. The process of fabrication, previously of interest only as a means, now displaced the product as the center of attention. From John Austin's "performative utterances" to Judith Butler's performance of gender, doing things with words and being gendered kept many a graduate program in business. J. L. Austin, *How to Do Things with Words* (Cambridge, Mass.: Harvard University Press, 1962); Judith Butler, "Performative Acts and Gender Constitution: An Essay in Phenomenology and Feminist Theory," in *Performing Feminisms: Feminist Critical Theory and Theatre*, ed. Sue Ellen Case (Baltimore: Johns Hopkins University Press, 1990).

41. Suzanne Lacy, *Mapping the Terrain: New Genre Public Art* (Seattle: Bay Press, 1995). Lacy also credits Judy Chicago as one of her mentors.

42. Lacy, *Mapping the Terrain*, 28.

43. If, with contemporary hindsight, we were to reflect upon the machinations that preceded and followed the installation of such stable works of public art as the Washington Monument, the Vietnam Veterans Memorial, and the classics of Europe, we would find them remarkably similar to those works now distinguished as processual. An exalted temporal slice has preempted their meaning, but it might have been otherwise and could be different once again.

Innovation in Public Art

They do not represent an interruption or suspension of daily life, as formal and classicizing public art does: They are brief emblems of the city rather than isolated monuments.

—LAWRENCE ALLOWAY

The aim of critical public art is neither a happy self-exhibition nor a passive collaboration with the grand gallery of the city, its ideological theater and architectural-social system. Rather, it is an engagement in strategic challenges to the city structures and mediums that mediate our everyday perception of the world: an engagement through aesthetic-critical interruptions, infiltrations and appropriations that question the symbolic, psychopolitical and economic operations of the city.

—KRZYSZTOF WODICZKO

Expanding the Public

There are few bystanders untouched by public art, although, as in warfare, the part played by ordinary civilians is often indirect and accidental. Caste and class constrict access to art both materially and psychically. Public transport is not available to many places called "open to the public," while other sites are socially forbidding due to cultural snobbery or to the observer's feeling of insecurity. Warranted or not, discomfort is real on other people's turf. Imposing architecture, like uniformed guards and handbag searches, is unwelcoming: such factors deter casual entry and drive away people whose business there is not pressing. Few people visit airports or courthouses solely to look at the art inside, and many are put off by the vaulted atmosphere even of "free" museums, libraries, and university campuses.

The public art found in privately owned spaces such as shopping malls and office parks, where the public comes to buy and consume, is an auxiliary diversion and is rarely the primary reason to congregate.[1] Moreover, this art is closely monitored, ostensibly to prevent mayhem but effectively to control ideological content. Controversy is not good for business. And since commercial property is privately owned, "disruptive" members of the public and their art can be evicted at the will of the owners. Private establishments are not wholly independent of public oversight since many receive some form of funding and/or tax benefits, but their obligations are minimal and hard to enforce. Court orders and injunctions take time to obtain, and citizens' groups aroused to petition for or against a display of art usually confront a situation over which—short of a major boycott—they have no control.[2]

Municipal and state-owned places are also not freely accessible. American streets are meant chiefly as thoroughfares; anyone alleged to obstruct passage by "lingering" or "sauntering" is viewed with suspicion. The same holds of parking lots. Expedition of traffic is the first objective, and while double-parked delivery vehicles and construction hindrances are not impeded, independent street entertainers must be licensed and demonstrators require permits. These are awarded selectively and capriciously.

In 1967, the National Endowment for the Arts (NEA) initiated a program called "Art in Public Places" not only to propagate art but also to promote cultural pluralism.[3] Included in Lyndon Johnson's Great Society plan, public support of art was part of a broad policy of "maximum feasible participation." Although supported by the conservative Nixon administration, its continuation was not aimed at the urban poor but at winning approval from a culture-friendly, middle-class electorate.[4] The NEA chairperson was given ultimate responsibility for grant-making decisions; however, the program works through a peer-panel system designed to distribute funds through tiers of state and local arts agencies.[5] The role of the "general public" should not be exaggerated: peer review panels that judge NEA proposals were initially composed entirely of arts administrators and artists. A later modification added some "lay" members of the public to the process of selecting proposals, but the chief beneficiaries of the program have been artists, not their audience. Nevertheless, where previously people had little choice but to live with, ignore, or throw eggs at a fait accompli that professed to speak in their name, now they held some degree of veto power. This was counterbalanced by the requirement that artists submit to direction by committee, and some, such as Richard Serra, creator of the notorious *Tilted Arc*, firmly rejected what he entitled creation-by-referendum as "art defeating."[6]

Mandatory set-aside funds for the embellishment of public buildings at the state and federal level grew increasingly popular during the twentieth century.[7] The guidelines encompassed sculpture, paintings, mosaics, pools, fountains, and grillworks—decorative features that would "lend dignity" to the urban environment. These so-called "elements of architectural design" were not to be sacrificed to budgetary cutbacks. An ad hoc committee during the Kennedy administration lobbied for greater quality consciousness in architectural policy,[8] and by the 1970s, private corporations such as the Chase Manhattan Bank were conspicuously commissioning work by famous artists for their headquarters. A quasi-collaborative public art-making was spurred by local and state percent-for-art programs that brought artists and public representatives up-front into the planning of public construction. Claiming to represent the public, a cohort of professional arts administrators, lobbyists, consultants, and community mediators emerged to work with the teams of artists, designers, architects, and planners. Enthusiasts hailed this technical and aesthetic collaboration as a renewal of civil consensus. However, far from the eighteenth-century public sphere that Habermas described as a forum for debate leading to rational conclusions, these twentieth-century conventions of "stakeholders" were bargaining sessions in which the winning proposal was usually no one's true choice but only the least objectionable one. Everyone yielded a bit for the sake of gaining something. This personal interest-driven approach to both politics and art prompted a pallid sameness of bland, user-friendly art that quickly filled urban plazas and office buildings.

As one critic objected:

> The problem is not that art is being integrated into our common, everyday environment, but that artists are content with the limits imposed on them by the established rules of their sites. The celebration of the ordinary that indicated a certain concern for public life twenty years ago—substituting human scale and "democratic

interaction" for the heroic pretensions of earlier public art—is now actively being restated as a celebration of the trivial and a passive confirmation of the status quo.[9]

He might have observed in addition that the fact of being presented "for" the public, or "with" public participation, does not automatically render a proposed project public art. The sheer exposure of art to large numbers of private consumers will not suffice to construct a public.

Other critics observed that the movement to exhibit art in public places was simply an extension of a disembodied museum zone, an aestheticization of absolutely everything without local attunement. Missing were the political bite and idealism that had brought artists into the streets in the 1960s. Political activists denounced the "collaborative" trend as a subversion of the social relevance of public art—which, although not a substitute for urban renewal, should be a part of it. It was noted that aestheticizing interventions, such as the construction of Lincoln Center and the renewal of Times Square, were less revivals of New York's public life than interruptions of it, allegedly as a means of quelling crime and unrest. Effectively, one public was being displaced for the benefit of another, more presentable one.

At the same time, a resistance movement was building inside communities grown conscious of their identity and unwilling to be submerged by compromise. Murals appeared once again in the 1970s, this time without benefit of government commissions, on city walls in California, Texas, Chicago, New York, Philadelphia, and elsewhere. This art, funded chiefly by grass-roots donations and created by nonprofessional residents of local communities, emerged wherever wall space was available.[10] The murals arose out of and solidified communities. Their production demanded local collaboration and generated collective discussion of subject matter, symbolism, and cultural heritage, enabling people to revive and reclaim traditions that had been diluted into the mainstream. Not satisfied with the right merely to reject and say "no," they were invigorated by the possibilities of "yes." Writing about the San Francisco murals, Timothy Drescher, their activist historian, distinguishes between public art that is "done for a general, undefined population . . . and commissioned by official bodies" and community art, including not only murals but also film, theater, dance, and performance art "created by or with a group of people who will interact with the finished artwork" whose standard of satisfaction is determined

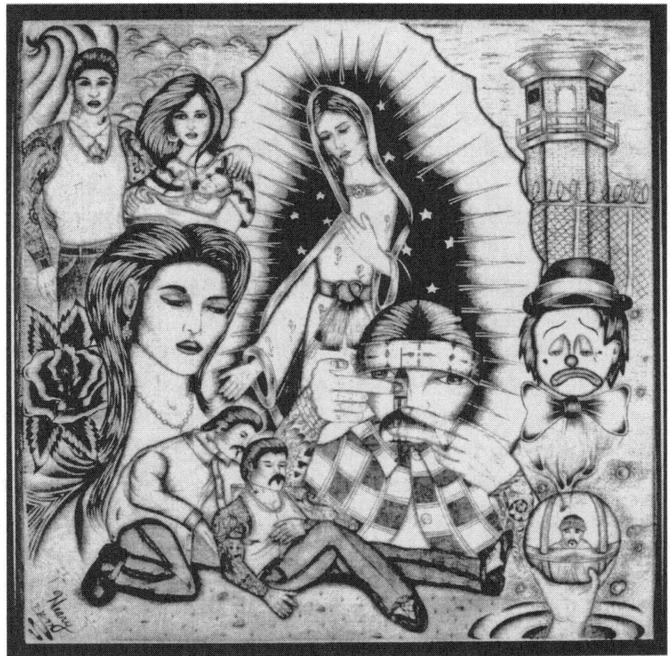

Heavy *Overdose* (1997), black ink on white cotton handkerchief. The Virgin of Guadalupe is incorporated into the contemporary anguish of Chicano prisoners. (Courtesy of The New England Center for Contemporary Art, Brooklyn, Conn.)

by acceptance within the community, not by the judgment of an outside audience.[11]

Public art was activated in these politicized communities as social practice, a medium of self-discovery in cultural context that, surprisingly, bears comparison with the lively debates of the *Federalist Papers*. Not to be confused with the escapist art condemned as kitsch by the modernist critic Clement Greenberg or with its avant-garde alternatives, community art was quirkily historicist. The San Francisco murals appropriated and mingled familiar images, such as the haloed Virgin of Guadalupe, beloved among Chicanos, and the emblematic eagle of the United Farm Workers. These were ironically merged and reinterpreted in contemporary and critical ways that helped to forge self-conscious and nonidealized cohorts of people poised for action in a world that typically disregards them. For this public, art was a medium not of individual self-affirmation but of integration of selves and their common empowerment.

What cannot be erased may be diminished by other means—by ridicule or by trivialization. The art world, finding its premises challenged by the new public art, ignored, then dismissed, and then finally incorporated the new art into its own domain. Public art began to attract attention competitively with the gallery system, sometimes, like outsider art, in its own alternative exhibition spaces, but more often at nontraditional art sites. People came together for street festivals and took part in art-initiated social projects. Some events even made their way into museums, stimulating debate over what truly belongs there. The pressure on elite institutions to be socially responsible and "relevant," together with an impulse toward aesthetic innovation, drove endeavors to decommodify art that succeeded chiefly in recommodifying it in slightly liquefied form.

The boundaries of art were eroding. Comic strips, earth art, urban murals—along with highly sophisticated sociopolitical analyses that mockingly revealed the stockholdings of museum trustees—all depart from the narrow confines of typical museum fare, yet all address it contingently and ultimately have found a place in the annals of art history and criticism. Obliquely, and not without guile, the art world embraced the barbarians at the gate and thereby defanged them. A compelling instance is the case of graffiti. Surreptitiously written words or phrases, spray-painted on walls, public sidewalks, and railroad cars, previously treated as unlawful acts of vandalism, were magically transformed by aesthetic fiat into art—thanks largely to their exhibition in the mid-1970s in avant-garde New York galleries. Complete with vernissage and catalogues, cleansed, and transposed to fixed canvases, the work of the "United Graffiti Artists" inaugurated a new genre, and some of its most proficient "writers" were enfranchised as "artists" under their individual names. It is hard to bite the hand that feeds you when the delicacies it proffers are so delectable.

This domestication of public art undermines its political energy by enhancing its aesthetic surface. An equal and opposite subversion, to reassimilate all art to its materially productive origins, had been the plan decades earlier of the Russian Constructivists. Goading his fellow artists to join the utilitarian world of social activism by deprivatizing art, Vladimir Mayakovsky issued an "Order to the Army of Art" that "the streets shall be our brushes—the squares our palettes." He intended, quite materially, that artists should follow revolutionary Leninist dictates and fuse their creative talents with the practical progress of technology and industrialism.[12]

Worker artists were to abandon their studios to join their brothers in factories, making useful, everyday things. As toolmakers, their inspiration would come from practice and would serve revolutionary society. In effect, artists were to abandon their romantic isolation and submerge themselves into the lives of the masses, once again as artisans, repudiating the bourgeois ideology that had exalted private art.

At the end of the twentieth century, interventionist artists again aimed to reverse bourgeois ideology and to bring about direct change in the material conditions of the world. These artists were less committed than their Constructivist predecessors to wholesale social reconstruction; however, neither did they confine themselves to attacks on art world politics and aesthetic mystification. They confronted immediate "real world" issues of homelessness, homophobia, domestic violence, sexism, health care, AIDS,[13] and environmental pollution. Individually and in small groups, they invented tactical devices for aesthetically enlivened acts of minor sabotage or mounted farcical performances in unexpected public places. Dozens of groups with whimsical names initiated educational programs, organized tenant groups to confront landlords, promoted safe sex, replaced hemorrhoid ads in transit systems with social service information, and created alternative recreational activities for youth at risk.[14] Some challenged the intention of public space by designing inexpensive mobile shelters for the homeless (Rudolph Luria) and reading rooms for the use of street people (Siah Armajani); others elevated the commonplace by way of ritual. Thus, Mierle Laderman Ukeles, by shaking the hands of New York sanitation workers in a 1979 installation called *Touch Sanitation*, sought to dispel their anonymity and make the social importance of their labor visible.[15] While these actions lacked both a unifying aesthetic and a single political program, their challenging presence on the streets, in churches and parks, and on public transportation may well have awakened the consciousness of some observers and helped them to see "that public life is more a matter of routine activities than dramatic events."[16]

"Art into life" is a slogan that calls for engagement within the public sphere but not necessarily for grand gestures. Whether figurative or abstract, traditional public art, when not purely decorative, dealt with "big issues"—conventional civic heroism and events of national import. The new public art is local and vernacular. Obsessively ordinary, it may be vulgar, irreverent, and even repulsive. It is suspicious of beauty as aesthetic affectation, a false friend, culturally relative, and maybe a distraction. Think of sunsets, a quotidian form of colorful pollution.[17] The detritus of industrialism is also seductive, especially to artists. Some create junk art and imaginative salvage projects that beautifully serve the interest of exploiters, lifting their burden of responsibility in the name of art.[18] We cannot assume that all artists, any more than their publics, agree on all topics. Social progressivism is not a prerequisite of public art; conservatism will do as well—but the construction of a public is a central ingredient and is usually intentional.

Publics, however, are fractionated and confused by a surplus of claims on their allegiance. They may infer different and unintended messages from a single text and are not always compliant. To rally a public, artists must therefore analyze it carefully, and this is a task for which few are prepared. Indeed it runs counter to modernist training to look inward for inspiration and to seek self-expression through aesthetic innovation. Striving toward engagement, artists risk appearing both crudely hectoring and cynically opportunist, their symbolic interventions indistinguishable from the manipulations of the commercial marketplace. Socially engaged artists, like all activists, must therefore undergo a social apprenticeship in addition to honing their aesthetic skills.

Ephemeral Objects and Pluralized Publics

Where mute objecthood once posed some limit on meaning, meaning now is pluralized by contextualization, and by a diversified public. Subtract the unifying swipe of abstraction, and a jumble of options remains with no saving hierarchy to rank them. Ironically, the decommodified object is well suited to an expanding free-market economy. Ideas are easily transported since they take up no space. Plasticity of identity opens new opportunities for shapers of opinion and makers of policy.

Without fixed meaning and their materiality vaporized, objects are reduced to their use. The free-standing object becomes a signifying remnant of one or another contextualized interpretation backed by persuasion. Advocacy entails a process, and so the social activism behind public art is also a stimulus to active art. When new-genre public artists of the 1980s abdicated the classic spaces of art to blend with life on the streets, they undertook a new order of public interaction that depended on dialogue. To be convincing, the art must induce confidence. Artists must, indeed, disarm themselves—lay down their brushes and palettes (the tools normally used to win entry into the art world)—and take up utensils unfamiliar as art, although otherwise all too commonplace.[19] Sometimes this tactic attracted media attention and, perversely, landed recommodified artifacts—now viewed as "Installation Art"—back in art world galleries. Occasionally the effort misfired: artists were rejected by the communities they hoped to represent.[20] The most successful instances, in a perverse sense, are those where an artist's work proliferates so deeply throughout a community that, as the Constructivists commended, it becomes indiscernibly a part of it. These are the instances about which we are least likely to know, since the art is lived, not noticed.

Like invisibility, impermanence is a quality that violates the ideals of traditional Western art but has become an eloquent feature of the new public art. Many works are temporary or even ephemeral, thereby escaping the neglect due to habituation that befalls more permanent public art. Among the more creative masters of this genre is the illuminist Krzysztof Wodiczko, one of whose works consists of images of itinerant homeless settlers in public parks projected upon the statues and monuments that are their usual residents.[21] The improbable cohabitants are forced into neighborly colloquy, and so is the public exposed to them. Using the Brechtian technique of estranging the familiar, Wodiczko's illuminations open a space for question and dialogue, without leaving behind a residue of forgettable objects. Like Hans Haacke's genealogical denunciations of corporate/art world complicity in exploitative practice, Wodiczko's ephemeral beams of light indict capitalist greed and abusive practice. But while Haacke produces displayable objects that can be sold at high prices by galleries, Wodiczko strikes guerrilla fashion, catching his audience off guard by briefly illuminating contradictions implicit in social spaces that we normally take for granted.

The assault on the familiar by disassociation is a technique that many artists have put to good use, but to be effective, it requires the support of a critical framework that must be constantly refreshed. In his account of the developing eighteenth-century bourgeois public, Jurgen Habermas called attention to the importance of discussion as "the medium through which people appropriated art" and hence the rise of the institution of art criticism.[22] Today's decommodified and conceptualized manifestations suggest that the discussion itself is the work of art. Public debate, dialogue, and analysis are the "substance" that purportedly outlasts artifacts and temporal events and may be renewed at will independently of authorial intention. Artists do no more than set the process in motion. Indeed, the aims of particular authors become secondary to subsequent elaborations, tailored to fit the times—a demotion that fits well into the democratizing ethos of public art. A conversation is launched that continues indefinitely. Having eliminated both the autonomous artist and the fixed object, only a ghostly process is left, to be maintained by a public, itself pulverized and in a state of flux.

Typically, and as Habermas suggested, it has been the task of institutions such as museums to define and preserve a legacy of cultural artifacts. That, however, assumes the existence of something preservable, even if we must think of it as more or less a stenographic note with multiple interpretations. Richard Serra boasted with characteristic immodesty that his sculpture would preempt and define the space around itself. His claim to dominance was arrogant but more rooted in the tradition of private art than was the self-effacing project of public artists a few years later, to seed and harvest art out of the loam of consensual communities. Many artists have pronounced themselves the tools (hollow reeds) of a power that creates works of art through them, but the subversion of agency is more radical among artists who insert themselves as catalytic agents that let loose the recumbent creativity hidden in publics not yet assembled. Art without artists or artworks seems improbable: Yet, somehow, spontaneous combustions ignite, fueled by contagion, and spread throughout the world.[23]

We might dismiss the short-lived efforts that blend artists with publics were there not comparable art routinely produced in cultural environments that never celebrated the artist as hero and where the concept of the artist as "professional" has also been alien. Using Western-influenced tools and techniques mingled with ancient indigenous symbols and materials, artists from Nigeria, Botswana, and South Africa[24] have recently produced art that seems neither "public" nor "private." Africa now has many internationally known and individually reputed artists, but traditionally art and art-making are integrated elements of utilitarian practice.[25] The idea of being "healed by art" (or haunted, punished, or killed by it) through its creation and ceremonial use is also still continuous with normal, social living—unlike its relegation in the West to a somewhat patronized (and feminized) lunatic fringe of therapeutics. Transplanted into the American gallery scene, this embedded art becomes detached from its roots and so requires explanation.[26] It was not made to stand alone, but in that stripped-down environment its aesthetic form and the talent of its individual producers are showcased, while its socially functional aspect is subverted. It approaches private art.

The African illustration suggests the artificiality of a sharp division between private art and public art. Perhaps their apparent divergence is a byproduct of the conditions of their reception. Art of the future may be sufficiently ambiguous to dissolve the distinction altogether. Even now electronic media permit private engagement in public interactions on a scale heretofore unimaginable, and nothing is more public than television, which most people experience in the privacy of their homes—often alone. Economic constraints limit universal accessibility but not more so than other obstacles to widespread experience of public art in the past. The village common has always been inaccessible to some shut-ins. If McLuhan's "global village" is not quite a reality, our ability to "reach out and touch someone" is virtually worldwide, and fellow members of any public can now be continents apart. I stand by my declaration that public art, unlike private art, sets out intentionally to construct a public, but members of such publics may be widely dispersed and unknown to one another. Conversely, connoisseurs of private art may enjoy their subjective experience in closely packed quarters, and so actual instances of the art forms can be externally indistinguishable.

I have admitted that all art is public in the sense that it transcends its creator by way of a publicizing vector, but this does not render it "public art."[27] All art is at the same time private in the sense that it evokes experiences uniquely constructed by and adherent to the person who has them. John Dewey subscribed to a pragmatist theory of art comparable to that of the Constructivists, though less materially reductionist. Like them, he wanted to close the gap between art and daily life. Dewey also wished to raise the experience of ordinary life to the level of art. He regarded art as a source of knowledge that was not propositional or generalizable but was transferable. He made no distinction between private art and public art, believing that "art as experience" can expand the ways in which we absorb things through senses outside our own and thus augment our perceptual capacity. Dewey held, in addition, that art breaks down the barriers imposed between feeling and cognition, revealing that knowledge is steeped in emotion, and that feeling is thereby cognitively enriched. He does not claim that people partake of the identical experience collectively, but in Dewey's experiential sense, art organically conveys and integrates our comprehension of the world and enables us to live our lives with deeper understanding of one another.

Certain Western artists, notably Christo and Jeanne-Claude, have also bypassed conventional dichotomies of private and public, replacing the standard legitimizing institutions of art with aesthetically nontraditional ones. In terms of its funding and initial conceptualization, Christo's work is typically private, not public. But in another, more basic sense, the art is freely accessible outside the museum. Reaestheticizing such familiar public sites as the Pont Neuf, the Berlin Reichstag, or the coastal highlands of

Northern California, the Christos enlisted the collaboration of national and local government bodies, engineering and construction agencies, inspectors, workers' groups, legal and technical advisors, and individual neighbors, all of whom become actors in realizing the art. Their enablement through formal petitions and site-approval hearings, public referenda, and information sessions is as vital structurally to defining the boundaries of this art as proscenium arches and raised platforms are to delineating conventional theater or as curators and guards are to the museum. As Christo said of *The Gates*, the long-awaited New York Central Park transformation would be "festive . . . invitational, and . . . very private."[28] The self-assembled public of the installation preceded and outlasts its brief moment of visibility. Yet it too is ephemeral.

A sense of place was thought indispensable to achieving the "environmental intimacy" characteristic of much of the historically laden public art of the 1970s, but this did not imply stability. Stasis is the very condition that would have hindered its endurance, for neighborhoods and their populations are volatile, as are the events that excite them. Protest, in particular, responds to specific circumstances that are current, emotionally charged, and usually localized. Protest art relies for its significance on the power of immediacy. Its shock effect, a potential invitation to action, is premised upon public awareness of the controversy at issue. Once that is forgotten, the public function of the art is gone, and it reverts to aesthetic objecthood, prone to neglect and casual abuse. Even in the absence of deliberate vandalism, lack of the maintenance and conservation that only museums can provide suffices to obscure and destroy the integrity of art. To say this is not to recommend imposing time limits on all public art but suggests that endurance is not invariably an asset and that public art is not well served by the fiction of art's immortality.

The Contrivance of Meaning

Historically, the public for all art has become both wider and more individuated. The Vietnam Veterans Memorial, explicitly mandated to conciliate the public, was designed by Maya Lin to generate individual, not collective, experiences. It is not a monument to one transcendent idea but reaches below politics and ideals to the personal pain of loss and waste. "This is a memorial to human beings, not a military symbol," said its progenitor, Jan C. Scruggs.[29] It is about people and for people, and its very nonspecificity is meant to avoid the divisiveness among them that any "realistic" depiction would foment. The prologue of the chronological list of the dead affixed to the memorial reads:

> In honor of the men and women of the armed forces of the United States who served in the Vietnam War. The names of those who gave their lives and those who remain missing are inscribed in the order that they were taken from us.

The memorial is intentionally nonideological and not about war. Maya Lin addressed it to those who grieve

> "to resolve or come to terms with this loss. For death is in the end a personal and private matter and the area contained within this memorial is a quiet place, meant for personal reflection and private reckoning.[30]

Yet this privately funded art that is addressed to healing private grief has become a prototype for all subsequent public art.

People, rather than a featureless public or disembodied spirit, now are the focus of much contemporary memorial art. Monuments that glorified abstracted figures and events have given way to structures meant to heal and make us whole. These often take the form of parks and gardens or soothing environments for meditation, where people come for personal renewal.[31] Many react intuitively, freed of the reverential posturing they were taught to associate with traditional public art. The absence of artificially distancing devices can also be puzzling to patrons who find a landscape too familiar to elicit respect.

Nondeclamatory art evokes a certain skepticism, derived from preconceived notions of what (and for whom) art should be, and is frequently expressed in the question "But is it art?" Immateriality, activism, collaboration, interactivity, ordinariness, and ephemerality—those features discussed here—have been alien to art. The derisory remark—"my five-year-old could do as well"—implies that "real" art requires genius (or at least a special talent) and assumes the creation of objects that endure. The new participatory art forms sometimes fail that test. But the question "Is it art?" confuses identity with quality. The question betrays its poser's discomfort with the new direction that (some) artists have taken and the breakdown of traditional boundaries that—to whatever end—kept art and non-art firmly in their separate places.

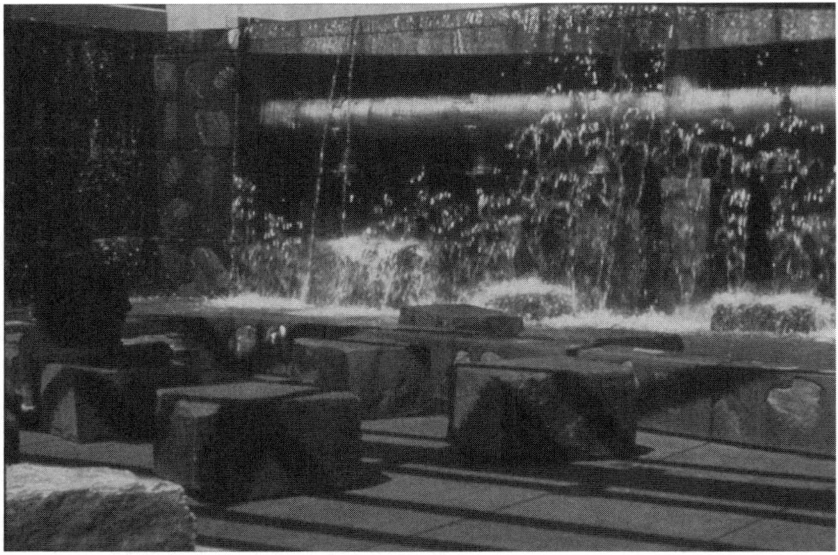

Mags Harries, Lajos Heder, and Steve Martino, 56th St. & Indian School Rd., Salt River, Arizona Falls (2003). Restoration of *WaterWorks*, Phoenix, Ariz. Art that serves a utilitarian purpose is often enjoyed by a public that ignores its identity as art. (Photo by the artist.)

The traditional equestrian statue in the square is indubitably art, regardless of its aesthetic merit or politics. The Vietnam Veterans Memorial stretched the paradigm of public art in the 1980s but was well within the pale of a modernist aesthetic of private art. It passed the test, though not without assailants. Episodic spectacles such as parades, illuminations, and Caribbean Carnival festivals are much farther afield. If these popular participatory events qualify as art, then why not annual Christmas tree lightings and the competitive home decorations that now accompany even minor holidays such as Halloween and St. Patrick's Day? What degree of solemnity distinguishes these from the antics of postmodernist irony? I do not pretend to answer that question. I do believe that not every spectacle is public art and that not all public art is spectacular.

The gentle amenities and "corporate baubles" found in office buildings and industrial parks are, in their own way, socially active. They deliver a message: users of these ritualized spaces are advised that they are conditionally approved "guests" of a benignly disposed establishment. The art speaks ambiguously but clearly enough to command implicit consent of a public that rarely contests it.[32] Should there be defiance, that too tends to be ritualized as counter-art. But such responses are problematic: if applauded by the art world, they lose popular credibility; if rejected by it, they are subject to police action. Public art lacks a history or science of criticism proper to itself. There is need of a critical theory with terminology that distinguishes public art from private art and makes its principles comprehensible to the publics it addresses.

The business of criticism, although commonly held to be primarily evaluative, is less to make normative judgments and set standards than to sharpen perceptual acuity. A theory appropriate to public art would explain its social function and amplify the meaning of constructing a public. Critics bring qualities that seem marginal to the center of consciousness and highlight features of art that, in some sense, are perfectly evident: they place these in less obvious contexts that are frequently disputable. Initiating public controversy may be the most useful thing a critic can do, for it enlivens the art and empowers the public. Mediating dialogue, critics foster understanding between publics. They bridge the gap between observing something and appreciating its contingency. Not by way of explaining what is but by enabling perceivers to "grasp" what might be, the critic is also a social activist.[33]

Merging Public and Object

Circumstances independent of its production affect the reception of all art. Public notice alone can move works of private art into the public domain without rendering them public art.[34] Some artists, for example, having been excluded by the art distribution system, have banded together to form alternative gallery space in public places such as storefronts, parks, and schools. Their work thereby achieves exposure. It does not become public art, although the performance of its display might qualify as that. However conceived to begin with, and to what end, private art is vulnerable to appropriation of its auxiliary and accidentally public features. It does not follow that all art that carries a political message is public art simply in virtue of its relevance to public concerns. Much originally political art is now enshrined in private homes and museums, and its political reference is known to relatively few observers.[35] The public and the political intersect, but they are not coextensive.

Publics do not endure indefinitely. What once was public can pass into the private domain, and it is doubtful that anything like the rational public

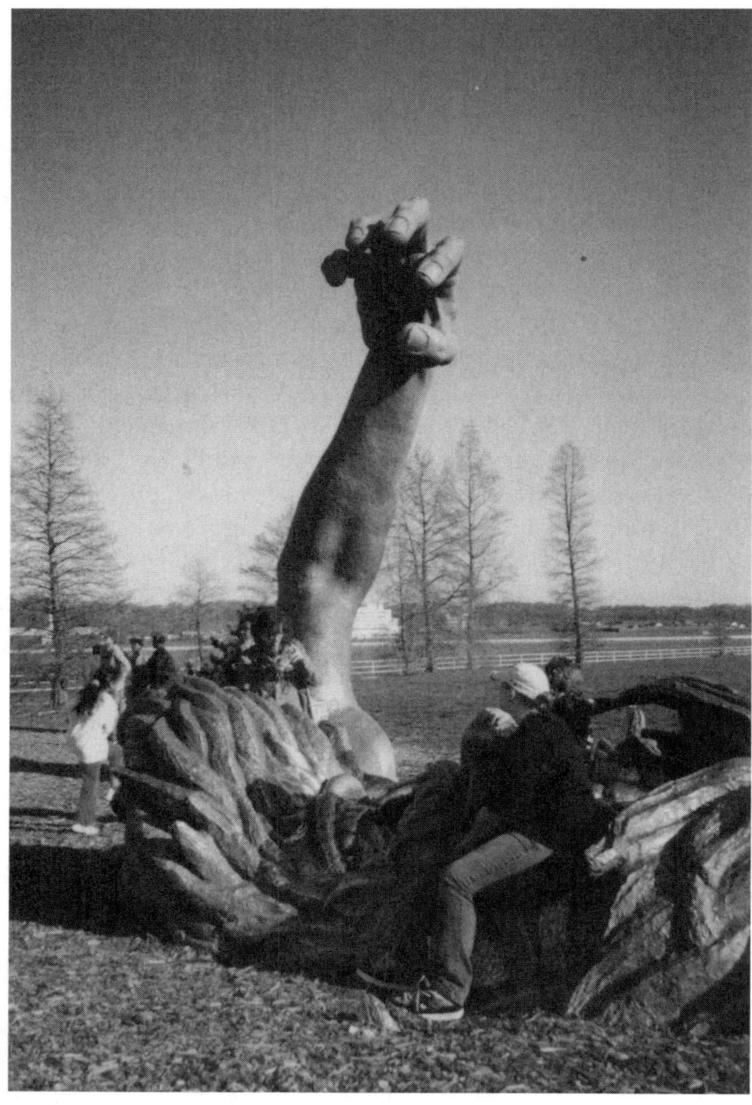

J. Seward Johnson, *The Awakening*, five-part aluminum sculpture, East Potomac Park, Hains Point, Washington, D.C. (1980). International Sculpture Exhibition. Art sometimes becomes public by acclamation as a site of public interaction. (Photo by Hilde Hein.)

sphere described by Habermas exists today. There are many publics. They are generated and quickly dissolved as circumstances warrant. They are composed of individual persons who affiliate according to habit, pressure, and choice, defining themselves in terms of the cluster of publics to which they adhere and the public-making issues that matter to them. Public art is one among other devices that recruit and construct publics, and as the character of publics changes, so must that of the art that convenes them.

Contemporary public art thus differs in almost all dimensions from the public art that preceded it. To begin with, artists no longer fill the central creative role in its production but become enablers of others. The vacuum left by the artist is sometimes entered by administrators, who stand in as representatives of a presumed public. Conceptually, artist and public merge, and the work of art comes about through a process of multiple enactments.[36] Thus dematerialized, its stability is a function of duration. Virtual space specifies its geography. An inconstant and discontinuous public effectively comprises creator, site, substance, audience, and critic. The history of past public art resonates only faintly in the mobility of social focus, and this scaffolding, too, yields to modification imposed by the present.[37]

Publics are easily mistaken for markets, inviting attempts to convene them that have the appearance of salesmanship. But where markets advance the private consumption of goods and experiences and profit from its increase, publics are mobilized to bring about public ends. Communication within and among them is vital, and public art works to bring that about. Discourse is the engine that drives publics. Enforced agreement and the suppression of difference bring it to a halt no less than does conflict fanned into violence. Public art motivates individual engagement with a social organism perpetually in motion.

I conclude this chapter with an incident that reveals the unstable complexity of contemporary public art. In 1993, an exhibition entitled Revelaciones/Revelations: Hispanic Art of Evanescense at Cornell University's Herbert F. Johnson Museum was co-curated by Chon Noriega, professor of film and television at UCLA.[38] The exhibition included an installation by Daniel J. Martinez, an artist well known for his inflammatory art project, *In Public: Seattle 1991*, jointly sponsored by the Seattle Arts Commission and the newly opening Seattle Art Museum. Martinez's contribution to the earlier event was a series of banners placed throughout the city's downtown business area that highlighted disparities between groups of inhabitants—those, for example, who deliberate over investments and those who choose between buying food and paying rent, or between candidates to Ivy League schools and students who cannot read. The exhibit prompted the city's business association to demand the removal of the banners and a newspaper editorial proposing a reduction in local arts funding. Extensive media coverage and hundreds of letters and phone calls to the editor by ardent partisans on both sides of the issue followed. There were spin-off enterprises by community activist organizations that put out their own banners and a few privately inspired imitators who turned out on the streets with message signboards. In the end, the installation was disassembled several weeks prior to its contractual conclusion in order to avoid distracting from the "cheerful decorations" of the holiday season. But the project did have consequences; it generated a colorful citywide dialogue that addressed both contemporary art and urban life, giving voice to some who had been marginalized. As one letter-writer put it, this was "mental art" and the artist had "stripped Seattle of its mellow manners and forced (us) to re-examine our lives."[39]

For his Cornell installation, Martinez set up eight-foot-tall, tar-painted plywood walls lining the main Arts Quad between the university museum and the administration center; and on the day before the official opening these were surmounted by Styrofoam forms imprinted with pithy sayings.[40] Even before their placement, students, some of whom had worked as volunteers constructing the walls, had used them as a "blackboard" for their own expression, and a war of epithets ensued revealing a history of class and racial hatred. Students rallied and demonstrated, winning support from Latinos throughout the country. On campus, the Latino students organized a sit-in that resulted in concessions by the administration of the privately and publicly funded university but not without further factional conflict.

As in Seattle, Martinez galvanized attention to the meaning of "public." Voluminous correspondence revealed that the Arts Quad is not seen by the students and faculty who cross it as an "open" space but rather as a conduit between private destinations. Some students claimed "property rights" on the basis of tuition payment, while others argued for a "public" right of free expression. Martinez was a lightning rod, attracting sparks even after his physical departure from the scene, which drew to a climax of simmering generational, class, racial, and aesthetic conflicts. Fault lines within the university bureaucratic structure showed up in the debacle that followed. No one was able or willing to assume responsibility for what happened. Noriega lists no fewer than six agencies, not counting the curators, artists, and students, that had a role in obtaining and implementing the exhibition. Each operated from within its limited bailiwick and chose to remain there, disowning involvement in the events that took place. Their disclaimers were enabled thanks to the aura of art, which had inhibited anyone's challenging the purpose of the installation at the outset—for the Quad would not have been made available for any less exalted use.

Martinez offered to make a permanent donation of his artwork to the Cornell museum, which, not surprisingly, declined the offer. The students negotiated some changes in the university; and life eventually returned to normal. Perhaps some behavior patterns were altered and some minds expanded in the process. We cannot really measure that. Some Cornellians will remember the social effects as due to art; others will recall the event as merely an uncivil disruption—this is a matter of perception. For better or worse in this instance, its official status as art at the time served as a shield, permitting the exposure of fissures hidden in the university structure. Protected by the aura of art, thoughts could be and were expressed that, however hurtful in the moment, might lead to a healing purge.[41]

Traditional Western aesthetic theory, with few exceptions, is wary of art that "does" anything, but according to the critic Patricia Phillips, something becomes public art, not in virtue of where or when it is but precisely in terms of what it does or purports to do. Moreover, what it does is public, although initiated and perpetrated through myriad private efforts and arousals. By those criteria, the Cornell installation was public art, regardless of whatever intentions might once have motivated its hosts and its curators. Its brief duration and ephemeral character do not inhibit its agency, which indeed is perpetuated in this very writing.

Rejecting the passivity promoted by conventional aesthetic and critical theory that pertains to private art, we may revert to an earlier claim that art is transformative: it can change your life. Public art is distinguished by the scale of this aspiration. Not content with merely affecting subjective experience, contemporary public art aims to change the world through multitudes of public events.

If I am right in holding that the museum is approaching the condition of public art, or at least that public art might be its model, then the tide that subordinates matter to process and displaces things with experience—which distinguishes contemporary public art—could also cast light on the commotion currently taking place in the museum.

Notes

1. Restaurants have discovered that art is good for business; people enjoy it, but they come to eat.

2. Organized economic resistance has been interpreted by local officials as constraint of trade and can lead to punishment of the organizers.

3. The original legislation, known as the National Foundation on the Arts and Humanities Act (20 U.S.C. 951ff), was enacted in 1965. The subsequent change of subheading to "Visual Artists' Public Projects" reflects a belated awareness that more conversation was necessary between artists and local audiences.

4. Quoted in Grant Kester, "Rhetorical Questions: The Alternative Arts Sector and the Imaginary Public," *AfterImage* (January 1993).

5. This proliferated structure was created to avoid some pitfalls of the New Deal, especially the suggestion of a federal ministry of culture with policymaking power. This is not to say that the NEA is free of political intervention. Appointment of its officers is in the hands of the president. Budget cuts have seriously undermined the original vision, rewarding the already well-endowed arts establishment and thereby jeopardizing the survival of the local and experimental alternatives. Controversy over specific grants, such as the Mapplethorpe, Serrano, and Finley affairs, led to compromises in the reauthorization of the NEA that further restricted eligibility for grants and tilted support in favor of arts groups that are ostensibly apolitical.

6. Serra's immense steel sculpture was commissioned in 1979 by the U.S. General Services Administration under its Art-in-Architecture program and was installed in 1981 in New York's Federal Plaza. Under the relevant legislation, the sculpture was owned by the federal government, and the local community was not consulted in its selection. Four years later, a highly controversial public hearing was held, resulting in the removal of Serra's sculpture, allegedly at the demand of the public.

7. The Philadelphia Redevelopment Authority in 1959 was the first city agency to require private developers to expend one percent of the construction costs of their projects on art. The phenomenon gradually spread to cities throughout the United States.

8. The President's Ad Hoc Committee on Government Office Space was chaired by Labor Secretary Arthur Goldberg. Its final report was published in May 1962.

9. Hafthor Yngvason, "Art Into Life: Contradictions of 'User Friendly' Public Art," *Sculpture* (May–June 1992).

10. The work was usually overseen by artists but carried out by local people, either as employees paid through grants awarded to the artist or as volunteers. viz. Judith Baca, *Guadalupe Murals* (California) described by Erika Doss, *Spirit Poles and Flying Pigs: Public Art and Cultural Democracy in American Communities* (Washington,

D.C.: Smithsonian Institution Press, 1995). Baca was also responsible for *The Great Wall of Los Angeles*, which depicts the history of California from the dinosaurs to the beginning of the civil rights movement. It was painted by teams of local teenagers under her supervision.

11. Timothy Drescher, *San Francisco Murals: Community Creates Its Muse, 1914–1990* (Pogo Press, 1991).

12. The movement's name "Constructivism" was no metaphor. It was to be taken literally. It glorified the work of engineers and applauded rational, standardized production processes like Henry Ford's assembly line.

13. The ubiquitous and too commonly copied folded red ribbon associated with the AIDS epidemic was an eminently successful public art inspiration conceived by a group of artists called "Visual Aids."

14. Paper Tiger, Gran Fury, Godzilla, Red Herring, REPOhistory, and Act Up, to mention a few that existed during the 1970s.

15. Ukeles's later projects, *The Social Mirror* (1983) and *Flow City* (1988), are more ambitious. Still focused on sanitation and maintenance, they point to such unglamorous circulation systems as the vulnerable core of urban vitality.

16. Patricia C. Phillips, "Waste Not," *Art in America*.

17. There are alternative modes of "reclamation," and not all of them are artistic. The ruined sites that beckoned to earth artists in the 1970s were equally attractive to dirt bikers and gun clubs, who relished the "unspoiled" landscape for recreational use and resented the complaints and pieties of environmentalist elites.

18. Ironically, although Robert Morris, one of the originators of "earth art," claims it was motivated in part to avoid the "raging commodity use" of the gallery, in fact there was no escape from "the crassness of the marketplace." His own reclamation project near Seattle was funded by the King County Arts Commission on the condition that the cost of the art must be less than restoring the industry-wasted land to its "natural" state would be. viz. "Earthworks: Land Reclamation as Sculpture," in *Critical Issues in Public Art: Content, Context and Controversy*, eds. Harriet F. Senie and Sally Webster (Washington, D.C.: Smithsonian Institution Press, 1992). See also Erika Doss's discussion of Michael Heizer's *Effigy Tumuli*, "a local mogul's private folly and tax dodge" meant to cover up the strip-mining damage left by the Osage Coal Company near Ottawa. The artist was inspired to "reactivate" an ancient Indian tradition of animal-shaped mound building. *Spirit Poles and Flying Pigs*.

19. The process resembles Dadaist appropriation of ordinary objects (toilets, brushes, and bottle racks) only in externalities. Dadaism was an outburst of aesthetic anarchism, protesting conventional forms through ridicule: this movement is a positive quest to articulate meaning through a vocabulary constructed of the marginalized paraphernalia of the dispossessed.

20. A case in point is that of John Ahearn and Rigoberto Torres, who received a commission from the New York City Department of Cultural Affairs to design a

park near a new police station in their own South Bronx neighborhood. Ahearn made sculptures cast from his neighbors, intending the realism to honor them, but the community was outraged at what it perceived as racial stereotyping. Embarrassed by the misunderstanding, Ahearn removed the sculptures voluntarily, a reaction very different from that of such art world figures as Serra and Oldenburg, who responded to similar rejections with lawsuits.

21. *Homeless Projection: A Proposal for the City of New York* (1986).

22. J. Habermas, *Structural Transformation of the Public Sphere* (Cambridge, Mass.: MIT Press, 1989), 40. He maintains that museums, like the concert and the theater, institutionalized the lay judgment of art. While eighteenth-century curators were caretakers in a more literal sense, today's curators have a great deal of creative license and authority akin to that which Habermas assigns to early critics.

23. The critic Eleanor Heartney has cautioned that such short-term collaborations "smack of another kind of paternalism which assumes that artists with a superficial understanding of a community's needs and history can supply the conceptual tools to solve its problems." She wondered: "Isn't there something disingenuous about the claim that these works are addressed to a general public rather than to the artworld proper?" Since the existence of the art is preserved only briefly and "through the intervention of the art media that documents, memorializes, and explains them," who, outside the art world, bothers to understand them? Why do they matter? "The Dematerialization of Public Art," *Sculpture* (March–April 1993): 45–49.

24. The incorporation of art in collective social practice occurs on all continents. Lucy Lippard, writing of the political struggles in Central America in the 1980s, reports: "For better or worse, Nicaraguan artists are being deprived of separation from daily experience; they are forced to 'stay in touch,' to make objects whose purpose is to communicate as well as to decorate, to reinforce communality as well as individuality. Yet most of their art is not identifiable as 'political' because its consciousness is embedded in forms and conventions that are just beginning to change." *The Nation*, 28 January 1984.

25. "Excavation and Reconstruction in Contemporary African Art," a symposium at Brandeis University, 23 October 2004, featuring the work of Kim Berman (South Africa), Victor Ekpuk (Nigeria), Neo Matome (Botswana), Stompie Selibe (South Africa), Paul Stopforth (South Africa), and William Kentridge (South Africa).

26. By now, the recontextualization of objects in museum displays is commonplace, but in 1988, an exhibition called Art/artifact at the Center for African Art (in New York) was galvanizing, for it not only addressed the question of contextualization but forced the museum public to pay attention to it, since this was the subject of the exhibition. It was, as museum director Susan Vogel announced in the catalogue, an examination of the extent to which our perception of other cultures is conditioned by our internalization of our own. The same object that

tells a story in a museum of anthropology tells a very different one when placed on a pedestal in a museum of art, and neither story approximates the fullness of the object's incarnation outside any museum.

27. viz. Chapter 2 discussion of Hannah Arendt. Language, the conventions of grammar and writing, and the use of technology necessarily bring thought into the public realm. The Hegelian notion that art is inherently a self-alienation or projection of an other that limits the self is a first step toward becoming public but does not entail a public or the aim of constructing one.

28. The long-awaited proposal was finally realized a quarter century after it was initially proposed. It was initially rejected by Gordon J. Davis, commissioner of the New York Department of Parks and Recreation, who professed to be concerned about the cost and security risks involved. One must wonder what he might have said after 9/11. His chief grudge, however, appears to have been Christo's end run around the California Coastal Zone Commission, which had not granted permission to the Christos to extend the final portion of *Running Fence* into the ocean in 1978. They did it anyway, knowing that, if an injunction were served, they could comply with the law by removing the artwork within its projected duration. It was this "cheating" of the law that ruffled the commissioner's order of priorities. viz. Calvin Tomkins, "Onward and Upward with the Arts: The Gates to the City," *The New Yorker* (29 March 2004): 74–85.

29. Jan C. Scruggs and Joel L. Swerdlow, *To Heal a Nation: The Vietnam Veterans Memorial* (New York: Harper & Row, 1985), cited in Harriet Senie, *Contemporary Public Sculpture: Tradition, Transformation and Controversy* (New York: Oxford University Press, 1992).

30. Lin's original entry statement is cited in Senie, 37. Her mission did not include a tribute to the Vietnamese whose lives were lost, but they too were people, as were those who grieved them.

31. These are radically unlike formal gardens, such as Versailles or the imperial gardens of Japan. Gardens in general are sometimes treated as "applied" art, a notion that seems singularly misguided unless specifically applied to vegetable gardens. As Mara Miller describes them, gardens create virtual worlds, embodying actual time and space, where they can mirror social relations as they are, or according to the gardener's vision of what they ought to be. Mara Miller, *The Garden as an Art* (SUNY Press, 1993).

32. A bubbly 1994 review advises: "Think of the 'public sphere' as an immense gray matter, where ideas flow in a phantasmagoric parade. You can think of the public sphere as an adventure in channel surfing with a TV remote control. Ideas flash by . . ." Karin Giusti, "Signatures in the Public Sphere: Temporary Public Art, New York, Summer/Fall 1993," *Public Art Review* (Spring/Summer 1994). This is far from the serious deliberative body imagined by Habermas. The public here evoked is numbed and stupefied, more like a mass.

33. Arnold Isenberg, "Critical Communication," *The Philosophical Review* 58 (July 1949). This excellent and still-valid examination of criticism and its function is all too rarely cited.

34. Two illustrations of such mutated identity are (1) art made notorious as a result of its theft or sale for outrageously high prices, usually to private purchasers, and (2) pornographic art, purportedly for "personal" delectation, which is denounced as a public incitement to violence against women. The first is public by virtue of its commodification; the second, because it incites the commodification of others. In both instances the art remains (much publicized) private art.

35. Picasso's *Guernica* is private art, as is Goya's series of *Disasters of War*. Both are also political works that are endlessly referenced in derivative forms of public art—films, skits, posters, etc. These secondary works may or may not be public art, but that does not affect the private art status of the originals.

36. Not coincidentally, the Conceptualist movement, a late-1960s rebellion against the commodity-driven, object-centered art then fashionable, had a significant influence upon the new public art. Conceptual artists aimed both to democratize the art world and to break down the barriers between art and life. In fact, their art stayed mostly within the private art fortress, a puzzle to those without, but its challenges to aesthetic exclusivism had a formidable impact on the art world that eventually affected the "real world" as well. viz. Nina Felshin, ed., *But Is It Art? The Spirit of Art as Activism* (Seattle: Bay Press, 1995).

37. Thus, Colonial Williamsburg now includes Negro inhabitants, and there are women depicted among the foot soldiers of the Revolutionary War.

38. Chon A. Noriega and Jose Piedra, eds., *Revelaciones/Revelations: Hispanic Art of Evanescence* (Ithaca, N.Y.: Hispanic American Studies Program, 1993). A documentary on the exhibition is available through the Cinema Guild, New York. My information is taken from *Daedalus: Journal of the American Academy of Arts and Sciences*, special issue on America's museums 128, no. 3 (Summer 1999): 57.

39. Tony Uribe, *Seattle Weekly*, 20 August 1991.

40. One, taken from the Greek philosopher Diogenes was: "In the rich man's house the best place to spit is in his face."

41. Aristotle declared tragedy cathartic, and several other aesthetic theories have celebrated the purgative value of private art. Generally, these theories are endorsing individual therapy achieved through personal aesthetic experience. The proposal hinted at by Noriega is not psychological but social cleansing. New-genre public art works through individuals but aspires to bring about concrete social change.

Old Museums and a New Paradigm

It was my monomania to make the museum the town wonder and town talk. . . . I studied ways to arrest public attention; to startle, to make people talk and wonder; in short to let the world know I had a museum.

—P. T. BARNUM

One day the museum building opens, and there is a flurry of national publicity, followed by a succession of expensively mounted and critically acclaimed shows. . . . All too soon the community has a deteriorating monument on its hands.

—KARL E. MEYER

Being one of the most philosophical institutions of Western culture, museums are apt to react to every dilemma of cultural identity and so every form of cultural criticism has a direct bearing on museum life.

—SANDOR RADNOTI

The End of the Museum and a Beginning

The end of the twentieth century coincided with the end of the grand master narrative. There is no longer a place for master narratives at all, wrote Arthur Danto: "Ours is a moment of deep pluralism and total tolerance. Nothing is ruled out." Nothing except museums as we have known them! If the kind of art that the museum defined has "had its day," then the museum itself may fall away or become aesthetically marginalized. Recalling the transcendent experiences that sometimes occur in the presence of art, Danto suggests that "it was the perception of artworks as fulcrums of meaning that inspired the temple-like architecture of the great museums."[1]

It is not architecture alone that links museums to holy spaces. Sacred groves and forests are likewise invoked,[2] but the spirit that once dwelt therein may have abandoned these shrines for other environments. The metaphors that elucidate the museum are persistently spatial, if sometimes less reverential. Among the comparisons are secular palaces and treasure houses but also tombs, graveyards, and mausoleums, where dead things are buried.[3] Museum representations often stress shelter and preservation, carefully indexed as in libraries and archives, practical as in a warehouse, disorderly as in "the nation's attic,"[4] or commodified, as in department stores. The market place or bazaar is an alternative trope, where things and ideas compete in wanton proximity. Since selectivity is imperative—otherwise, the museum would simply duplicate the world—a talent for organizing is enjoined in analogies such as the microcosm and the mosaic. Likened also to a theater or a mirror, the museum is imagined as a site that reveals by mimicry and, if in reduced format, as a script or frame. I have suggested the model of the laboratory, where sections of the world are exposed to experiment and explored.[5] Others have proposed the university as a model, where education and scholarly research are foremost. Less concretely, museums are described as gathering places not merely for things but for their representations, according to multiple categories and systems, yielding countless patterns of patterns decoded by sophisticated analytic devices. Museums are also described as "congregant spaces" for people to come together for diversion, amusement, inspiration, or instruction, or to be thrilled in relative safety and comfort.[6] The images have gone from concrete to abstract and from passive containment to institutional promotion, but almost all of them imply that a museum is where something is or happens. Only rarely does the museum appear to be an agent that brings something about.

No model fits the institution perfectly or applies to all instances, for museum history is peppered with their variety. Historians disagree over which of the proposed ancestors rightly merits the name of museum: to declare a direct line of descent would imply consensus on something like a definition. But each representation captures some facet of an institution continuously in flux and seeks to tie present uncertainty to a legendary past. Priority as a public museum is generally awarded to the Louvre, which, in 1793, turned what had been a royal collection into a nationalized public museum with free admission to everyone. Other nations soon emulated the French Republic, but the meaning of "public" was not everywhere the same. In eighteenth-century England and well into the nineteenth century, for example, only "well-born, educated men of taste" who were, not incidentally, land owners, were admitted to public galleries.[7] What now seems private and exclusive then appeared publicly accessible and was heralded as part of a glorious movement to expand citizenship.

The museum is thus inevitably as much an expression of the spirit of its own time as it is a willed recovery of an absent past. But while the latter project is usually conscious and deliberate, the former is less transparent. It is manifested rather than articulated, exemplified in practices rather than pronouncements. We overlook ourselves in our productions, but they reveal us to others, if not to ourselves. "Now," unlike "then," lacks the dignity of history, although it compensates with the immediacy of unguarded gesture. We need to consider museums in terms of these current gestures instead of as receptacles in which frozen events are memorialized in things.

Museums are often said to be transformative. People who say this are generally thinking of the effect on individual hearts and minds produced by certain objects contained in the museum but not by the museum as such.[8] The overwhelmed individuals, in turn, are moved to bring about transformations in the world apart from the museum. The museum thus initiates a chain reaction: it is a catalytic agent that transmits change but is only distantly responsible for what happens. In another context I depicted the museum as a suprapersonal entity, larger than any individual person, yet like people, subject to moral imperatives and responsible for its effects.[9] My aim there was to attribute a moral persona to the museum, separate and different from its personnel and derived from a human-like capacity to create meaning. I argued that this capacity, while it entails intentionality, does not assume consciousness of that intention—for museums are not conscious, sentient creatures. If you prick them, they do not bleed, but their actions are purposive and have moral consequences. I challenged museums to acknowledge the remarkable power they possess, as institutions, to affirm and deny value by using inanimate objects and the animate persons under their influence. There, I was making an ethical claim. I wanted to emphasize the agency of the museum that supervenes that of the individuals who compose it: here, I again point to the museum's supervenient agency but strive to understand it aesthetically. I want to consider the museum as a work of art, a complexly crafted artifact with the power to transform its constituent materials, including the things and people that compose it.

A few museum theorists have approximated the proposal that I will defend here. The observation that the museum is a grand and very complex work of art that houses other works of art could refer to the architectural extravagance typical of contemporary museum construction, but this is to mistake an inessential part of the museum for the whole. Some critics of flamboyant museum architecture charge that it "upstages" the museum's content and prevents visitors from properly experiencing it.[10] The objection is made that, where it should interlace exhibitions with spaces, the fancifulness of the receptacle creates conflict between them instead. This criticism obscures the fact that architecture has obligations not only to the environment inside the museum but also to the community outside. Setting up a dialogue with that community, whose members might never set foot inside the museum, is of mutual advantage. The physical design is but one element of the museum, inseparable from its total composition. Architecture does not "make" the museum art but pervades every aspect of what the museum is and does.[11]

As an integrated totality, the museum is both compound and complex. Its attributes are in constant transition. Like a garden, a museum is continuously buffeted by external elements, which it absorbs and incorporates into sustenance and growth. Objects pass into and out of collections. Some are reevaluated and may be deaccessioned. Others are reassigned or distributed among different institutions. Their identity is metamorphosed, for example, if items once designated "natural wonders" are reclassified as "rarities," "specimens," "works of art," or "ethnographic artifacts." Within a single museum, the placement of objects follows current trends in curatorial practice and exhibition design.

Alfred Barr, the first director of the New York Museum of Modern Art, had a vision of its collection as a single, complex, but coherent and longitudinal (i.e., art historically conceived) work of art that articulates modernism with impeccable, single-minded artistry. Julian Spalding, former director of the Glasgow Museums and Art Galleries, holds that museums should not tell one history but rather facilitate many concurrent stories. In his book *The Poetic Museum*, he proposes that the museum be something like a self-generated poetry anthology, permissively equipped with stimulating artifactual props. Unlike Barr, he encourages visitor/curator collaboration in the reimagining of exhibits, but the two directors do agree that the museum's collection is the kernel that integrates one or many works of art.

Carol Duncan somewhat ambiguously considers the museum both as a site of ritual, namely, a space in which ritual takes place, and as a performance of ritual. She seems more interested in the first option, since she concentrates on the ritualized conduct that visitors (and nonvisitors) are coerced to enact under the subtle influence of the museum structure.[12] Duncan's second alternative is closer to my proposed approach toward the museum as itself performative—the dancer and the dance.[13] We agree that the museum is not only a structure but that it constructs. Duncan cites with approval the words of Philip Rhys Adams that the museum is "the controlling intermediary who sets the scene, . . . then bids the actors take the stage and be their best artistic selves," noting only her reservation that Adams believes that "objects rather than people are the main performers." I believe that both of them are correct: the museum is a performance in which objects and people participate.

Some museums combine the memorializing of events with dispensing information about them: the National D-Day Museum, in New Orleans, is a multimedia facility that continues to collect vast quantities of data, artifacts, and reminiscences from participants on all sides of World War II. It does not spin a single thread but aims to combine and reassess with continuing historical hindsight the tangle of perceptions that compose an "event." Visitors to the museum are overwhelmed with impressions, jostled from one idea to another, shifting abruptly from space to space, attitude upon attitude, and confronted by partial conclusions. One does not come away with a sense of wholeness but rather of loosely cemented fragments brilliantly illuminated and left to the synthesis of visitors.

The U.S. Holocaust Memorial Museum took an alternative route, deciding upon a single dominant narrative and carefully selecting materials to construct it. Its aim is to memorialize the Holocaust by conveying one story. Achieving the unanimity to accomplish that left many dissident parties outside and unreconciled. The story, relentlessly rendered through artifacts and images, determined the selection of the mediating devices, but these, in turn, influence its telling. Effectively, every shadow, space, and object, and their location in the museum, reinforces the story. It is kinaesthetically and emotively insinuated even as the visitor processes and absorbs factual accounts cognitively. The museum demands engagement that is not compartmentalized but responsive to the whole, and the exhibits are not intended to be experienced independently but—like the ingredients of a stew—suffused by each other's savor. Of course, one can resist the whole, as any work of art can be resisted. My point is that the experience of this museum is holistic. Its single story is meant to be absorbed. That is its program.

All of these museums achieve their diverse ends aesthetically, making visitors complicit by drawing them into different contexts that cast them as the principals of distinct scenarios. We underestimate contemporary museums—or what they have come to be—if we consider them merely as gorgeous shells in which a dramatic production takes place.[14]

The Museum as Work of Art

In the previous chapters, I discussed public art as a phenomenon distinguished by what it does, not where it is. I differentiated between private art and public art on the basis of the latter's implicit construction of a public. I showed how the conception of that public has changed and how, in conjunction with that change, public art has undergone massive transformations. Museums have followed a similar path, never without an addressed audience, but radically reformulating their idea of its character. That alone would be insufficient reason for assimilating museums to art, but there are other grounds for doing so.

One is their shared multidimensionality: notwithstanding the disciplinary focus of some museums, or their dedication to the illumination of a single topic—bicycles, basketball, or Bayeux tapestry—the presentation is never linear but invariably multisensory and multifaceted. To the dismay of traditionalists, many museums have become multimedia arcades festooned with electronic gadgetry. But even a modest storefront display center combines arrayed artifacts with photography, text, occasional lectures, video, music, and collaborative public programs with invited celebrities. Lest this appear a shallow concession to contemporary fashion, I note that museums have ever rejoiced in the latest technology, of moving images, lights, sound recording, and reproduction, by whatever means their resources allowed. Even glass cases were once a novelty. In these concessions to fashion, museums are motivated as much by experimental curiosity and love of spectacle as by practical need.

If multidimensionality is an asset, so is open texture. As a principal ingredient of art, ambiguity lends itself to renewal and reinterpretation. It also contributes to the vitality of museums. The monotonous voice of authority, long associated with didactic schooling and the conventional curator-interpreted museum, has given way to visitor-centered museums, with options that encourage the public to create meaning. Inviting debate, museums become sites of controversy. At the same time, there must be critical standards. Minimally, the museum must have defensible grounds for the positions it takes. Surprisingly, though not without dissent, there is considerable agreement on what the great works of art are—if not on what makes them great. History and science are more disputable and engender controversy inside and about the museum. Such disagreement invites further discussion; it does not foreclose it.

The challenge of assessment is comparatively new to museums. It comes with their reliance on public funding rather than on the personal idiosyncrasy of benefactors or the judgment of the marketplace. Charitable foundations and government agencies have formulated criteria for the distribution of funds, and recipients are held to standards of achievement beyond mere accountability.[15] To be "transformative" in the vague sense affirmed a half-century ago is not good enough. Museums learned quickly to police themselves internally and to spell out goals and procedures that have to do with improving the quality of people's lives. They have thus become part of the public service sector. While the precise nature of their obligation remains somewhat murky, there is at least a consciousness within the museum world that something is owed in return for support and that being of service to the public by running a museum is both a duty and a privilege.

Like works of art, museums are sometimes loved, sometimes hated, and too often ignored. The standards by which they judge themselves are generically like those applied to art. Is there an overall coherency maintained by skilled execution? Is it arresting? Illuminating? Convincing? Is it true to itself?[16] Clarity of purpose is not incompatible with alternative ways of understanding, but its lack precludes them, leaving only confusion. Integrity has long been a value attributed to good art and is surely requisite for museums as well. The term "integrity" implies obvious imperatives like proper care of objects, commitment to truthful representation, and the prohibition of counterfeit or illicit acquisition, but integrity also relates to subtler conduct at the fringes of decency and criminality. It applies to judiciously probing influence, assuming responsibility for choices, pressing for answers to difficult questions, and attending to unforeseen consequences of behavior.

Just as no single standard applies to all works of art, so must museums be judged according to their differences. Completeness and excellence of collections, for example, are irrelevant to museums that do not own collections or that obtain artifacts temporarily for specific exhibitions. Originality is valued in some arts, but in others, adherence to ancient canons is more prized. A quality that enhances one work can be a defect in another. And so it is with museums: their mission must be adopted with care and periodically reviewed. It must be appropriate to their circumstances and the resources available. Contemporary museums do not have the luxury of gratifying only their creator but must consider the potential for reception. An artist with independent means may stack her work in her studio forever and command its destruction upon her demise, but museums are compelled to reach beyond temporal and physical perimeters to interact with the world. They must analyze that world and address themselves to serving it without culpable compromise.

The Museum as Public Art

And so we come to public art, which, I believe, illuminates the conceptual heart of the museum. Public art entails communities smaller and more distinct in character than the universal "mankind" sometimes alleged to be the beneficiary of great private art. The public addressed by public art is specific and has discernible attributes.[17] In preceding chapters, I discussed historic differences in the constitution of that public and consequent changes in the art that serves it. Public art has become less material, more processual and more directly involved with the public it addresses. It absorbs creator and created in its process and embraces the participant-observer. Detachment and disinterested affection, the responses that classical aesthetic theory deemed appropriate to private art, are rejected by this view of public art, for it demands engagement.

Also repudiated is the defense of art's heroic autonomy. The classic equestrian statue in the square may seem quite isolated on its pedestal, but it carries a load of civic baggage that, I have argued, is eloquently revealed by people's instinctive understanding of the language of desecration and selective vandalism. It is not bulk that immobilizes public art but rather a social network that fades over time and is ultimately dissipated. While it lasts, however, it anchors the art and protects it. Public art engages in vital dialogue with its environment, and its removal can paralyze or destroy it even without harming the art physically.[18] Its location, implying more dimensions than latitude and longitude, is important to it because of its significance to the community that claims "ownership" of it.[19] A bust of Beethoven is at home in front of any Symphony Hall, where it is understood to be a tribute to a music immortal, but it would be out of place at a football stadium or a bank even though some patrons might be music lovers.[20]

Museums can be similarly out of place. Sometimes a city grows around a museum, changing its demographic environment. Urban residents move to the suburbs, leaving the inner city to commercial or industrial development. Once fashionable museums, caught in the middle, can then seem inaccessible or uninviting to their former audiences while failing to welcome their new neighbors. Correspondingly, museums that change their location thereby affect their character. The decision to move the Barnes Foundation from its exurban site in residential Merion, Pennsylvania, to Museum Row in downtown Philadelphia cannot help modifying its eccentric personality, part of which derived from the pilgrimage it required of its patrons.[21] Museums are well advised to reflect upon their relationship with the communities in which they find themselves unintentionally as well as those with which they interact by design. Neighborliness is more than grounds maintenance and traffic control; it also includes providing jobs and adjusting to the habits of the habitat.

The editors of a groundbreaking book on *Museums and Communities* (1992) observe that "When people enter museums they do not leave their cultures and identities in the coatroom. . . . They interpret museum exhibitions through . . . membership in multiple communities."[22] The editors also acknowledge that to identify those who enter the museum as "their" (i.e., the museum's) communities is to illegitimately assume possession. Indeed, museums are not so entitled; interaction is a two-way affair. Moreover, even those communities left out of the museum interact with it indirectly. Sometimes they actively resist inclusion because the compromises expected of them in return are too extreme. Sometimes they are intimidated by what Elaine Gurian calls "threshold fear," which may be induced by physical design features such as monumental facades. Other deterrents are less tangible—an attitude displayed by museum staff or confusing signage.[23] It is also the case that museums are simply not part of everyone's universe—a stop on the subway, perhaps, but otherwise meaningless. That might be unimaginable for those of us who love museums, but we too have blank spots—not purposefully disregarded but simply outside the range of our horizons. Museums must learn to acquiesce courteously to indifference that is not meant as affront, just as they must avoid affronting those whose interest they fail to enlist. Excessive zeal to win everyone's hearts and minds is misguided and looks more like self-aggrandizement than goodwill. Again, like public art, museums effect limited social construction, not universal conquest.

There is an abundance of examples of successful community building where museums have been locally specific and, upon yielding authority to the communities they inhabit, have been happily integrated by that community. Those discussed in *Museums and Communities* include the Brooklyn Children's Museum, recommitted to a new environment following major demographic changes in its neighborhood, a museum on the Ak-Chin Indian reservation in Arizona that revitalized its Hohokam ancestry, several museums of black American history, and a New York museum of Chinese-American history that critically examines its own vibrantly mixed constituency. A contributor to the volume points out that "what is an ethnographic collection in one context (abroad) is often considered a historical collection in another context (at home)." She observes that displays of ethnographic objects generally promote the idea of strange and romantic customs of an alien "other," while exhibitions of the same things kept at home are seen with more cultural sensitivity. They are still relatively romanticized, however, insofar as they concentrate on another sort of "other," namely, the past, from which present descendents are alienated.[24] She applauds the recent trend among museums to use the objects in their collections to reacquaint members of contemporary communities with the culture of their own predecessors. This diversion from artifacts as oddities is symptomatic of both a dematerialization of the museum and its social reintegration. Objects become, once again, items for use instead of musealized treasures to be hoarded. Although they cannot revert to their prior function, their functionality is made imaginable.

Constructing a public does not invariably confine museum outreach to a given geographic neighborhood. Electronic communication technologies have orbited far beyond Malraux's photographically facilitated "museum without walls." They now offer worldwide access to museums interactively, replacing physical contact and one-way communication with intangible lines of exchange. Thermometer buffs need only click on to the website of the tiny, privately owned thermometer museum in Onset, Massachusetts, to learn about obscure thermal measuring devices and confer with fellow enthusiasts. Although it challenges the museum's transcendent status, this vast public outreach comes at an opportune moment, since the burden of collections has become an albatross.[25] Coincident with the turn to narrative that subordinates objects to storytelling, museums now are able to combine their resources with those from other quarters for shared exploration. They benefit from one another's collections and become partners in research. Some use their exhibits to gather fresh data directly from visitors and code information into ongoing data analyses used to investigate subjects such as genetic individuality, olfactory sensitivity, or the impact of lifestyle on the environment. Exhibits display the real-time phenomenon recorded from the visitor's input together with an analytic representation.[26] Spared the risk and expense of packing and shipping expensive objects, museums can open their laboratories and storerooms virtually to anyone's query and for whatever reasons. The problem of "threshold fear" may not be entirely eliminated by these procedures, since some people are uncomfortable with sophisticated electronic equipment, but for those not so impeded, the "virtual museum" can be an avenue to information exchange unformatted by the authoritative voice of the museum. "Virtual visitors" to some museums now exceed actual ones numerically. They can freely rearrange their downloaded treasure and shape it into "collections" of their own devising, however and in the company of whomever they like.

Like the emerging public art, whose identity lies in its process, the "virtual museum" is ephemeral. Its vitality lies in the capacity to meet contemporary needs with contemporary means. While it seems anomalous to couple survival with discontinuity, many other institutions are also doing just that.[27] They perpetuate their history through recurrent self-recreation, prolonging the past in memory through metaphors that once had literal reference.

In the 1980s, museums met critical assault with self-criticism. Charged with managing the past they were created to preserve, they enlisted the help of their attackers to turn themselves into testing grounds of the present. Blossoming under siege, they overcame opposition by inviting it into the museum. Everyone had a tale to tell, and everyone was encouraged to tell it. No doubt this was a concession on one side to the logic of musealization and on the other to confusion and popularization. It was a strategy of pacification—but all parties benefited to some degree. The layers of narrative that entered the museum as a result are sometimes simplistic, and their transcription falls short of the transcendent experience promised (and often achieved) by the superceded traditional museum, but the taste of diversity delivered instead is real, if muted somewhat by a gnawing sense of formulaic trivialization.[28]

In an ultimately optimistic essay subtitled "The Museum as Mass Medium," Andreas Huyssen ponders the astonishing popularity of museums in the spectacle-glutted latter decades of the twentieth century. Admitting their radical departure from their nondemocratic ancestral form, Huyssen insists that they have not (yet) descended to the level of "cheap thrills." They still offer the epiphany of aesthetic illumination and "genuine" experience. How, he asks, is this possible? What is it that museums have done to make it happen? Rejecting alternative theories—that museums offer pockets of compensation to those who grieve a world gone awry or, conversely, that museums have capitulated to the simulation mill—Huyssen proposes a pragmatic explanation of what museums are doing right. The museal gaze, he says—and he insists it is the gaze that endows the object with its aura—"revokes the disenchantment of the world." The museum offers multiple transitory and dependably repeatable narratives of meaning at a time when all metanarratives have lost their persuasiveness. A danger remains that museum representations co-opt, repress, and sterilize the stories they relate, but the impetus is there "for the cultures of this world to collide and to display their heterogeneity, even irreconcilability, to network, to hybridize and to live together in the gaze and the memory of the spectator."[29] This is a slim message of hope.

If all this seems too redolent of preaching the peaceable kingdom, ask yourself what makes you happy. Is it not an occasional and momentary sense that things are right with the world? Those moments are rarely delivered through mediation. Most of them come from direct encounters that can be emended but not fixed by secondary elaboration. It has taken some effort to figure out how a mediated experience can substitute for a primary one without considerable loss of intensity. But our friends are working on the problem. The world has accomplished this before, notably with the distribution of the printed word, and again with more advanced communication systems. They offer their own reward, but they do not displace "real experience." Museums held out against invasion, professing to preserve directly accessible "real" things, but it is now generally admitted that these too are mediated even prior to their definitive "musealization" when they enter the museum. The signifying gaze that picks something out as noteworthy excises it from the life stream and sends it on its way into history. In the museum it gains another kind of "presence," no longer a thing but an object.

There can be no reclamation of an "original" state; the aura-conferring gaze rests upon an object's musealized presence. Presence does not depend on materiality, but it rarely arises from transmitted, programmable simulations—providing, of course that these are recognized as such.[30] Huyssen suggests that "it may be precisely the isolation of the object from its genealogical context that permits the experience via the museal glance." Mundanity is no obstacle to presence; ordinary things placed before the museal gaze acquire a new dimension. Indeed, museums as readily estrange the familiar as they familiarize the strange and remote. It is not their exoticism nor any other more earthy property but the encounter actualized in the museum that evokes a "transitory reenchantment" that feels almost like joy.[31]

No museum experience guarantees enchantment, but that is not the issue at hand. Animated dinosaurs are as likely as Vermeers or old tools to produce it. The point is that museums have been looking for legitimation in the wrong places. Having invested heavily in building collections, they reasonably assumed that these and the scholarship that accompanied them were sufficient to justify their being. They were then at a loss to defend themselves against the charges of commodification and selective bias. Decentering the revered object to foreground narrative instead, they focused on techniques to tell and distribute stories, loudly, diversely, and dramatically. But in this they are no match against well-funded media or Disneyland. Their much underestimated strength is not in their yarns but in the capacity to inspire the museal gaze, which ignites the sense of presence.[32] Infusing that is a collaborative phenomenological enterprise: the museum positions the gaze, sweeping musealized objects, events, people, memories, and ideas into its ambit as a newly constituted, fleeting experience.[33] Achieving that is, once again, the power of art.

The gesture the museum makes is broad, and its limits are indeterminate. It incorporates timely tools and techniques adapted to a receptive landscape of the present. Most new or renovated museums bristle with interactive devices. They have diminished storage area and increased convocation spaces designed to be public centers, not sanctuaries. Yet they differ from concert halls and theaters, where people also assemble simultaneously to attend performances. Programs prepared for the latter are more easily enacted elsewhere (though not without some adjustment to the venue). They rely less integrally on audience interaction. In contrast, museum attendees often come in groups, and while members of crowds can be a nuisance to one another, their experience with exhibits includes and is validated by the unscripted participation of other people.[34]

It is still possible in the museum to commune alone with a work of art or a science exhibit, just as one can enjoy a parade from an isolated vantage point, but the others are there implicitly and are a part of the event. Critics are quick to complain that uninterrupted meditation is hard to maintain since the "museum experience" has become busy and convivial. It frequently includes lunch and a tour through the gift shop. The museum's persona is nevertheless present throughout, as menus and sale items are coordinated with exhibition themes, along with related music and sound effects. Like it or not, the museum presents itself as a compound aesthetic totality that beckons the public with banners outside and gimmicks within. It is a multimedia performance whose authorship blends with its matter and assimilates its public.

The character of this whole changes with the succession of exhibitions and supplementary programs. Visitors come and go; staff members are replaced, galleries renovated, and departments reorganized.[35] An exhibition is an elaborate ballet in which things change places or are specially fabricated. Temporarily and with much preparation, the museum dons a new costume, but fashions pass, and apart from their documentation in catalogues, videos, souvenir items, and monographs, each apparition has a limited and discontinuous duration. What could be more ephemeral or more public than a traveling exhibition? The particles that compose it are assembled and disassembled to coexist briefly in dozens of places, to figure together with local luminaries in assorted programs and civic sites, and finally to be dispersed and returned to their separate domiciles. Transported from museum to museum, they appear in different environments at different times and are viewed by different audiences. They are profoundly inconstant, and so is the public response to them. The "same" exhibition that provokes an uproar in one city may elicit only mild curiosity in another, but often its reputation travels ahead and preempts its identity.[36]

The itinerant museum exhibition arguably differs only in scale from mobile multimedia installations sometimes referred to as "Border Art." One ambitious example was a 1988 collaborative project by David Avalos, Louis Hock, and Elizabeth Sisco called *Welcome to America's Finest Tourist Plantation, San Diego Bus Poster Project*. This publicly funded enterprise, sited on advertising space on the back of San Diego's public buses, depicted brown hands scraping plates, cleaning houses, or bearing handcuffs—typical postures of undocumented workers. This public spectacle disclosed a civic scandal that set in motion a public discourse covering immigration laws, labor exploitation, oversight of tax revenue allocation, the limits of free speech, racism, Mexican-American history, the tourist industry, and politically correct language. By clever design, the installation mimicked the elusiveness of its subject. It was not only mobile but of limited duration. However, by way of video, poster, and book, it achieved a sort of aesthetic transubstantiation, entering into the institutional world of the museum. Indeed, it metamorphosed into an exhibition that traveled from the Los Angeles County Museum into the international museum circuit. Admittedly, it lost a little of its bite in the transition to relative stability. No longer a tool to incite public discourse on the streets and through the mass media, it became a pedagogical instrument becalmed in the museum. But the impact on the public of such restrained educational ventures should not be underestimated.[37] Evidence shows that museums are becoming significant learning centers and that the "free-choice" learning that happens there ripples outward over time and throughout communities.

Inadvertently, perhaps, museum exhibition generates factions that may be politically divisive. Museums are inevitably political in several dimensions. They are subject to internal power relations among their staff and sponsors. These are present in any institution and are not unique to the museum, but they affect its judgment and aesthetic style. If the museum receives public funding, whether municipal or national, it is part of a patronage network that has political goals and responsibilities. Its survival hinges on the skills of diplomacy, which can compromise specific collection and exhibition strategies. Gesture and tone extend from membership solicitation to the treatment and conduct of guards and cafeteria workers and contribute to political harmony or discord throughout the museum population. Whether exhibitions should declare explicit political messages is always a contentious question for museums that finds passionate supporters on both sides. Arguably, there is no escape from political commitment, since its avoidance is also, effectively, a political statement. Except for those museums whose foundation endorses a particular political conviction, most museums prefer to stand apart from overt political advocacy, but the measure of their success is in the public's perception. Thus, a science museum exhibition that displays embryos in progressive stages of development using fertilized chicken eggs may be picketed by antiabortionists, and an exhibition on the fragile beauty of the Arctic can be charged with political propagandizing by proponents of regional oil prospecting.

Like some of the instances of public art discussed in previous chapters, museums become more controversial as they seek to diversify their outreach. Moving away from familiar fare to introduce uncommon themes, they shock traditional audiences and sometimes upset the very communities they hope to include. An iconic example of such a dual catastrophe was the Metropolitan's 1969 exhibition Harlem on My Mind, which followed shortly after the Harlem school strike and riots in 1968. Intended to mark the museum's wedge into "relevance," it turned out to be an ill-conceived disaster that worsened relations between blacks and Jews and fomented rancor throughout the city. The incident came close to costing the museum its municipal funding and soured relations between its newly appointed director, Thomas Hoving, and his board. It is hard to judge what effects it might have had on intracity race relations or whether it paved the way to an increased black presence among the Metropolitan audience. Ultimately, the museum's original intentions are insignificant.[38]

A far less notorious exhibition that successfully diminished rancorous racial strife took place at the Brooklyn Children's Museum in 1991. In the wake of violent clashes between black and Hasidic communities following a tragic accident, the museum became a reconciliation site where local neighbors could meet and address the long-standing issues that divided them and work out problems peaceably.[39]

Museums have become more socially audacious in the intervening decades, and the public has come to accept controversial challenges. The passing of a generation of lordly directors and museum boards has also affected the working of museum governance. Women and minorities now carry weight in decision making and the design of museums. They are not inherently more liberal or democratically inclined than their predecessors, but they bring new ideas and sensibilities to the institution, and they are open to untried experiments. Perhaps they are less wedded to stability and tradition and ready to welcome process and change.

Innovative Museum Practice

I conclude this chapter with some examples of radical museum transitions that temper reverence for objects with their diversion to programmatic ends. These, in turn, disperse as things become tales, tales become tellings, and tellings dissolve in a shower of interpretation.

When the National Museum of the American Indian, at the Smithsonian Institution, ceremonially opened its handsome new building on the Washington Mall in September 2004, its aim, in the words of Director Richard West, was as much "in-reach" as "outreach." It was to be of use to the millions of native peoples who inhabit the Western Hemisphere.[40] The soul of the museum is not on the Mall, however, but a bus ride away, at the Cultural Resources Center, in Suitland, where the collection is maintained. External storage centers are not out of the ordinary for large institutions with more objects than room to display them, but this one is different. It is more correctly described as a "home" where native people care for and commune with sacred objects that "need to breathe and be fed and be blessed." It is therefore conscientiously designed and fitted out with conveniences including a stone fire pit for use in "smudging" ceremonies and facilities for ageing visitors to rest and spend time with items from the collection. In other words, the objects are being reanimated for use and exhumed from the museal gaze—to the extent possible—to participate in traditional spiritual observances by communities that have not relinquished ownership of them to the museum.[41]

Although the objects do not reside in their traditional environments but in museum space, their community comes to the objects like grandchildren making a family visit and renewing ancestral connections. Undoubtedly something is "lost in translation," but the museum is perceived, and acknowledges itself, as preserver of meanings and practices kept alive in the reunion of things with people.

Other museums are likewise finding ways of crossing secular borders to share objects that have devotional significance for a particular public. Thus, in 1990, the Dalai Lama consecrated a new Buddhist altar for the display of Tibetan sacred objects that had been in the Newark Museum's collection since early in the twentieth century. As a result, the now-sacralized museum site became an accessible place of worship for Tibetan Buddhists living in New Jersey. Another passage from sacred to profane status and back again took place in Moscow, at the State Tretiakov Gallery, upon the resurgence of the Orthodox Church after the demise of the Soviet Union. The ingenious compromise achieved here was to accord curatorial status to the Orthodox patriarch of Moscow. As a museum professional, he was entitled to handle and use the sacred twelfth-century Icon of the Virgin of Vladimir to ecclesiastical purpose. The icon remained part of the museum's collection and continued to reside there, where it was displayed as an object of secular scientific and aesthetic interest; but from time to time, on festive occasions, it is removed and venerated in liturgical incarnation, presided over by the curator-patriarch.[42]

The assignment of dual identity, in one instance, to objects and places, in the other to a person, without causing physical or spiritual disturbance recognizes the fluidity of meaning that supervenes objective stability.

Museums are stepping in to ease difficult transfers, exercising their unique capacity to entertain diverse meanings and keep them operationally afloat. From the museum's perspective, in these examples, the object remains central, but its multidimensionality is accommodated in a manner that partially detaches the object from the museum context and dematerializes it. The performance of certain ritualized acts by appropriately empowered persons sanctions a temporary demusealization of the object and its reinsertion into the life stream. A reverse border crossing then restores the object to its secular museum presence, and it continues, with the help of necessary rituals, to oscillate between its several identities.

Another sort of border crossing dispenses with the conventional display of objects altogether but not with the manifestation of their acquired significance in certain socially defined contexts. The case at hand was an objectless show called The Status Project at the New Museum of Contemporary Art in New York. A pair of artists employed the standard rules of formal logic to set up relations of status-inclusion and exclusion in a database (p or not-p). The aim of the show was to explore, abstractly, how people pass from one social position to another. Accessing a virtual road map to identity construction, computer users could follow step-by-step instructions through a process that led to procurement of false credentials—student ID cards, drivers' licenses, credit cards, and passports.[43] The trail might lead to beer or to stealthier adventures. The intention of the British artists who created the project was politically idealistic rather than criminal, but its implications were not lost on U.S. authorities. American customs officials, wary after September 11th, barred one of the artists, a veteran of documented illegal treks, from entering the country on a charge of "port shopping." The artist was therefore unable to attend the opening of the exhibition at the museum, but his physical presence would have been superfluous anyway. The guests, using alias-identities, would be logged onto faraway virtual adventures, and their face-to-face encounter would seem an anachronism.[44]

If this example brings the ranked world of social licensing into the museum virtually, another stretches the museum's reach outside its premises symbolically to claim areas beyond its official domain. The construction of the architecturally radical Kiasma Museum of Modern Art in the center of Helsinki provoked aesthetic, as well as nationalist controversy in the 1990s, stimulated in part by the proximity of the site to the equestrian statue of Finland's distinguished former president, C.G. Mannerheim. A plywood fence protected the building site, revealing the construction in progress to curious onlookers through strategically placed slits. Viewed as a "temporary environmental art work wrapping around the vibrations of the construction work," the fence could be taken as the museum's first work of art. It was painted a shocking pink (magenta) and left free of commercial announcements, but the portion that surrounded the presidential statue was painted a "neutral grey," presumably out of deference to the dignity of the national leader. The fence thus insinuated an influence beyond the museum perimeter to affiliate itself visibly with the seat of government. At the same time, it offered civic entertainment and advertised the future glory of the museum—to be fully disclosed once its beguiling wrapper was removed.[45] Aestheticizing the temporary building site drew attention to the museum as performance, a species of street theater with peepholes that presaged the unconventional artwork it would eventually display.

To be dignified and sexy, powerful and cute is a tall order for museums to fulfill. They are striving to reach new audiences, but that goal is coupled with the more fundamental objective to redefine themselves. "From being *about* something to being *for* somebody" is the title of Stephen Weil's 1999 contribution to an essay collection on America's museums.[46] Taking their responsibility to the public seriously has become a rallying theme for museums and underscores the extent to which people are central to the museum's identity. Objects and their collection presuppose someone's interest and attention, someone's longing for enchantment through the museal gaze.[47] The museum has always been a medium that excites and gratifies this yearning. Defining museums in terms of objects exaggerated their priority but has worked to distinguish museums from other institutions that also profess to please, serve, and educate. Schools, libraries, hospitals, banks, communication networks, and even judicial systems connect people with things beneficially. This is hardly distinctive, but the museum does it differently. It recenters our presence among things, revealing our mutual dependency. The interaction is physical to the degree that it entails sensation, but it is also spiritual, as the traditional metaphors suggest. Today's secularized museum language is diminished to "experience"—aesthetic, emotional, or just plain "wow." That does not exclude mystical encounters or religious awakenings but fastens upon their phenomenological intensity, which is notoriously unstable. Contemporary technology, although replete with hardware, softens the insistent physicality of most human interactions. As a potentiator of experience where public and private, subject and object, meet, the museum converges with public art by fusing things with thought, and thought with action that merges into a public world.

Notes

1. Mellon Lectures of 1995, see *After the End of Art: Contemporary Art and the Pale of History* (Princeton, N.J.: Princeton University Press, 1998).

2. S. Dillon Ripley, *The Sacred Grove* (New York: Simon & Schuster, 1969).

3. According to Paul Valery, if not dead upon arrival, the things in museums will eventually kill each other. "The Problem of Museums" (1923).

4. Smithsonian Institution.

5. *The Exploratorium: The Museum as Laboratory*; see also Fabrice Grognet, "Ethnology: A Science on Display," *Museum International* 53, no. 1 (2001), cited in *Museum Studies*, ed. Bettina Messias Carbonell (Oxford: Blackwell, 2004). Speaking of the Musee de l'homme, ". . . the museum was defined more by its professional scientific dimension than by its cultural and educational dimension."

6. Elaine Heumann Gurian addresses the consistently narrow demographics of museum users despite apparent efforts by museums to widen their outreach. Using such popular attractions as zoos, libraries, shopping malls, and for-profit events for comparison, she lists the qualities of places organized so that strangers may safely interact while pursuing their own ends—seeking access to information and experiences in the case of museums. "Threshold Fear," address to meeting of American Association of Museums, 12 May 2004. Regrettably, the designation of all such spaces as attractions to terrorism inhibits their ability to be welcoming and hospitable.

7. As Carol Duncan observes, "Our notion of the 'public' dates from a later time, when almost everywhere in the West, the advent of bourgeois democracy opened up the category of citizenship to ever broader segments of the population and redefined the realm of the public as ever more accessible and inclusive." *Civilizing Rituals: Inside Public Art Museums* (London: Routledge, 1995), 36.

8. "The museum experience" refers rather vaguely to an entire visit of some duration, but a transformative experience usually takes place in a single, overwhelming moment.

9. Hilde Hein, *The Museum in Transition: A Philosophical Perspective* (Washington, D.C.: Smithsonian Institution Press, 2000), 103–7.

10. Frank Lloyd Wright was accused of deliberately interfering with optimal sight lines at the Guggenheim in New York and forcing visitors to view paintings from an awkward angle. Frank Gehry has come in for similar criticism, especially for the Bilbao Guggenheim Museum. It is worth noting that classical museum architecture was also impressive and often intimidating. Frequent museum-goers today are so habituated to fluted columns and grand stairways that they perceive them as neutral, but they were meant to be impressive. The understated architecture of the "modern" art museum (e.g., MoMA) was a direct reaction to the grandeur of the nineteenth-century style and a rebuke to its implicit rhetoric.

11. In the same essay quoted in the previous note, Elaine Gurian discusses the inadequacy of museums' architectural program planning. Too frequently the

objectives of architects and those of bodies responsible for the museum are not meshed; much less so are the interests of users.

12. See Duncan, 1995. These cues and their concomitant behaviors have been well explored in the past decade both within and outside the museum, thanks in large part to critics in the 1970s, including Duncan and Alan Wallach, "The Universal Survey Museum," *Art History* (December 1980), and "The Museum of Modern Art as Late Capitalist Ritual," *Marxist Perspectives* (Winter 1978).

13. I am taking the term from its usage in linguistics as a "performative utterance" first articulated by J. L. Austin, *Philosophical Papers* (Oxford, United Kingdom: Clarendon Press, 1961). Certain expressions, such as "I thee wed" or "I promise . . . ," are not descriptive of something but are the actual doing of it. Likewise, if I shout "Wake up!" when you are asleep, I am not issuing a command but am waking you up. In this sense, the museum is a doing as well as a doer.

14. Even a shell is not merely a domicile. It grows and adapts its form to its occupant, which shapes it with its own secretions. Museums, likewise, are neither neutrally external to nor dominant master of a "content" but are one with its substance.

15. Stephen E. Weil, "From Being *about* Something to Being *for* Somebody: The Ongoing Transformation of the American Museum," *Daedalus* 128, no. 3 (1999). Describing the standards set by the National Endowments for the Arts and Humanities, Weil makes the interesting observation that no agency "took into the slightest account the museum's external impact on either its visitors or its community." Those were the balmy days of peer evaluation and professional courtesy.

16. Not all museums make literal truth claims, but all of them subscribe to a standard of authenticity appropriate to their subject matter. In some cases that means reliable research and verification of fact; in others it refers to certain qualities of the objects displayed and the experiences evoked.

17. There are exceptions. World-renowned artists commissioned to create art for public centers sometimes produce works better identified as "private art in public places" than as "public art." Their celebrity is the attraction, and what they create, while it may be good art, is often considered irrelevant and lacking a sense of place. This charge was leveled against Picasso and Alexander Calder, respectively, for their Chicago and Grand Rapids sculptures.

18. Although some critics refused to take his defense seriously, this was Richard Serra's response to the decision to remove *Tilted Arc* from the New York Federal Plaza, where it had been commissioned. He meant it to be site specific and intentionally disruptive. And indeed it was, which is why its detractors wished its destruction.

19. One might argue that, following Andy Warhol's *Brillo Box*, private art is as dependent on environment as public art, for the same box in a supermarket would not be art. For further discussion of this thesis, see Arthur Danto, *The Transfiguration of the Commonplace: A Philosophy of Art* (Cambridge, Mass.: Harvard University Press, 1981). His point is metaphysical rather than geographical, namely,

that the existence of art depends on certain institutions such as the museum and the art gallery.

20. For a variant claim, see Danielle Rice's discussion of the series of *Rocky* films, which climax with the ceremonial placement of a statue of the prize-fighter at the top of the steps of the Philadelphia Museum of Art. As Rice notes, the museum is used here as a stand-in for "the state" over which the hero triumphs. The "art" stays safely outside the building (as does the public), for its function is less aesthetic than celebratory. "Museums: Theory, Practice, and Illusion," in *Art and Its Publics: Museum Studies at the Millennium*, ed. McClellan (Oxford: Blackwell, 2003).

21. Opponents of the Barnes's relocation understood this instinctively. Writing in *The New Yorker* (16 and 23 February 2004), art critic Peter Schjeldahl amplifies my thesis: "Altering so much as a molecule of one of the greatest art installations I have ever seen would be an aesthetic crime. . . . The Barnes is a work of art in itself, more than the sum of its parts. . . . As you test the virtues of the collection, they test you, probing the depths and exposing the limits of your perceptive powers. You don't view the installation so much as live it, undergoing an experience that will persist in your memory like a love affair that taught you some thrilling and some dismaying things about your character." The removal of the Barnes to its downtown destination has since been decided. Dr. Barnes might have enjoyed presiding over the scrappy struggle but would, no doubt, have been furious at its outcome.

22. Ivan Karp, Christine Mullen Kreamer, and Steven D. Lavine, eds., *Museums and Communities: The Politics of Public Culture* (Washington, D.C.: Smithsonian Institution Press, 1992).

23. Karp, Kreamer, and Lavine, eds. Lack of transportation and high entrance fees are major obstacles to public use, but these are practical rather than fear-inducing limitations.

24. Adrienne L. Kaeppler, "Ali'I and Maka'ainana: The Representation of Hawaiians in Museums at Home and Abroad," in *Museums and Communities*.

25. Stephen E. Weil, "Collecting Then, Collecting Today," in *Making Museums Matter* (Washington, D.C.: Smithsonian Institution Press, 2002).

26. viz. Exploratorium exhibition on memory.

27. Marriage and the family are prime examples.

28. As Steven Weil pointed out in his 2004 AAM lecture in New Orleans, nearly every museum opened or rededicated in the past decade, whether public or for profit, has been "bottom up" in its topical interest and processual in practice. Among his examples: the National Health Museum focuses on patients, not doctors; the National Museum of the U.S. Army addresses the experience of troops rather than foregrounding grand strategy or military hardware; the Newseum's emphasis is on news-gathering and editing rather than on sensational machinery. Even the privately owned International Spy Museum, which does feature glitzy paraphernalia, also concentrates on the techniques of spying as a craft that any of

us can apply to our neighbors. These and other newly emergent museums cast many of the old museum truisms in doubt. They are thriving for the moment; it remains to be seen how they will prosper.

29. Andreas Huyssen, "Escape from Amnesia: The Museum as Mass Medium," in *Twilight Memories: Marking Time in a Culture of Amnesia* (New York: Routledge, 1995).

30. This is not always the case. To those unfamiliar with the historical Joseph McCarthy, the use of actual tapes from his hearings in the George Clooney film *Good Night, and Good Luck* was insignificant. They saw only an actor exaggeratedly performing his role. The distinction between appearance and reality that preoccupied ancient philosophers is not a pressing concern to a generation that thrives on simulation.

31. With the Brillo box, Andy Warhol brilliantly revealed this quality that is not ordinarily apprehended in the supermarket, where Brillo boxes are routine. Effectively, he has made narcissistic anthropologists of the ordinary of us all.

32. There are, of course, unsuccessful endeavors. Inferior museum exhibitions are sometimes described as "books on walls," and artworks can degenerate into didactic screeds. This is why I stress the capacity, rather than the fulfillment of potential.

33. Huyssen identifies the longing for that achievement as a kind of fetishism but certainly not commodity fetishism, for it has no exchange value but only "memory value," which is real enough. Speculators more enterprising than Huyssen have, in fact, sought to commodify and market "immersive experience" that amazes as it educates beholders. viz. advertisement for BRC Imagination Arts. These projects are much indebted to the research of two economists, B. Joseph Pine II and James Gilmore. See *The Experience Economy: Work Is Theater & Every Business a Stage* (Boston: Harvard Business School Press, 1999).

34. People also attend theater and musical performances in groups, but (apart from rock concerts) they are expected to remain in their seats quietly until intermission, when they are allowed limited mobility.

35. The role of the curator, as the name connotes, was formerly to care for collections. Today it has a very activist significance, and curators have become public figures whose hirings and firings are front-page stories. At the same time, there is a flattening of eminence throughout the museum hierarchy as all strata bend to public service.

36. Robert Mapplethorpe's 1989 photographic retrospective *The Perfect Moment* is a perfect example. The Corcoran Gallery cancelled its exhibition, although it had appeared in several other cities without incident. It caused hardly a stir when it appeared at the Boston ICA, but when it reached Cincinnati, it cost the director of the Contemporary Arts Center, Dennis Barrie, his job and nearly landed him in jail. It is true that the public reacted to only a few pictures, but the exhibition was conceived as a whole, and not a single curator accepted the option of merely expelling the offending images from it.

37. C. Ondine Chavoya, "Collaborative Public Art and Multimedia Installation: David Avalos, Louis Hock, and Elizabeth Sisco's 'Welcome to America's Finest Tourist Plantation' (1988)," in *The Ethnic Eye: Latino Media Arts*, eds. Chon A. Noriega and Ana M. Lopez (Minneapolis: University of Minnesota Press, 1996).

38. A pivotal point of discord was a passage quoted in an essay in the catalogue by a young black woman affirming that "blacks may find that anti-Jewish sentiments place them, for once, within a majority. Thus, our contempt for the Jew makes us feel more completely American in sharing a national prejudice." Cited in Thomas Hoving, *Making the Mummies Dance* (New York: Simon & Schuster, 1993). The author of the essay later admitted that the inflammatory passage was quoted from Daniel Moynihan and Nathan Glazer's book *Beyond the Melting Pot*. The curator chose to express the words without attribution for greater dramatic effect, which he undoubtedly achieved.

39. Mindy Duitz, "The Soul of a Museum," in Karp, Kreamer, and Lavine, eds.

40. W. Richard West, "A Song Made Visible," *Museum News* (September/October 2004).

41. Bob Thompson, "Spirit Lodge: The Indian Museum Storage Facility Feels Less Like a Warehouse and More Like Home," *The Washington Post* (2 August 2004).

42. Ivan Gaskell, "Sacred to Profane and Back Again," in McClellan, ed.

43. In reality, the credentials are not false but are obtained without legal entitlement. The process is logically sound and, if followed without error, may achieve its forbidden end.

44. Elizabeth Bard, "How to Cross Borders, Social or Otherwise," *The New York Times*, 27 October 2004.

45. Timo Kopomaa, *Ars Longa, via brevis, Tyomaat katukuvassa* [*Building Sites in the Streetscape*] (Helsinki: Edita, 2000). The book concerns Helsinki urban culture.

46. *Daedalus* 128, no. 3 (1999).

47. An interesting spin on what is thought the backward gaze of the traditional museum is a "history of the future" that is the subject of the recently opened Science Fiction Museum and Hall of Fame, in Seattle. This museum has no lack of objects, many of them memorabilia from movies and television series, such as *Star Wars* and "Star Trek," as well as drawings, first-edition books, and copies of science fiction magazines. This museum, however, adapts the concept of "alternative realities" beyond the pluralistic viewpoint of caste, class, and culture or winners and losers among museum users. It aims at the possible, or the not yet realized. It is a museum of what has been imagined. This museum bypasses truth and authenticity to mingle fiction with fact and to diminish the distance between what is known and what can be imagined. viz. Edward Rothstein, "Sci-Fi Synergy: A Broad Look at the History of the Future," *New York Times* (24 May 2005).

Why a New Paradigm?

The board of a museum is not a House of Lords, nor yet an exclusive social club. The present incumbents must let down the bars gradually. There must be less emphasis on wealth, old family and big game hunting, and more on representing great masses of people potentially interested in the museums and their work.

—ROBERT MOSES

It's a cultural war to destabilize the mainstream. The question is why institutions of the center should join this crusade to do themselves in.

—JOHN LEO

Without things, we would stop talking. We would be as mute as things are alleged to be.

—LORRAINE DASTON

The commodity is not one kind of thing rather than another, but one phase in the life of some things.

—ARJUN APPADURAI

What Are Museums Good For?

Explaining oneself to others is seldom easy. Institutions are hardly suppler than individual people at justifying their existence and bear the added burden that their purpose alone is their soul. People can be good for nothing; institutions cannot. They are measured by their purpose and how well they achieve it. Museums are obliged to declare their raison d'être up front and must stay current within its guidelines. Yet, mission statements commonly lack specificity. They are bland and hopeful announcements of good intentions standard in the literature of every institution that courts public attention.[1] They are needed to evaluate whether or not an institution successfully does what it sets out to do and are helpful to applicants choosing among alternatives—colleges, for example, or foundation grants. It is as important to know what is not said by a mission statement as to know what it does include. A college committed to training foreign missionaries, for example, is not a likely choice for the study of high-energy physics. But this is common sense. Once you have visited them, you do not need to read their mission statements to distinguish between the aims of the Metropolitan and those of the New York Tenement Museum. The institutions are obviously dissimilar, yet as museums they are taken to have something in common. Is there, then, a mission that all museums share?

Stephen Weil, who seems to have the last and best word on all things museum-wise, observed decades ago that not all museums are created equal and that their prodigious differences should be celebrated, not suffocated. And yet, the temptation persists to seek the common essence, a Platonic ideal perhaps, whose realization in our world can be approximated but is never perfect. Weil himself succumbed to the platonizing urge in a 1990 rumination on a new paradigm, in which he expands upon the meaning of "communication" as a two-way interaction rather than a one-way transmission of information. This insight coincided with a movement or, more correctly, an invasion by newly emboldened transmitters of meaning into and outside of the museum. Exhibition/interpretation—a moderately tidy dyad that still awards pride of place to things—led, in time, to a virtual renunciation of materiality. That had to be an embarrassment to a profession that, for centuries, had defined itself in terms of its solicitous care for the now-ambiguated objects that filled its galleries and storerooms. There was no rush to their deaccession and barely a pause in acquisition; it was the univocal meaning of objects that was devastated. Was this proliferation of meanings an enrichment or a devaluation?

Confusion reigned and rightly so, for museums attribute special, value-importing qualities, such as uniqueness, typicality, historical priority, or outstanding beauty to the objects they collect.[2] Their claim to irreplaceability was already under stress thanks in part to the advent of science centers and museums that dispense with collections in the strict sense and treat the objects they possess as vehicles to teach and illustrate ideas. If its relation to material things is not what distinguishes the museum but is merely a means to performing its function, then the museum appears in danger of becoming a superfluous entity.

Reinvention is thus less optional than imperative. With collection moved to a subordinate role, many museums shifted their attention to public service, an exceedingly vague and general obligation that, even if correctly assumed, lends itself to imitativeness and banality. It translates poorly into action. The adoption of public service as an aim, moreover, gave rise to bitter and distracting controversies over who the public is and the definition of "service." One merit of these discussions was their foregrounding of ethical and political questions that had previously been obscured. Museums were compelled to recognize that possession of inanimate objects neither entails automatic objectivity nor protects the holder from clashing subjectivities. Ironically, their repudiation of objects forced museums to wrestle more closely with their worth. Things had never been so complex.

I believe that, in their zeal to redefine themselves, museums have bounced from one extreme to another, from the reputedly stable world of physical things and their properties to the subjective world of consciousness, where private experience is supreme. I propose an alternative conceptualization of the museum that borrows language from the philosopher Karl Popper and amplifies his thesis. Popper declares that the traditional dualism between thought and matter is insufficient to explain the complexity of the universe. He posits a (regrettably titled) third world of *objective contents of thought*.[3] This is not a compromising substitution of a "happy medium" between the two more familiar realms of thought and matter or an opportunistic synthesis of them but a rationally derived metaphysical postulate. Popper's interest is chiefly in theoretical systems and problem situations that ground science, but his arguments to substantiate the third world also fit the dynamically amplified museum. Like many collective nouns, such as "university," "state," or "disease," "museum" denotes a complex variety of related entities, some material and some immaterial, discontinuous in time and space and largely conceptual but with significantly physical aspects and affective consequences. Museums are composed of thought and actions, perpetuated by concrete persons who are thinking and doing, but also of objective realities that are thought and done. These persist whether or not anyone is currently aware of them. The museum, like Bishop Berkeley's tree in the forest, is there in the absence of staff and visitors not because of its (unseen) building and collections but as the gathered actions and memories that led to their accumulation and multiplied their meaning.

Some ideas exist as sheer potentiality, never to be realized. Some cultural concepts are, or ought to be, obsolete—suttee, for example. Absent in practice, they are present in Popper's third world as objective content of thought. We come to know or understand such contents through the mediation of a variety of verbal explanations, formulae, imagery, technological projections, and dramatic demonstrations. We can conjecture how or why someone devised or discovered those contents and imagine how they might have gained currency or suffered rejection. We are then contemplating a subjective process—how someone might think—as I am doing at this moment and you too, dear reader, if you are trying to follow my argument—but the existence of what is thought is independent of our thinking.[4] We can discover and describe relations between such thought contents and illustrate them with the help of physical representations that might enable others to grasp them. Suppose, for example, that a sumptuous, traditional Chinese yellow robe is used to symbolize imperial divinity (let *x* represent *y*) and is exhibited next to a plain wooden ballot box, representing popular sovereignty (and let *w* represent *z*). The abstract contents (imperial divinity and popular sovereignty—*y* and *z*) really do exist independently of robe and box, as does their incompatibility. They might have been symbolized by other things—a crown and a stone, for example. The robe and box are physical things that can and do coexist. They are not incompatible as physical objects, but in the (supposed) museum exhibit, they stand for conditions that exclude one another. Under other circumstances, these same physical objects might play entirely different roles that museum visitors would be expected to understand with the help of appropriate guidance. The robe might figure in an exhibition of dragon imagery or silk manufacture, while the box could exemplify carpentry skills or eighteenth-century furniture. The business of museums is not to cause people merely to undergo private experiences of thinking and feeling but to render this (third-world) realm of objective thought accessible.[5]

Popper holds that the third world is autonomous, although it is produced by human action and influences human behavior. Its study throws light on how humans think and behave and affects their further conduct. The contents of the third world are not fully determinate. Many are realized only when certain ideas are actually thought or put into practice. When that happens, unexpected (third-world) features that existed only dispositionally are divulged. It is as if all potential consequences of an action were inscribed in its nature, although some of them will never be actualized and which ones these are is unforeseeable. If coffee beans had never been plucked and consumed, their energizing capacity would be unknown, but it would not be absent.

Museums often depict historical developments, arranging exhibits from a vantage that would have been impossible for those who lived through the events described. They could not have perceived that sequence in spite of undergoing its stages, for its trajectory emerges as such only to historical hindsight. The evolution of a style in literature or painting, likewise, appears only after the fact. Once identified, antecedent and pivotal moments appear evident to observers, but their implicit dynamic could not be recognized as such, even by the agents who knowingly follow their lead. Impressionism did not spring full blown out of anyone's head and was given its name by a critic (unsympathetic) who confronted a body of independent expressions. The linkage among actual, potential, and extraneous phenomena is an abstract relation that, according to the thesis I am endorsing, emerges conjecturally some time after several noteworthy events have taken place and someone chooses to connect these while discounting others. Museums reveal such sequences through the arrangement of exhibitions and often do so intentionally, but visitors also apprehend orders of relationships unprompted by exhibition planners.[6]

The subjective act of thinking is a private experience, and Popper holds that psychological description of such acts is less fruitful for understanding the world than discovery of the autonomous third-world structures that underlie and legitimate the thinking process. The immediacy of the personal experience is psychologically compelling. It inspires art and literature that resonate with those who appreciate it. We empathize with and sometimes gain insight from that experience, but it is not explanatory. Explanation is a public phenomenon. Like scientific investigation, which normally proceeds from anomalies or "problems" to seek "objective knowledge" that would resolve them, museums also direct thought from perceptible objects to the construction of plausible stories. From Galileo's telescope we cannot recover his experience of elation upon observing the heavenly bodies or the agony that must have accompanied his recantation, but it is possible to reconstruct the logical reckoning that would follow upon his discovery of the moons of Jupiter.[7] The public thought can be verified; the private, only imagined.

I am suggesting, along the lines of Popper's reasoning, that the museum is a locus of thought, quite apart from the actual thinking of individuals—those whose ideas are collected in the museum as well as those who mount exhibitions or guide school groups among them. This is not to deny the reality of these people's subjective experiences or to minimize the importance of the conditions that induced them. The museum, however, is reducible to neither, although it is a product of human agency and could not exist in the absence of either matter or consciousness.

In further agreement with Popper, I believe that the objective realm of thought affects subjective thinking: That is why it is possible to learn from and be inspired by museums. More postmodern, however, than Popper, I also admit some reverse causality; subjective thought affects the objective realm. Museums are materially dependent on and must be responsive to subjective judgments that have generated new objective realities. Their current self-critical stance, albeit partially pragmatic, is an indicator. More is at issue than the need to meet public demand. Museums bear the mark of massive changes taking place within the third-world structure of thought itself. Science is also beginning to succumb to that pressure. The changes are a consequence of the technologies that represent thought. Computers, to name a powerful force, no less than language, cut deeply into our conceptual foundations. They do not imitate how we think but legislate thought; under their spell we learn to think differently. Like other cultural institutions that have adopted the technology, museums exhibit the consequences.

Moreover, if *memes*, the cultural equivalent of genes, are recombined and passed from one generation to the next, we must assume that today's cognitive procedures, moral values, and aesthetic values, are mutable. Third-world contents will change, and their alterations will be replicated by successor generations to the same extent as somatic traits. The transformation of the museum is therefore neither an aberration from an ideal state nor an approach to one but registers a process of adaptive change. Its trend toward dematerialization and pluralization can be seen, in retrospect, as part of a longer process in which abstract ideas, along with productive and reproductive technologies, commercial enterprise, war, disease, law, personal ambition, and idealism, have all played a part. While adaptation has been conducive to the museum's survival thus far, we cannot call it progress since there is no discernible endpoint and since the goals in view are themselves transitional states prompted by circumstance.

If there is neither progress nor regression but only and inevitably adaptive conformity to environmental pressures, one might question the logic of judgments of value. I affirm them on the ground that we human beings are both subject and object, the environment and also that which is environed. We exercise causality and observe it in the museum. The museum mirrors and reproduces us to ourselves, and through it our interactions reverberate. In this book I defend a model of the museum that, unlike the prevalent static models, takes these dynamic exchanges into account. Here I emphasize the museum's objectivity to counterbalance a currently modish celebration of subjectivity.

The Mutable Museum and the Volatile User

A remarkable book by Ivan Gaskell, with the beguiling title *Vermeer's Wager*, uses a single painting to make a case oddly parallel to my own. Gaskell argues that a painting, in this case Vermeer's *Young Woman Standing at a Virginal*, cannot be understood simply as pigment on canvas or as whatever Vermeer might have been thinking when he painted it or as what the perceiver of the moment happens to experience upon contemplating it. Those are certainly significant way stations in the process that is the painting but neither its end nor its beginning. The whole, if it is one, is structured more like a chambered nautilus, cycling ever outward in a pattern due less to fate than to a constantly shifting productive and reproductive environment. Its history is itself. Typical of Vermeer's domestic scenes, this complex work includes paintings within the painting, hence, implicitly, paintings that preceded it, which beg their own prior iconographic scrutiny. *Young Woman Standing at a Virginal* is further analyzable according to a number of curatorial and scholarly art historical strategies. Beyond these is a history of industry, ownership, display, and preservation practices with tangential forays into the art and science of influence, authentication, derivation, forgery, and copying. The work thickens next in light of presentational custom, which engages not only aesthetics but also the sociology and economics of bourgeois acquisition, museums, and the conditions of donation. Vermeer's painting is also qualified (enriched?) by subsequent associations and appropriations, often through popular culture. What, in the end, was Vermeer's wager? Perhaps faith in the human capacity and desire for continued and renewed resonance that would validate his effort.

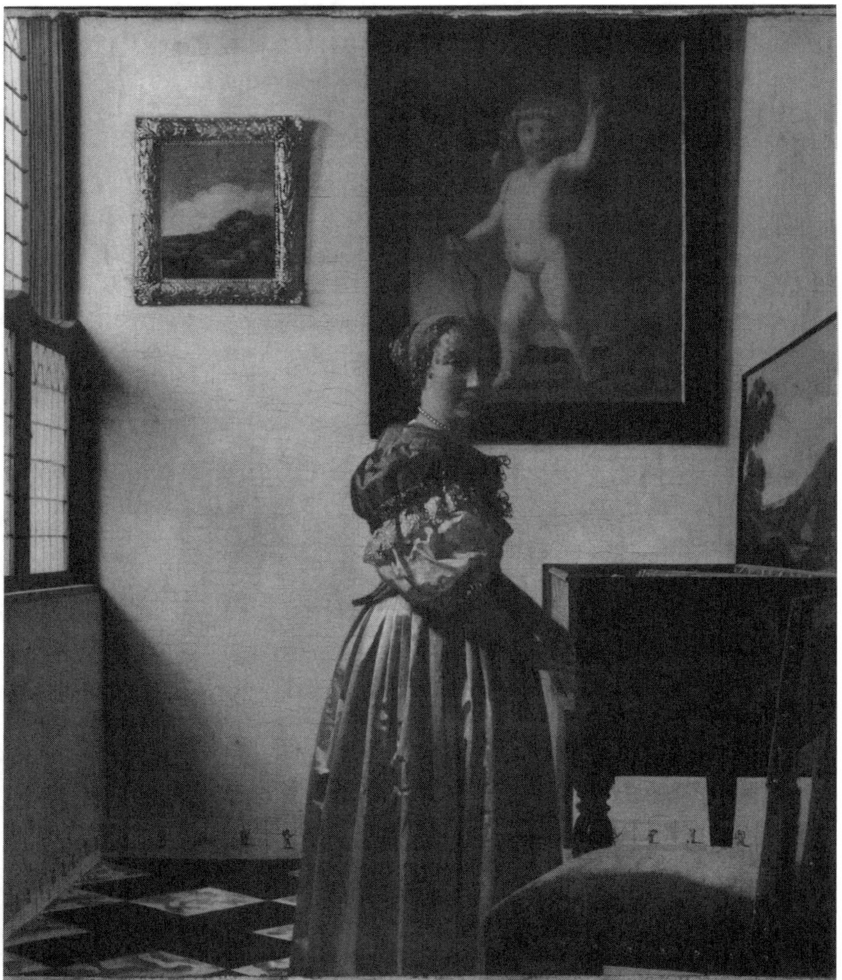

Johannes Vermeer, *Young Woman Standing at a Virginal* (ca. 1670). (Courtesy of National Gallery, Picture Library, London, U.K.)

That same trust in some kind of perennial truth or shared human reality, however elusive, seems to motivate the pursuit of knowledge and the creation of art. Vermeer is betting on something's endurance beyond himself.[8] The painting places us within the scheme of continuity.

Gaskell's analysis of works of art applies also to the museum, a form of art writ large. Whatever such works meant to those who made and initially used them, our ability to enjoy them today is largely determined by what has befallen them since their origin, which could not have been anticipated. My approach to the museum in terms of a public rather than private form of art, which Vermeer's painting arguably is, is meant to underscore the quality that the museum itself now chooses to emphasize, namely, its concern with the public interest. I have argued (see chapter 3) that the presence of sociality is not an essential ingredient of private art, where, in the sense under consideration, the public may well be damned—but there can be no denying the public dimension of public art.[9]

Public art is not regulated by mission statements, as museums arguably are, but restrictive conditions of a competitive selection process frequently do apply to it. Implicit in public art's identity and sometimes explicitly declared is an affiliation with a public that the artwork constructs. The specificity of this public is significant. It is not a featureless universal. Its character grows and changes together with that of the art. Publics sometimes emerge spontaneously and sporadically, and often they are short-lived, enduring responsively throughout an incident or provocation—a worker strike, for example, or an epidemic. If the public ceases to exist, the art that constructed it may revert to private status or even cease to be art at all. Sometimes it is destroyed.[10]

Even a comparatively stable and static work of public art, such as the Vietnam Veterans Memorial, has been altered by circumstances independent of its initial conception. Not the least of these was the ideological struggle and political regime change that followed the acceptance of Maya Lin's abstract design. The conflict led to the compromising appendage of Frederick Hart's populist sculpture and the U.S. flag. An unofficial factor that has shaped the character of the monument spontaneously is its daily accretion of memorabilia delivered by visitors.[11] These are regularly collected and preserved elsewhere, yet they belong to the memorial. The monument has also been affected by changes in its environment. At the time of its dedication, it sank, like a great gash into the ground, between the two memorials to the founding struggles of the republic to which it pointed (the Washington Monument and Lincoln Memorial).[12] Now the Vietnam Veterans Memorial is one of many tributes on the Mall to heroes and wars of unequal magnitude, and its stark style has many imitators. The monument's creator, moreover, has matured to achieve fame and fortune as an artist, thus altering the memory of the slight Asian-American architecture student whose powerful concept bowled over the male-dominated 1970s arts establishment. Today, the Vietnam Veterans Memorial is one of

Washington's most popular tourist attractions. As the memory of that war recedes into history and is superseded by more recent conflicts (which do not yet have memorials of their own),[13] the meanings affixed to the Vietnam Veterans Memorial must take on a different hue.

We are conditioned to think of museums as more or less permanent fixtures, but this is to confuse the stability of some parts for the whole and to miss the fluidity of the entire gestalt. Heraclitus observed that you cannot step into the same river twice, and in a sense, this is also true of museums. Both you and the museum will have changed in the interim.

A Chicago installation commissioned for six months' duration illustrates one museum's effort to turn itself literally into an ephemeral work of public art. The project Between the Museum and the City, realized in 2003 by Garofalo Architects, was a collaboration between the Museum of Contemporary Art and the College of Architecture and the Arts, University of Chicago. Initiated as part of the museum's program to display the work of living artists, the project was designed to animate the somewhat forbidding stairway and plaza that connect the museum to the street. This was not the first use of the museum façade as art; its windows had been the site of shadow puppetry by Redmoon Theater in 2001 and of images of visitors in 1999. Christo and Jeanne-Claude wrapped the building's entire exterior in cotton drop cloth in 1969. But the 2003 project was different in that unchoreographed public behavior was to be an ingredient throughout the duration of the construction. Envisioning various options for seating and reclining, casual gatherings, performance spaces, and a weekly farmers' market, the artists set out flexible props made of texturally odd and inviting materials and waited to see what people would do with them. There were notable impediments such as Chicago's high winds and the prohibition against permanently attaching anything to the building or the plaza, but public creativity soon revealed itself: "The skateboarders came first, testing the curves on the underside of their boards, and when the sun came out, sunbathers appeared seemingly out of nowhere." Wooden decks worked as platforms for yoga practice or impromptu orators, and soft islands woven out of industrial materials sometimes attracted young couples at night "to engage in ten minutes of private activity." Attendance also increased in the museum galleries, as the gulf that had divided the institution from the city and the public was mended by the socioarchitectural weave.[14]

This story of a museum's temporary self-transformation into a work of public art relates a cautious experiment. Notice that it was of fixed and limited duration and that the museum remained safely coiled within its property lines.[15] Public art is frequently more transgressive and ventures farther into "public space." Museums ordinarily do not resort to physically radical makeovers beyond altering a few walls and hanging some banners.[16] Some have gone so far as to open branches in accessible places such as department stores. A few plant corn or wheat fields around their perimeter, complying with the spirit of a particular exhibition, but their basic outcroppings tend to be programmatic and organizational rather than physically intrusive. Their community ingression is through people's conduct, which is increasingly proactive. Inviting the involvement of neighborhood children, community groups, resident artists, scholars, subject specialists, and local interest groups tends to build islands of attention and short-term affiliations, a few of which coalesce into permanent attachment. One motive is certainly to gain long-term fidelity measurable in repeated visitation, donation, and active membership.

Loyalty is hard won, however, and easily dissipated where its object is inconstant and there is much competition. If it is not hated by a public on which it is imposed, public art sometimes attracts a different kind of loyalty. There is a benign acceptance that Harriet Senie's students observed among regular passersby, who live with certain works of public art in the routine of their everyday lives. They interact with these works without reverence or sentimentality, assuming an attitude of familiar disrespect—leaning on them, adorning them with seasonal decoration, affixing Post-Its on them, using them as meeting places, climbing into and on them, and giving them wondrously imaginative names that reveal an unsuspected aesthetic sensibility.[17] Echoing the voices of urban critics Jane Jacobs and Kevin Lynch, Senie notes that "audience use of public art highlights what people find missing in our urban environment: places to sit and/or play, humanizing elements in general, place markers, and a sense of civic identity." While the use made of the object may not be what its author(s) had in mind, it has a place in the life of a community like a ritual presence and would be missed if it were absent.[18]

This type of public art eludes media attention, which goes to the catastrophically offensive, expensive, and controversial, but it is noticed and, by and large, enjoyed by segments of the population, especially children, the homeless, and many working people, who never set foot in museums and are rarely consulted about anything. Interestingly, of those asked by interviewers, few had objections to spending taxpayer dollars on public art.[19] Museums would do well to study the route by which such generous affection is gained.

Some museums actually are monuments, if not monumental, and a number of monuments now support auxiliary museums. These pose interesting questions, for while the two facilities are meant to reinforce each other, the tasks they perform, as memorial and as museum, are not the same. My discussion of the Son My Memorial visited at fifteen-year intervals (see chapter 4) illustrates this point, and its description applies to other situations—the Statue of Liberty, the Jefferson Memorial, the St. Louis Arch, all of which have small museums attached. Each of these works of public art was constructed to prolong the memory of or celebrate an occasion or person. The structures serve to honor their subject and maintain its place in history. For those who lived through or witnessed an event, a commemorative object might revive aspects of an experience or animate a nostalgic memory. Such revival is not possible for nonparticipants, who cannot relive what they have not endured. For them it is only history. Original experience inevitably disappears with those who experienced it and can at best be approximated by mediating devices. The museum, therefore, can only supplement the experience the monument recalls with evidence and information. It can amplify, enrich, and elaborate upon the subject, even illuminating those people who underwent the experience, but it cannot regenerate it.[20] Nevertheless, museums attached to memorials do win a derivative affection as a result of their association with the memorial. Visitors appreciate learning about the memorialized event as well as the construction of the memorial itself and usually come away with good feelings toward museum facilities that tend to be rather nondescript according to professional museum standards.

In a comparable way, a modest museum with a distinct neighborhood reference is a source of pride to a community that is validated by it. While visiting a tiny fishermen's museum in Gloucester, Massachusetts, I was once startled when a small boy rushed in with great excitement. Cupped in his dripping hands was a live sea creature that he had caught in the harbor and wanted the director to put on display immediately. His impulse was legitimate, for much of the museum collection consisted of fishing tackle and old gear that had been collected from the attics and garages of local inhabitants. It was "their" museum, filled with their stories, and it was alive with their energy. The boy was making proper use of "his" museum. Neighborhood museums inform newcomers to a region and are affirmative to old-timers whose memory warms to the community's history.

Impressive buildings or "destination sites" can obstruct that vitality. Not a few museums have grown glamorously sclerotic in well-secured comfort after vigorous beginnings. Overwhelmed by accumulation and its burdens, they become bureaucratically obsessive and lose their original dynamic. This is a major problem for large museums with huge collections and territorialized departments, but it can also be a risk for small museums with limited resources and an entrenched agenda. In their eagerness to upgrade, they succeed in becoming boring. More damaging than physical ossification is the intellectual desiccation lampooned by critics who scoff at museums' pretension—or at least their ambition—to know and impart the correct order of things, whether the authentic story of art, of historical fact, or of the advance of science.

The reactive Foucaultian assault on museum orthodoxy ridicules every attempt to reduce heterogeneity to homogeneity, dismissing them all as ill-disguised manifestations of the will to power. Thus, Douglas Crimp assimilates the museum to other disciplinary institutions, such as the asylum, the clinic, and the prison, which strive to socialize people to fit a prevailing prototype.[21] Crimp finds support in Flaubert's satirical novel *Bouvard and Pecuchet*, in which two zany social misfits who come into an inheritance seek but fail to find comprehensive order in one scientific and practical pursuit after another. Eventually, they construct a private museum guided by the principle that an ordered display of artifacts metonymically represents the whole of human reality and history. When this venture also fails, they conclude that "the museum was a doomed institution from its very inception." This, according to Foucaultian critics, is because the metaphysical ambition to create an ordered representation of reality is misplaced. The master narrative has been discredited; what remains is a proliferation of fables. The museum, they claim, contains only an arbitrary collection of "bric-a-brac" that somehow struck someone as evocative. Attempts to understand the nature and essence of objects rationally are thus anthropocentric, and faith in the possibility of any material representation of natural order is delusional. They conclude that the learned pretension of the museum is a narcissistic fraud.[22] Worse yet, it may be a fascist plot.

Flaubert's characters express an extreme of epistemological nihilism. No museum could tolerate without protest their description of its treasures as "senseless fragments without a memory . . . (whose) history is nothing but vain fabulation." Responses to such denunciation have varied from right to left. There are those who cringe with horror at the relativist conclusion that, if there is nothing but facts and phenomena, then "anything goes; everything is equal," but there are others who greet the same judgment with delight. (If God is dead, then anything is possible.) If one story is as good as another, they rejoice, then whichever is most persuasive wins the day. Herein lies the problem, for persuasion is not always a victory of logic or even aesthetics, and so we come to the hidden persuaders, namely, politics and coercion.

The exposure of overt and hidden agendas in museums and elsewhere has become a popular pastime, and by now it is generally understood that every story reflects a point of view. There is no omniscient seer, much less a teller of universal truth. It does not follow that every speaker is a liar, but neither should we conclude that every speech is equally valid. This is a call for standards. Museums are hit hard by the dilemma. The authenticity of their collections has been the bedrock of their authority—indeed of their legitimacy—which devolves to their profession of knowledge and judgment. Like all institutions, the confederacy of museums has been deeply compromised. But, as James N. Wood points out, "The line between being authoritative and authoritarian is one that separates trust from coercion or intimidation."[23] How reliable are the collections? How collected? By and for whom? To what end or benefit? Museums are far from above the fray. Their past, present, and future are on the line. Wood quotes Alexis de Tocqueville, who put the question plainly: is it possible to democratize high culture? As an aristocrat, de Tocqueville feared the tyranny of the majority, but today's conflicts are not between an entrenched ruling minority and a faceless majority. Rather, there is a plurality of points of view, each warranted by standards of quality that are fervently defended by their partisans, and often mutually incompatible. To claim supremacy for any one seems indefensible, and so they pale to equal vacuity. How can the museum avoid the cacophony of the marketplace or profess to remain nonpartisan? Instead of neutrality, the museum should strive for transparency and integrity—clear objectives, honestly delineated with conviction, by museums with distinct, admittedly fallible, and yet determined points of view.

Unlike commercial business, the business of the museum is not making a profit, and as Philippe de Montebello observed, running a museum in a businesslike manner is not the same as running a business. The commodities, services, and experiences purveyed by the museum are not subtracted from a definable inventory.[24] Users of the museum bring their own expectations, and what they take away with them does not deplete the museum's resources. The exchange that takes place is not of material goods. It subsists in the realm of thought and values, where contraries and contradictions can coexist peaceably and be vigorously scrutinized.

In proposing public art as a paradigm for museums, I do not have specific works in mind as models but am directing attention to developments in the field that have changed the perception of what public art is. Instances of new-genre public art are everywhere—illuminating trees and clouds, shown on buses and traffic signs, cleansing rivers of their waste, and posted on the tiny screens of cell phones. There are enormous differences among its manifestations, in substance as in subject. My aim here is to normalize the variability, impermanence, and limited scope that have become acceptable in public art and to urge their adaptation to the museum.

The Convergence of Museums and Public Art

Museums and public art have already begun to converge to a considerable extent. Many museums no longer have the resources to add to collections and lack sufficient display space to exhibit everything they own. They have little choice but to become more dynamic. Going virtual is a risky option that entails a major investment in technology. Moving into the streets is another alternative, and museums are sending forth tendrils to airports, shopping malls, resort hotels, and casinos, as well as mobile units that travel to schools, senior centers, and public parks. At the same time, public art programs are including peripheral workshops and educational events much like those typically offered by museum education departments. Public art proposals, maquettes, and sketches are also appearing indoors as museum exhibitions.[25] Museums and public art projects are equally promoted on public television and radio stations. Both enlist audience participation, not only in the selection and enjoyment of art but in its creation and sometimes performance. Moreover, the same funding agencies award grants for museums and the production of public art.

Designated the perpetuators of culture, museums have traditionally been charged with passing values from one generation to the next. Now they are experiencing pressure from outside and within the profession to become social activists, shaping today's world and influencing what is to come tomorrow. What formerly seemed commendable disinterest is denounced as shirking responsibility or, more strongly, as evading complicity with the partisanship of the past. Public art has a different but no less complex history to overcome. Detachment was not its burden; on the contrary, the mythologizing of heroes and victims was its clear purpose. But agreement on who they might be and what they accomplished was presumed to be beyond dispute, and that confidence is no longer possible.[26] The notion that a single rational public sphere exists is obsolete as a utopian ideal. In its place we have a proliferation of locally generated and temporary publics and counterpublics, each clamoring for the validation of its own cultural expression.

Much of the new public art is vigorously partisan and highly contested but also brief. Its moment onstage coincides with occurrent interests, and its short duration gives it a sense of urgency that protects it from indifference and habituated disuse. I believe this was a factor in the enthusiasm that greeted Christo and Jeanne-Claude's installation of *The Gates* in New York. Had it remained in Central Park for much longer than its allotted sixteen days, it would have been just another canopy decoration—pretty but inconsequential. Enthusiasm would have ended in indifference. Staged as a happening, it attracted hordes of visitors who came expressly for the experience, and its buoyancy uplifted them. The artists' genius was in anticipating this, yet persevering for twenty-six years to realize the evanescent moment.[27]

Where short-term public art, especially that which arises from within a community, can afford to be unequivocally promotional, museums, especially those with public funding, are more restricted. Their cumbersome lack of agility prevents museums from responding in timely, relevant ways to major events in the world even when the knowledge and means of doing so are available to them. It is no simple feat to upgrade a "permanent" exhibition that may be sadly out of date. Equivocal waffling is not an option, but many museums are finding ingenious ways to make themselves current. There is agitation for museums to be forums for debate, to serve as "the new town square," where people come together safely to be informed and to exchange ideas.

Exchange value dominates the marketplace, and its rules are not adequate to describe the museum. The market consists of goods and interested parties and the system that regulates their coexistence, but it has no personality, no will, and no ethical function, although it certainly has ethical consequences. By contrast, the museum is a "third-world" personality that supervenes the individuals and things that compose it. It filters and transmits ideas, rarely initiating them. There are insiders and outsiders, and the museum has interests and obligations to both, irreducible to the will of those currently employed by or directly involved with the museum. These people are instruments through whom the museum's principles are enacted (or violated). Because it is a moral being[28] capable of doing good or evil, the museum is embroiled in countless internally specific moral controversies and is implicated in a variety of broad societal ones.[29] That situation alone warrants recognition that the museum must be more than its preserved collections, whether of things, meanings, or experiences. The museum's moral identity suffuses all that it undertakes and makes nonsense of the notion that museums ever were or could be neutral bystanders.

What, then, is the museum's mission? What could it mean to be about something and for someone? I return to the classical language of integrity and authenticity—the real thing, the genuine article. How do these words translate into the syntax of ephemeral public art? What can be salvaged after the demise of the solid object and the fractionation of interpretation? Were we to fabricate our own meanings at every turn, there would be an end to communication altogether. Meaning would be meaningless. We depend upon mutual agreement and conventional understanding for survival. Note that this also permits—indeed entails—difference, for block unanimity obviates discussion. With absolute unison there is nothing to discuss, no recognizable issue to agree or disagree about. Recall the critique of mass art in chapter 2. There the mass was described as an undifferentiated aggregate of units "who respond passively to the suggestions given to them . . . (and who) do not even act out of genuinely personal interest, let alone that of the whole." Such creatures are hardly moral beings, for they are denied the capacity of moral reflection. Agencies that intentionally render humans into such identically programmed automata are themselves immoral. Museums have, on occasion, been the instruments of such agencies.

Mindful of that charge and of their past culpability, museums have become shy of universalizing (except in the most bland declarations) and fearful of making any direct judgments. Instead, they proffer alternatives, assuming a pose of liberality while leaving it to the public to decipher and choose among options.[30] We cannot forget, however, that the museum is the *metteur en scene*. It controls the range of choices. More important, the museum decides the arena in which choices are to be made, a tactic that easily confounds people and works to disempower them.[31] Subtly compelled by agendas not of its choosing, the public is diverted from articulating other interests. "Distraction" is an ambiguous concept: At times a therapeutic refreshment that renews energy, when externally imposed distraction is an assault that robs one of dignity and autonomy. In a culture of distraction, we lose the ability to differentiate among the clattering demands made upon our attention and are reduced to dithering incompetence. We accord them equal weight, and everything appears both exaggeratedly important and depressingly trivial. Museums are in danger of becoming mere distraction. Visitors learn to navigate within the buzz of paraphernalia and to encapsulate themselves defensively. Success at closing out interference comes at the cost of conviviality and ordinary courtesy. This is a strange way to build community and raises doubts about the ability of congregating spaces to provide sanctuary of any kind.

Yet people do come to museums seeking regeneration. They stand, uncomfortably, in the presence of other people, whom they stolidly ignore, raptly attentive to the objects before them. Since most arrive voluntarily, we may infer that their quest is to some degree satisfied and that a part of the benefit they gain is the sociality of their experience. Many individuals might prefer to commune in solitude with a single object—that would be a different but no less museal experience. The one typically undergone surrounded by people and objects appears, in spite of its inconvenience, to gain strength from implicit sharing. The consciousness of others is a reassuring affirmation of solidarity that avoids conformity while remaining short of the ideal advanced by Habermas, "that important cultural experiences should take place in a public space where we find ourselves side by side with large groups of unrelated strangers who make up, together with oneself, the social category of the public." I hazard the guess, in addition, that most people are not altogether secure in their judgment whether of objects or experience and welcome some authentication from an external presence. Thus, even wonder, surmounting the anguish of indifference, needs ultimately to be shared.

Stephen Greenblatt, the author of the essay "Resonance and Wonder," describes resonance as the power of an object to "reach out to a larger world, to evoke . . . the complex, dynamic cultural forces from which it has emerged . . . ," but this does not happen in a social vacuum. Recalling his own paradigm instance of resocialization, inspired by a collection of articles of worship confiscated by the Nazis and preserved in a cluster of synagogues in Prague, Greenblatt describes a memorial complex wherein one senses not the aesthetic surface of the objects but the resonance of "a felt intensity of names, and behind the names, as the very term resonance suggests, of voices: the voices of those who chanted, studied, muttered their prayers, wept, and then were forever silenced. And mingled with these voices are others . . ."[32] It is comforting to find oneself among the many others who also resonated with those objects and not altogether alone. Perhaps just such a concilience of voices would be the redemption of Vermeer's wager?

Wonder stretches our reach beyond solitary indulgence and distraction to reconcile us with what has been and still might be. Greenblatt cites a passage from Dürer's journal, in which the artist wonders at the objects from Mexico sent to Charles V, king of Spain, by the conquistador Cortes: "I have seen nothing that has gladdened my heart so much as these things, for I saw amongst them wonderful works of art, and I marveled at the subtle *ingenia* of men in foreign lands." Greenblatt understands Dürer's emotion as at least partly independent of the structures of politics and the marketplace and finds its origin in genuine respect and admiration for the *ingenia* of others that the art awakens. I agree with him and with his further observation that this respect is a response worth cherishing and enhancing. Respect for the *ingenia* of others connects us to those others. It is a civilizing, as well as socializing, sentiment. Museums should strive to instill it in the publics they construct.

Let me linger a bit longer with this feeling of wonder, for it needs to be distinguished from the private experience with which I began this book. One can be stopped in one's tracks with astonishment by a "wow" experience. When that happens, we are momentarily aroused, intrigued—and usually we collect ourselves promptly to go on about our business. We are briefly invigorated, mildly curious, but not particularly enlightened. Some wondrous happenings, however, are transformative. They propel us to go further, to want to know, to understand, to communicate, or to resonate with something larger than ourselves. Aristotle, having observed that sensation acquaints us with particulars—*that* fire is hot—but not with the *why* of it, goes on at some length to explain: "For it is owing to their wonder that men both now begin, and at first began to philosophize. . . . And a man who is puzzled and wonders thinks himself ignorant . . . whence (he) is, in a sense, a lover of wisdom." Aristotle believed that, in order to pursue such wisdom, a man must have secured the basic necessities of life and exist for his own sake, not for another's—meaning that he must be free to take part in the public sphere.[33] For, Aristotle continues, the "divine science" (that which it would be most meet for God to have) is not only an end in itself but is further productive and empowering.[34] Wonder is the beginning of knowledge because, with intense urgency, it makes us want to know. It drives us from private experience to public understanding.

Aristotle seems to have believed that wonder is a good starter but ceases once understanding has been achieved.[35] If that was his intention, I think he was mistaken. We can continue to wonder at what we have come to know with increased perspicacity. Indeed, most things become more interesting and more wondrous once one has learned to perceive the complex detail that is invisible to the untutored mind.[36] Museums initiate and reward the wonder that renews itself as it uncovers more to wonder at. They open avenues to further understanding but do not carry the knower to its end. That requires effort, far beyond the initial (and too often terminal) "wow" experience. More resources than the museum possesses are needed, and the museum is not in competition with the agencies that provide them. On the contrary, the wonder the museum arouses incites desire for wisdom and steers the individual to pursue it, wherever it might be found.

I do not mean to preach such exalted aspiration to all museums at all times or to judge them solely by its achievement, which is anyway hard to gauge. Life is not so serious—lunch is OK. Yet I believe the stretch from private stirrings to the public juncture I have tried to elucidate informs the museum's mission. It entails respect for the *ingenia* of others and is implicit in the very notion of the museum. This can be sensed even in the most modest instances; the little fishermen's museum in Gloucester, which has long ceased to exist, and the private thermometer museum in Onset. The sense of wonder is obscured in museums that become ponderous teaching machines, determined that their message shall be learned, but also in those that fear having any message at all and therefore emit merely a random array of disassociated blips.

Museums join with and are kin to public art that reconfigures ideas and places them in new contexts. With ethnic murals, wrapped buildings, giant jackalopes, gay pride parades, and Little Ducklings, publics meet and redesign themselves. Small museums identify themselves similarly through emblems—saddles, quilts, firefighting equipment, or wetlands preservation data, excising their chosen commitments from the mundane run of people's lives to be celebrated museally. Both major and minor museums thus convert the trivia of living into instructions for response that calls a social world into being.

Extending beyond the capabilities of material things alone, museums are able to confront the third world directly. Old and new museums now explore abstract concepts such as tolerance, civil rights, spying, sex, and news, further dematerializing but not fundamentally refining their approach to objects.[37] Notwithstanding their abstractness, these topics are eminently vernacular. They touch us all selectively and in every aspect of our lives.

Putting them in the museum affirms their common interest and instructs a public to pay attention. Although abstract, the themes are site specific, varying as publics differ in distinct environments. Abstractions, of their nature, have concrete instantiations that are not alike. In the museum, they become further detached from the actual circumstances under which they normally intersect our lives, but they are not without a context.[38] Confronting these framed and etherealized realities, people are drawn into dialogue with themselves and each other as by public art. The interaction is meant to be constructive, but it is not inherently or necessarily harmonious—nor should it be. Discord, judiciously confined, provokes reflection. Silenced or suppressed, it fosters impotent rage and violence; approached with respect, it is a gateway to greater understanding.

Following the lead of recent public art, museums are well placed to explore the clash of opinions. There have been angry reactions to public art that crosses taboos and arouses uncomfortable memories, but impermanence and local relevance sharpen interest and can diffuse incipient aggression. Museums, too, can be safety zones in which difficult ideas are subject to cross-examination. Hosting controversy requires more tact than certainty, but a lack of conviction comes across as insincere. Relinquishing the infallible voice of authority is hard to do, but museums are doing it. Now they are suffering a crisis of confidence and too often seek popular acclaim from a public that formerly regarded them with reverence.

Their present popularity and the proliferation of new museums are misleading signs of the museum's vitality. Its true outreach will be found in the recognition that what is abstract, immaterial, and temporary can be exhibited and is not without consequence or significance. Entrusting itself to these ephemera, the museum approaches public art.

Notes

1. Museum insiders invariably proclaim the importance of "distinctive organization with a unique mission." But consider the data: a typical bottom-line goal is "to further innovation in America." Another example: "The mission of the XXX History Museum is to encourage the inquiry and exploration of XXX within the broad context of American history." While the statements are generally true, they are not very informative.

2. Libraries sometimes possess rare books and original manuscripts, but in preserving and displaying them, they function as museums.

3. Karl Popper, "Epistemology without a Knowing Subject," in *Objective Knowledge: An Evolutionary Approach* (Oxford, 1972). Susan M. Pearce, in *Museums,*

Objects and Collections: A Cultural Study (Washington, D.C.: Smithsonian Institution Press, 1992), cites the same essay and draws much the same conclusion from Popper that I do. The difference between us is that, where Pearce would add "museum collections and exhibitions" to Popper's third-world contents of "journals, books, and libraries," I introduce the museum as an institution, replete with its architecture, staff, programs, and people. Still, our understanding of the museum is very similar, as Pearce goes on to say: "The museum worker makes a selection from the materials to hand, both tangible and intangible, that form part of his (sic) social practice and which will include elements of Popper's objective knowledge. He (sic) orders these into museum narrative which will be judged by those who come to it. He (sic) is taking part in a rhetorical project of persuasion, but he (sic) does this as part of a participating community" (Pearce, 263). I call the entire production described by Pearce a (public) art performance.

4. A common mistake is the confusion of a historic event, e.g., Newton's thinking about the apple, with the objective content to which he was led, namely, the laws of gravitation. They would have existed even if Newton had never been born.

5. History museums face the greatest challenge to accomplishing this task. Archie Bunker's chair, Henry Morgenthau's cables revealing the Turkish massacre of Armenians, and the striped uniforms of Nazi concentration camp inmates are all materially substantial and emotively evocative. Their place in history, however, is due to what they represent, which transcends their immediate specificity, and that is why they are preserved in the museum. The museum does not prove a point. It is not about evidence or impact, although it offers both to those who seek them. In declaring that their primary business supervenes both matter and thought, I do not mean to underestimate the role of subjective experience in the museum, but to portray it as the museum's mission is both presumptuous and vacuous.

6. Developmental sequences can become discernible through museum exhibitions, even where that was not the conscious intention of exhibition designers. Visitors sometimes bring a logic altogether different from that intended by the museum to exhibits. Speaking from personal experience, a visit to the Merrimack Textile Museum (since renamed the American Textile History Museum) taught me, through its displayed sequence of machinery, the rationality of industrialism and the rationale of Marxism. It was evident from their appearance that the earliest mechanical looms replicated the activity of human labor and multiplied it. What one arm did could be amplified by dozens of mechanical arms linked by a bar and activated by a lever. Later, more-sophisticated instruments dissected the process, beginning with the end product and reasoning back to the most efficient means of achieving that end with less human labor. Byproducts and waste could also be channeled into value-producing materials automatically. No reading of *Kapital* could so clearly reveal the social and economic implications of mechanical intelligence, but I doubt that this was the museum's intention, since the accompanying signage and videos told an altogether different story. Yet my perception

was no mere subjective reaction. It extracted an objective alternative as real as the one the museum had chosen to deliver.

7. The common association of objectivity with truth is confusing here, but truth is not at issue; neither is utility or intention. A video or theater performance that simulates what Galileo might have said or done is confusing. It may predispose the visitor to sympathize with the man, but it is not a presentation of that about which he was thinking, which can be inferred from his diagrams and notes of experiments. These are schematic, physically accessible references to the third world.

8. Quoting at length from Gaskell's introduction, here is the wager: "First, that it is possible to embody systematic abstract ideas that constitute methodical thought in purely visual form exclusively employing representations of plausible contemporary material reality (i.e. domestic scenes rather than religious or mythological iconography). . . . Second, a further proposal that we apprehend complex pictorial abstraction purely visually by means of the operation on the heart or soul directly through the eyes, evading language, in the manner of love. . . . Thus, through the love proper to art, on the part of artist and viewer alike, art can offer its wisdom, solace and reflection. . . . Finally, relationships among objects, between people and objects, and among people mediated by objects are diachronic as well as synchronic. Without the past we cannot imagine the future. Those to whom the past is denied cannot change the world."

9. Obviously sociality is necessary to the survival of private art and, in Gaskell's terms, to its creation as well. But in that sense, all art is public.

10. But note that not all terminations signify an end of the art or the cessation of its public status. I have mentioned desacralization in previous chapters. There are also intentional closures such as the scattering of sand paintings and mandalas. As much as the act of construction, these ceremonial destructions are part of the art. They are not lapses of its public identity. In other types of public art, the meaning but not the matter of the work is lost, and it simply becomes incomprehensible. A bust of the founder of a defunct business might retain aesthetic value, but it has no public function to succeeding occupants of the building.

11. A quarter-century later, enough mementos have been collected to furnish a small museum. The Museum of Our National Heritage, in Lexington, Massachusetts, mounted an exhibition of these spontaneous offerings. In contrast, devotional objects are discouraged at the newly dedicated World War II Memorial in Washington, D.C. When left, they are confiscated and destroyed. An instant museum of found objects and tributes appeared almost immediately at the site of the World Trade Center catastrophe.

12. "We erect monuments so that we shall always remember, and build memorials so that we shall never forget." Thus, according to Arthur Danto, the Washington Monument celebrates a beginning, while the Lincoln Memorial meditates upon an ending. See "The Vietnam Veterans Memorial," in *The State of the*

Art (New York: Prentice Hall Press, 1987). Maya Lin's memorial is an ambiguous tribute that finds a beginning in the end.

13. A traveling exhibit, Eyes Wide Open, assembled by the American Friends Service Committee and composed of black military boots, began a nationwide tour in Chicago with 500 pairs of boots (the number of soldiers killed at that moment). By mid-March 2005, it reached San Diego, and the number of pairs, many of them donated by bereaved families had reached 1,513. On its November arrival in Boston, the number exceeded 2,000.

14. "Between the Museum and the City: Garofalo Architects," MCA and CAA/UIC (Chicago, 2003).

15. In fact, it did take a teensy-weensy step beyond the line, placing a single canopied steel "flyover" into the park across the street to convey a sense of civic connection.

16. New museums, as noted elsewhere, tend to allocate more space for public congregation and comparatively less private storage space. They also glory in spectacular external design but not to a greater degree than do their palatial predecessors within the limits of available technology.

17. Harriet Senie, "Reframing Public Art: Audience Use, Interpretation, and Appreciation," in *Art and Its Publics: Museum Studies at the Millennium*, Andrew McClellan.

18. viz. Bernard Rosenthal's *Alamo* (1967) in New York's Astor Place, near Cooper Union. Popularly known as "the cube," it inspires spinning contests among other regular uses. Temporary removal of the piece for repairs has caused some anxiety among the faithful.

19. In contrast, the public most closely affected had little to say about the fate of Richard Serra's *Tilted Arc*. Although the workers at Federal Plaza were exposed to the sculpture every day, their opinions were largely manipulated and smothered in the dispute between art professionals and government operatives who claimed to speak in the name of the public.

20. Theme parks that purport to lead us down memory lane are not reanimating our own memories but fabricating an image alleged to be of a reality. They offer a surrogate experience infused with referential meaning. Conceivably they also convey information, but they cannot revive an experience that did not happen. Instead, they synthesize a new one.

21. Douglas Crimp follows the path of Michel Foucault in examining the history of modern institutions, whose sophisticated means of surveillance and instruction exceed the more direct and obvious constraints of earlier times. See *On the Museum's Ruins* (Cambridge, Mass.: MIT Press, 1993). In principle, discipline requires the art of applying knowledge and not just the science of its transmission. Museums lack the instruments of reward and punishment that the institutions to which Crimp compares them possess, so they cannot guide practice with the same efficiency. But according to Pierre Bourdieu et al., they nonetheless do

a creditable job of reinforcing social stratification. See *For the Love of Art* (Stanford, Calif.: Stanford University Press, 1992).

22. The relationship between the order of words and the order of things is complicated enough. Compounding this with artifacts used metonymically as parts of nature representing the whole raises the ante considerably. The implication is that museums are even more delusional than are scientific reconstructions, which, the critics contend, are also suspect. See Eugenio Donato, "The Museum's Furnace" in *Textual Strategies: Perspectives in Post-Structuralist Criticism*, ed. Josue V. Harari (Ithaca, N.Y.: Cornell University Press, 1979).

23. "The Authorities of the American Art Museum," in *Whose Muse? Art Museums and the Public Trust*, James Cuno (Princeton, N.J.: Princeton University Press, 2004).

24. Except in the gift shop, whose enterprise is a separate matter.

25. A recent exhibition of works by Augustus Saint-Gaudens at the Smith College Art Museum included full-sized and diminutive models and studies of the artist's well-known outdoor sculptures and bas-reliefs, as well as $10 and $20 coins, memorial plaques, a medal in honor of Theodore Roosevelt's 1904 inauguration, and various architectural elements. Saint-Gaudens came across as a postmodern forerunner, working eclectically in multiple media. The display of his models and sketches meant for utilitarian purposes paralleled exhibitions of ancient relics and artifacts commonly shown in universal survey museums or museums of archaeology. Bringing this art into the art museum raises questions of taxonomy also suggested by exhibitions such as Art Deco 1910–1939, organized by the Victoria & Albert Museum, which (in the Boston MFA) encompassed models of skyscrapers, elevator doors, industrial design elements, and furniture, along with couturier fashion and domestic items. The line between private art and public art is here as obscure as that between art and non-art.

26. More correctly, those who disagreed with that assessment were discounted.

27. This work was also relatively nonpartisan, although countless meanings could be attributed to it. The artists avoided substantive claims but declared themselves followers of Olmsted's original plan for Central Park—that it provide refreshment and urban relief.

28. Let me be clear that to be a moral being is to be capable of moral agency. It does not mean morally good; only moral agents are capable of being good or wicked. Nonmoral entities (like tsunamis and bombs) can do a great deal of harm, but they are not evil. Blame and punishment (as well as praise) are rationally applicable only to moral agents. See my discussion of institutional morality in *The Museum in Transition*.

29. A list of the former would include the return of stolen art and sacred artifacts; examples of the latter are the perpetuation of racism and economic exploitation.

30. This is not a simple offer. It is cloaked in layers of rhetoric and interpretive information with invitations far in excess of what is exhibited. These take the form of catalogues, symposia, public statements, and scholarly references that may be

studied or ignored. The point is that responsibility is shifted to the perceiver to do as much research or as little as desired and to reach his or her own conclusions. The museum steers clear of definitive judgment in an equivocal and somewhat disingenuous gesture of antiauthoritarianism.

31. I cannot resist comparing this ploy to that used by the manufacturers of bathing suits, shoes, and other apparel. The variety available is astronomical, but the differences are microscopic. The bewildered consumer, overwhelmed by options, ultimately purchases something that is not quite what he or she originally had in mind but now despairs of finding. In this *embaras de richesse*, he or she succumbs, persuaded that surely it is he or she who is at fault in wanting something beyond the achievable.

32. Stephen Greenblatt, "Resonance and Wonder," in *Exhibiting Cultures: The Poetics and Politics of Museum Display*, Karp et al. (Washington, D.C.: Smithsonian Institution Press, 1991).

33. This, of course, excluded all women and eighty percent of his compatriots from that joyful potency, but we need not follow him there.

34. "For all men begin by wondering that things are as they are, as they do about self-moving marionettes, or about the solstices or about the incommensurability of the diagonal of a square with the side; for it seems wonderful to all who have not yet seen the reason. . . . But we must end in the contrary and . . . the better state . . . when men learn the cause." Aristotle, *Metaphysics*, book I, chapter 2. Learning the cause is Aristotle's equivalent to apprehending Popper's third world, a public enterprise.

35. The most honorable life, Aristotle believed, is that spent in quiet contemplation.

36. "They murder to dissect" is a taunt thrown at analytic critics, and it is true that the habit of analysis can interfere with simple enjoyment. viz. James Elkins, "We in the artworld never talk about art in terms of 'transformative power,' but as objects to be analyzed." *Pictures and Tears: A History of People Who Have Cried in Front of Paintings* (London: Routledge, 2001). But consider the passion that drives sports enthusiasts to assimilate reams of information that is deadly boring to anyone not so enthralled and the joy shared by true amateurs of music or art, as of every field, as they ponder the ever-deepening mysteries of their beloved subject.

37. Yes—these topics are abstract. Tolerance is not a manifesto, and sex is not a dildo. Museums cannot escape the use of physically perceivable things, but the subject explored is something else.

38. Imagine contemplating boredom as an abstract concept apart from the circumstance that bores you. Configuring boredom as a museum exhibition would be illuminating. Would it be boring? Should it be? A museum that deconstructs the architecture of prejudice raises similar perplexities.

Conclusion

I have turned to public art in order to break with conventional depictions of the museum as a passive site or container. Art has the power to affect the world by transforming perceptions of it. I concentrated on public art because its implicit sociality renders those originally private perceptions collective. Whether we locate their inception in the sacred groves of antiquity, the Renaissance cabinets of curiosities, or the Napoleonic public museum, museums have forged publics by inclusion and exclusion, profiling them as the current fashion dictated. In today's museums, a single public is replaced by defined clusters, enclaves of difference, interactively engaged with the museum and each other.

Supporting this robust pluralism is the museum's declared objective. Every day brings announcements of newly opened museums dedicated to an originator's passionate interest. Every month, *Museum News,* the professional journal of the American Association of Museums, publishes descriptions of niche programs or exhibitions directed to special populations or pairings of populations and meant to catalyze their mutual enrichment.[1] While these reports of clever partnerings and new supplemental resources are inspiring, they stand in sharp contrast to the advertisements in the same journal, which relentlessly picture slick and standardized individuals wielding acoustic guides as they contemplate beautiful arrays of sensuous things in glass cases.

I am nevertheless inclined to conclude optimistically that what is actually happening in museums is more interesting and humanly rich than what commercial advertisers persistently purvey. The stories that circulate within the profession reflect careful and labor-intensive stretches toward goals that museums pose for themselves. Their achievement, however, rarely meets the horizon of the typical visitor who comes to spend an hour or two browsing in the museum without expecting that experience to translate significantly into life. Exoticism keeps things at a distance, and the aesthetic that museums have cultivated over several centuries is a form of exoticism. Visitors are trained to expect insulated encounters and to reject what approaches them too closely or feels like inappropriate advocacy—but this could change.

I propose that, instead of turning to professional marketers to help them "package their product" and "brand" themselves more fashionably, museums make a more fundamental self-assessment. I take public art as a paradigm for change and urge museums to emulate its dynamic experimentalism.

Public art is inherently purposive. Statues of stone or bronze, cast according to a plan, are fixed in place but tend, nonetheless, to wander off base. A patina accrues and not alone of material encrustations. The meaning of even stationary objects changes with time, and yet the art rarely becomes wholly meaningless. Museum collection, too, meanders from its start but is not random aggregation. It increases selectively. Step follows step, and design emerges, modified by circumstance. Museum goals are adjustable as the practical conditions of their realization demand. Adding and culling, acquiring and restoring, museums reallocate and sometimes jettison, but barring wholesale demolition, a melodic continuity persists throughout their transformations.[2] Mission statements declare the obvious. They are too general to register departures from an agenda, too bland to fix a sustained character; but policies are revealed in a museum's actual conduct—their hirings, firings, and promotions—as well as accessions and exhibitions—and their purposes are refined in practice.

Museums assemble, blending things and ideas with people. They are experimenting with configurations new to their audiences and themselves. Where museums of the past sought to gratify a preexistent public whose expectations were predictable and to educate newcomers accordingly, museums of the present join with publics in the process of defining themselves. Traditional museums exhorted and affirmed with unchallenged self-confidence, but declining unanimity among the primary audience today, coupled with increased independence on the part of those not yet inducted, has undermined the simple paternalism of the original museum project. From patronizing amateurism at the outset, museums moved through a phase of skilled professionalism that remains influential to a stage of confused reactivity to external pressures. Faced with unprecedented standards of accountability and the obligation to benefit unfamiliar publics, museums were forced to reassess their public function. What are they good for? Rarely do they heal the sick, protect us against our enemies, put out fires, or collect refuse. Whatever they do must be distinguishable from the good works of other institutions that are also committed to public service. As I puzzled over this problem, what had appeared a figurative allusion turned into a model. Following the course of contemporary public art might loosen the restrictions that earlier models of the museum have imposed.

In this book, I have avoided discussion of the museum's legal and financial responsibilities and the areas of management and governance. Like the personalities of their founders, these facets of museum genealogy obviously affect the museum's character profoundly and to a degree that exceeds a parallel with most public art.[3] No single characterization can cover all aspects of the museum. My emphasis on innovative public art does not displace other analyses but is meant heuristically to encourage museums to exert forthright agency like that currently exhibited by public art. The idea is that museums mobilize temporary interactions among people and through things and export those combinations into social reality.

Like public art, the museum has become open-ended and processual. The relationship initiated among the people and things that museums combine is continuously in flux, effectively generating communicative circles or, better said, a spiral of understanding.[4] I call the museum art, and more specifically public art, to recommend emulation of an art form that departs from the usual presumptions—that the work is perceptibly physical, aspires to permanence, has universal value, and possesses fixed meaning (however inscrutable). The new public art rejects those classic verities. It enlists public engagement at every emergent point, seeking renewal throughout the creative process and the life of the work. It professes not to exist independently of that interaction. Effacing the (singular) artist whose finished creation is to be apprehended by other self-contained individuals, this art merges the creative act with its never-completed interpretation and reception. Yielding authority to the public, such art accumulates energy while denying the presumption of universality. Its appeal is temporary and conditional upon change. It does not promise unanimous approval, but no model can guarantee such an extraordinary effect. Art so conceived offers the relief of finitude. Its satisfaction is contemporary without disrespect toward the past or foreclosure of the future.

Attributing such ephemerality to the museum casts its conventional commitments in a new light. From this perspective, the museum is no longer seen as a palace that holds priceless treasures in perpetuity, yet the temporal appreciation of things that gratify and collaborate with us in what we do is preserved. The museum is not conceived as an empty stage where people and objects happen to coincide: nor is it a protected site in which to luxuriate in private experience, whether of objects or of induced brain states. Imagined as a work of public art, the museum acts upon, incites, and constructs publics, whose members spread as filaments stretched in an expanding web. So configured they redefine themselves and it and thereby alter their relationship to one another.

I close this book as I began, with a pilgrimage: the path led me, once more, to New York and to the self-described Nomadic Museum, temporarily bivouacked at a West Side pier on the Chelsea waterfront, an area itself in process—transforming from scruffy meat-packing warehouses to upscale clothing and jewelry stores. Dockworkers and deliverymen mixed on the street with wandering tourists, stiletto-heeled businesswomen, and gay flaneurs. This authentically deconstructible museum, although not a boat, was moored at the *Lusitania*'s embarkation dock and the intended landing site of the *Titanic*. It was designed by the architect Shigeru Ban and constructed entirely of recyclable materials: the walls a lattice of cargo containers, the roof of corrugated steel, and the supporting columns of pressed paper tubes made out of used teabags. Inside, on a bed of river stones, a planked walkway was laid, and on each side, suspended between support poles, were giant photographs by the Canadian artist Gregory Colbert, idyllically beautiful images of wild animals interacting with humans. Gentle illumination, a slight breeze with the scent of sandalwood upon it, and a background of soft musical sounds accompanied the slow progression of hundreds of pedestrians shuffling through the nave-like space to an open apse where a floating overhead screen animated the stationary scenes we had witnessed in passing. People of every size, shape, color, age, and class made their way along the route, mostly in awed silence, yielding to the tranquility of the environment. Some stopped to rest, nibble on lunches, and comfort children on stumps at strategically placed way stations. Most of the visitors did not seem to be regular museum-goers, but like the workmen who had built the structure and the initially skeptical locals, passersby were first intrigued, then attracted, then drawn into this peaceable kingdom.

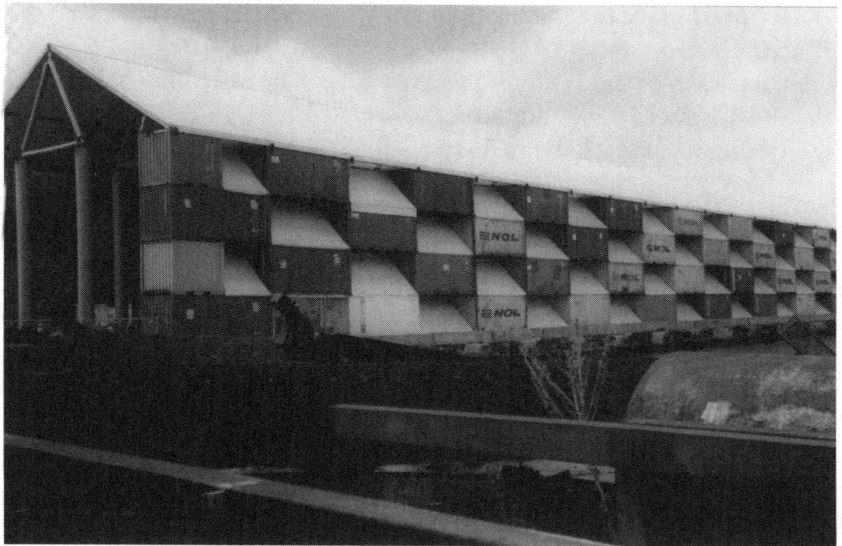

Nomadic Museum, Pier 54, New York City (2005), museum designed by Shigeru Ban. Composed of 148 shipping containers stacked in a self-supporting grid and other recyclable materials. (Photo by Hilde Hein.)

It would stay there only briefly, providing employment and diversion for a few months, before being deconstructed and moved on to other ports of call. Taking along only the irreplaceable necessities, packed up in a few cargo containers, it will be reconfigured wherever it goes—next stop, Santa Monica—supplemented with local materials and rebuilt by local laborers to conform to its new environment. Some adaptations will follow manmade legal and administrative regulations; others are a function of climate and geography. Its visitors will undoubtedly have a different character as well.

This is not a typical museum, and it is sure to evoke controversy within and without the profession. It is privately owned and funded—but so are many traditional institutions. It celebrates the work of a single artist—but others do likewise. It achieves a very theatrical ambience, as many others aspire to do. Its chief novelty is its ephemerality and recyclable structure. That enables it to move lock, stock, and barrel and to reshape itself to fit every venue. Like Christo's *Gates*, its novelty could wear off with excess exposure, arouse antagonism, or meet with practical opposition. Then, like the nomad it is, it can silently steal away, leaving behind no more than a memory. But that is enough.

Embracing ideas and making them accessible, along with the crowd of accumulated things, is not a new adventure for museums, but they can approach it with a new attitude. The reward will be revitalized encounters and experiments of brief duration and lasting interest. The new public art has led the way: museums are not far behind. Following this path can energize the museum to renew its mission and revive its soul.

Notes

1. Picking at random, the May/June 2005 issue of *Museum News* includes two reports of museum collaboration with medical school instruction, one of which is paired with a geriatric program. Another item describes a coalition pledged to support museums that are openly committed to social welfare activism and consequently face consignment to the fringe of museum respectability.

2. Did anyone really expect the newly reopened MoMA to change its spots? Reversing the chronological order of viewing is an interesting switch that revitalizes familiar and forgotten works in altered context; but the scent of Western European and American modernism still prevails and is not likely to be forfeited, whatever the height of ceilings.

3. The legal and financial constraints on public art are not negligible, however, for it too must satisfy funding boards and avoid offending civic bodies with the authority to deny or approve it.

4. In fact it resembles the hermeneutic circle, which declares all understanding to be interpretation that appropriates what is being understood to its own current situation. Not its originary source, therefore, but its trajectory into the present occupies the place of "truth" and links the knower with the known. This continuity of consciousness may have been the substance of Vermeer's wager, a hope-filled bet that the future will be resonant with the past and that the present enterprise contributes to the perpetuation of its meaning.

Index

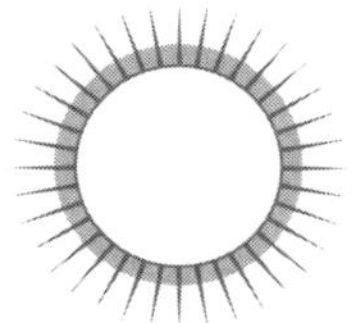

About the Author

HILDE HEIN is associate professor of philosophy, emerita, at Holy Cross College. Her previous books include *The Museum in Transition: A Philosophical Perspective* (2000) and *The Exploratorium: The Museum as Laboratory* (1990).